TRADITIONAL HOUSES
of SOMERSET

Jane Penoyre

with a foreword by
Peter Beacham

CONTRIBUTORS:

Landscape and Buildings
John Penoyre

Farms and Farm Buildings
John Dallimore

Conservation
Russell Lillford

Somerset County Council
2005

Somerset Books

First published in Great Britain in 2005

British Library Cataloguing-in-Publication Data
A CIP record for this title is available from the British Library

ISBN 0 86183 407 0

Somerset Books is a partnership between DAA Halsgrove Ltd
and Somerset County Council (Directorate of Culture and Heritage)
www.somerset.gov.uk

SOMERSET BOOKS
Halsgrove House
Lower Moor Way
Tiverton, Devon EX16 6SS
Tel: 01884 243242
Fax: 01884 243325
email: sales@halsgrove.com
website: www.halsgrove.com

Printed and bound by CPI Bath Press, Bath.

Contents

For my husband John, whose skilful drawings and great knowledge of buildings inspired this book.

Foreword

It is a pleasure to contribute to this splendid book. As someone born and bred in Somerset who spent the formative years of his working life in Devon, I have long wished to see an account of the local building traditions of my native county to put alongside those that have already been published for Cornwall, Devon, Dorset, Gloucestershire and Wiltshire. Our local buildings are vital to the definition of what makes one part of England different from another and are a major contribution to the regional identity of the South West.

This book does exactly what is needed. Drawing as it does on her and her husband John and many colleagues' work over so many years, Jane Penoyre has given us an account that truly deserves the epithets original and authoritative. She has pulled together all the knowledge garnered over the last half century and more to present a picture of how it all coheres, allowing us to see the distinctiveness of Somerset's buildings. It also links with the traditions of neighbouring counties and the national canvas.

At English Heritage I am presently engaged in the reform of our national system of heritage protection. We have high hopes of delivering a new system that will manage the historic environment in a more comprehensive way. But no system will work unless it promotes understanding of the buildings, sites and landscapes in which we live and work. There is no substitute for the thoughtful owner, visitor or enthusiast who sees how buildings have evolved over centuries. If we understand what we are looking at, there is some chance we shall care for our historic environment in ways that continuously enrich it to hand on to generations to come. It is this that Jane Penoyre's book helps us to do.

Peter Beacham
Heritage Protection Director
English Heritage
London, July 2004

Introduction

This book is concerned with the domestic buildings of historic Somerset, including South Avon, a subject which has gained enormously from the considerable quantity of research and recording done in the county over the last 40 years or so. Many individuals have studied buildings at a time when other researchers throughout the country were beginning to explore the new subject of 'Vernacular Buildings'[1]. These are the traditional houses and farm buildings of the countryside: the houses of the villages and some towns, all built of local materials, with the skills of local builders and craftsmen. They conform to the local style of building of their time.

Traditional buildings such as this in Somerset extend in date (on the evidence of the houses recorded so far) from the late-thirteenth century to the beginning of the eighteenth. After that, outside influences in design and fashion, combined with a universal distribution of cheaper building materials from other areas, resulted in a style of building common to the whole country rather than one particular county. Materials such as mass produced bricks and tiles which were easily transported, began to replace more traditional materials. The popularity of the fashionable Georgian and Victorian styles can be seen anywhere in the British Isles and no longer represent the local variations of the earlier periods. This book, therefore, will examine the houses built no later than the early eighteenth century.

The book is arranged into two main sections, Chapters 1 and 2 describe some aspects of the physical and historical backgrounds against which all the buildings are seen, while Chapters 3 to 7, deal with the buildings themselves. The chapters describe the smaller domestic rural houses, the larger high status buildings, features and decorations, some town houses and farm buildings. Finally, as an appendix, some examples of individual surveys of houses are included to show the method of recording in more detail.

House Surveys and their Recorders

Writers and artists of the early-twentieth century and before had often studied the picturesque appearance of rural houses[2]. The choice of materials and decorative styles were all examined, but the planning, construction and social context was not generally discussed. Our interests today have led to a detailed study of many hundreds of houses and farm buildings, by means of measured drawings and historical research derived from documentation. These methods, combined with a stylistic comparison of features of the buildings and their decorative styles, give a fairly reliable indication of date. However, more recently the science of dendrochronology (or tree-ring dating) has given us a method of precisely dating timbers. In the following text, to distinguish these more precisely dated buildings, the 'tree-ring' dates are prefixed with a 'd' and the dates based on stylistic grounds are prefixed with a 'c'.

The county of Somerset has benefited from the pioneering work of many people who have studied and recorded a great number of local traditional buildings. Most of these researchers, working in the mid- to late-twentieth century, were also members of the national group, the Vernacular Architecture Group (VAG).[1]

Among the many people who made these recordings, two individuals should particularly be named, R.G. Gilson and the late E.H.D. Williams, who were working in the 1970s onwards. They lectured, researched and recorded enormous numbers of Somerset buildings and published, analysed and compared the houses and made splendid drawings.[5] Some of us working in the field were fortunate in having at first hand the benefit of their wide knowledge and experience. They also made a pioneering study of early roof structures in the county and later, our own group, the Somerset Vernacular Buildings Research Group (SVBRG)[3] was able to contribute with more surveys and tree-ring dating of a number of medieval structures.

Some of the other recorders of Somerset buildings over the last 50 years are the late Sir Robert Hall, R. Taylor, L. Walrond, the late B. Hale, Mark McDermott and Chris Sidaway, as well as many members of the Somerset Archeological and Natural History Society (SANHS). Pamela Brimacombe and the Historic Buildings Committee of SANHS have compiled lists of the recorded buildings and the Somerset Record Office have stored copies of the surveys in Taunton, the records being available for viewing by interested people.[4]

The work of these recorders is referred to in the text, including that of our own group, SVBRG, and these recordings form the basis of descriptions and drawings presented here. Some of this work has been published in a rather piecemeal form from time to time in journals, so this book is intended to put the various studies together using drawings from different sources. Here, the buildings chosen (only a limited number, of course) will hopefully be of interest to many people; house owners, builders and craftsmen, students of architecture and the local authorities who do so much to conserve these buildings.

ACKNOWLEDGEMENTS

I would like to thank personally the following experts in their field for their help over many years relating to Somerset buildings: Dr Robert Dunning and Mary Siraut, *VCH* Editors, the County Archivist, Tom Mayberry and his colleagues, and the County Archeologist, Robert Croft. In all matters concerning books I have benefited by the kind help of David Bromwich of the Somerset Local Studies Library.

This book has been greatly helped by the Somerset County Council, and in particular the Architectural and Historic Heritage Department under the direction of Russell Lillford, whose enthusiasm and knowledge of the houses of Somerset is immense. My sincere thanks for their encouragement and help both to publish and fund this book.

Some of our work with SVBRG was concerned with the buildings of various villages of Somerset, Shapwick in particular, where our work was greatly inspired by Prof. Mick Aston and his former colleagues, Michael Costen and Jo Bettey of the University of Bristol, and Dr Chris Gerrard of King Alfred's College, Winchester. SVBRG's contribution on the standing buildings of Shapwick formed part of the 10-year Shapwick Project[3]. For expert advice from the Vernacular Architecture Group, I would like to thank John T. Smith for his encouragement and scholarship on structures and planning of vernacular buildings. Also thanks to Dan Miles and Mick Worthington of the Oxford Dendrochronology Laboratory for their patient work and knowledge on Somerset roofs.

My husband John and I joined the SVBRG group in 1982 and were greatly helped by the founder members, Clare Austin, John Dallimore and many others, who introduced us to the intricacies of the traditional buildings of Somerset and to the 'Village Studies' compiled by the group. The SVBRG members today have been generous in their encouragement for this book.

Finally, thanks must go to the publishers, Somerset Books, and their patient and helpful staff.

CONTRIBUTORS

The following people have personally contributed to this book: John Penoyre has written and illustrated Chapter 1 on landscape, building materials and regional styles. My grateful thanks are particularly due to John Dallimore for his specialist knowledge on farming and farm buildings, writing and illustrating Chapter 7; to Russell Lillford, of the Historic Environment Service (Somerset County Council) for Chapter 8 on the conservation aspect of traditional houses; to Tom Manning for his many drawings in Chapter 5 and John McCann for his expert photographs combined with a knowledge of the timber buildings. Geoff Roberts has provided some excellent photographs as has Isabel Richardson with her photographs and knowledge of the buildings of the Holnicote Estate in West Somerset (NT) in Chapter 7. Indeed, this book is illustrated by many hands, as I have used the recorded drawings of SVBRG members, those of John Penoyre and John Dallimore in particular. The photographs are chiefly my own, and were taken during survey visits and when I was merely a passer-by, and therefore they were not intended for publication as such. So the reader must forgive this patchwork of information which is put together under one cover here, to record the many aspects of Somerset's traditional buildings.

The following people have kindly read and made suggestions for the text: Steven Croad, Robert Croft, Robert Dunning, Ron Gilson, Mark McDermott and Gregory Penoyre. I am grateful for the help of Joan Dallimore, Mary Jackson and Kate Penoyre for their patient work of proof reading and indexing.

Finally I would like to thank all the house owners who extended their hospitality and interest while we surveyed, drew and recorded their houses. The reader is fervently asked to respect the privacy of these house owners, as only a very few well-known houses are open to the public.

Jane Penoyre

Notes
1. The Vernacular Architecture Group (VAG), a national organisation.
2. Books by Sydney R. Jones and others, published by Batsford.
3. The Somerset Vernacular Building Research Group (SVBRG) is concerned with recording and researching old houses in the county. (SVBRG was previously known as SSAVBRG to include South Avon). SVBRG has also published various "Village Studies" of the Vernacular Buildings of some villages in Somerset including Shapwick.
4. The Somerset County Record Office have kindly stored these surveys in Taunton Record Office under the title "the Vernacular Architecture Files".
5. Gilson, R. and Williams, E.H.D., work published in the Somerset Archeological & Natural History Society (SANHS), Proceedings (see chapters for references) and other journals.

ONE

Landscape and Buildings

by John Penoyre

Fig. 1.1   Summer in the Somerset Levels.

THE COUNTRYSIDE

Somerset is a large county extending over 60 miles from east to west and 40 miles from north to south, with a coastline bordering the Bristol Channel (fig. 1.2). It is essentially a rural area of well-watered open countryside, traditionally devoted to dairy farming, cider and sheep.

The Somerset hills which punctuate this lowland agricultural scene are scattered, well defined and, with the exception of the Brendons and Exmoor, give the appearance of being isolated. Most famous, in the north lie the Mendip Hills, bare and a little desolate on the top, scarred by long-abandoned lead-mining and, like their limestone counterparts in the Pennines, concealing many dark and labyrinthine caves and underground streams. Their bare uplands are mostly pasture with some drystone field walls or, where the underlying Devonian rocks form the summits, are covered in heather and bracken. Deep clefts in the limestone, such as Cheddar Gorge on the south and Burrington Combe on the north, make dramatic vertical-sided rocky chasms leading up from the low-lying surroundings.

South-eastwards the Mendip Hills fade gradually into the very different limestone country of the extreme southern extension of the Cotswolds where, in sharp contrast with Mendip, there are many villages and small towns which owe their late- and post-medieval prosperity to quarrying, sheep raising and above all to the woollen cloth industry. In this area of flat-topped limestone hills are many steep sided valleys and small streams which powered the fulling mills, used to 'full' or pound the woven cloth to the required density. Here the hills are bordered by no well defined west-facing scarp as further north in Gloucestershire and rise to no great height. The hills form an eastern boundary stretching from Bath in the north to Yeovil in the south.

In the west of the county the Brendon Hills merge into the high mass of Exmoor, both formed of exceedingly ancient rocks. The Brendons give rise to a scenery strongly reminiscent of Devon, with small isolated farm groups and irregularly shaped green fields covering the steep lower slopes, giving way to the splendidly open heathland summits of Exmoor proper, which plunge vertiginously down to the sea to the north with narrow tree and fern-choked valleys. Farms on Exmoor, unexpectedly high up towards the open moors, are typically marked by the straight, well maintained beech hedges that border the lanes and define the large rectangular fields.

North of Taunton, the Quantock Hills form a conspicuous free-standing north–south ridge of the same ancient rocks with similar deserted tops and wooded valleys.

Surrounding the Quantocks on all sides lies the vale country, a gently undulating landscape of pale green fields and strikingly red soils, giving way

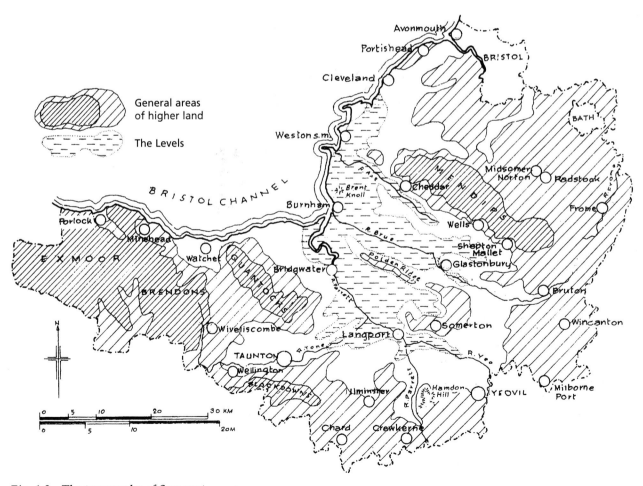

Fig. 1.2 The topography of Somerset.

eastwards beyond Bridgwater to a huge area of flat land, a large part of which lies virtually at sea level. These Somerset Levels have been subject to flooding for centuries past and still every winter large areas are inundated. Completely flat, the Levels were in only the very recent geological past covered by the sea and form today a countryside of summer pasture and peat moors that have been artificially drained since medieval times and before. The Levels provide some of the most enchanting landscapes in the county, their lush willow-fringed meadows deep in buttercups with yellow flags and sedgy reeds along the wide drainage ditches (fig. 1.1).

Three principal rivers drain the Levels, the Parrett, the Tone and the Brue. Water from the Levels is pumped up into the rivers which now run between high embankments, the fast-flowing water in flood time alarmingly level with their tops. Such streams, and many more even smaller, afforded vital transport routes from the coast to well inland until at least the early years of the nineteenth century. This fen-like scene is always relieved by a backdrop of wooded hills, quite unlike the East-Anglian and Lincolnshire fens whose geometrical ploughlands seem to go on for ever and have no neighbouring high ground to define their limits and relieve the eye. Sandbanks left over from the ancient sea still rise a few feet above the Levels as little dry islands of raised ground called Burtles. The area of the Levels is bisected by a narrow south–east to north–west ridge of hills called the Poldens. Although rising to only 98m (320ft), the hills seem larger than they are as they rise steeply from the flat moors on their south side. On their other side they slope down more gradually into the moor and support a number of stone-built villages along their line of springs.

Beyond the Mendip Hills, in the north of the county towards Bristol, is another very different area of small hills and broken countryside of confused geology, where every few miles a different sort of stone underlies the green fields. Among these humpy hills lie the Somerset Coalfields – small in extent and output when compared with South Wales or the Midlands but still productive into the twentieth century. The pits, now abandoned, gave rise to towns such as Midsomer Norton and Radstock with terraces of miners' houses standing as a reminder of Somerset's recent industrial past.

Along the southern boundary of the county around Yeovil and Chard lies an area of deep sandy soils where wheeled traffic along the lanes has in centuries past worn the surface down into gorge-like tracks, with vertical fern-clad sides studded with projecting concretions of harder sandstone called doggers. These deeply cut 'hollow ways' are a notable feature of a district which until the latter part of the nineteenth century, had for some 200 years, supported a cottage industry of flax cultivation and linen cloth production that resulted in largely heavy-duty sail-cloth being sent to Bridport, much of it for the Navy.

The vale country south of Taunton is abruptly terminated along the south county boundary by the high ridge of the Blackdown Hills whose north-facing scarp dominates the vale; too steep for agriculture, the hills are deeply wooded, marked at their highest point by the Wellington memorial which stands above the town as a fine pencil of stone to commemorate the Duke and Waterloo.

The Somerset scene is not all-of-a-piece. It comprises many different regions, each with its own very different landscape character, and therein lies the interest and beauty of the county. That this diversity is the outcome of the widely varied underlying rocks is obvious, but wherever you go in Somerset, with the exception only of the alluvial silts, clays and sands around Bridgwater, the land provided abundant stone for building, each region with its own recognisable stone that lends the houses their varying character.

In the following descriptions pride of place is given to stone, and this is quite right in such a stone-dominated county as Somerset. However, other building materials do appear; brick around Bridgwater and cob sporadically throughout the lowland areas, but chiefly in the south and west of the county near the border with Devon and Dorset where cob is far more at home. Both these materials are briefly described later in this chapter.

REGIONAL BUILDING STYLES AND MATERIALS[5]

The style of small traditional rural building throughout the greater part of Somerset is extremely simple, relieved by the varying colours and textures of the many different walling materials and roof coverings. The only notable departures from this rather austere character are in the extreme north-east and extreme west of the county, as will be described in their appropriate places in the account of the nature and distribution of building stones which follows the very generalised description below of the typical building style.

The straightforward appearance of the ordinary buildings of most of the county is striking. There are no deeply overhanging eaves or verges and few dormer windows; eaves are narrow, straight and uninterrupted; chimneys above the roofs are almost always built or rebuilt of brick, whether placed off-centre on the ridge or at the gable ends. Windows are stone mullioned wherever good freestone could be had (Plate 1).

Such houses as seen today are plain rectangular structures, mostly of two full storeys, their straight eaves parallel with the street. Houses from the medieval period, where an upper floor has later been introduced over an open hall, have a storey in the roof which requires dormer windows, but that is by no means general, nor is it how they were originally constructed. Any medieval upper room (or solar) was lit from an end window in the part-gable of a half-hip, not from the side.

Although there is no doubt that in medieval times the roofs of small houses were hipped or, more commonly, half-hipped at the ends, gables were introduced when end chimneys were added. Subsequently, gables became the pattern of building and it is rare indeed to see a sixteenth- or seventeenth-century Somerset house with anything but gabled ends. Until clay tiles (and later imported slates) became popular for their lightness and improved fire-proofing qualities, say from 1700 onwards, thatch was the universal roof covering except for stone tiles (for which see below). If the house had a storey partly in the roof space, the thatch was humped up over the low-set windows as 'eyebrows'. In good-sized farmhouses (and many still retain their thatch), this feature can be seen, almost the only one that contributes an element of cosiness to the Somerset building style (Plate 1).

Wings are usually, but not invariably, additions, built to accommodate a dairy or an extra parlour. Where the house was built L-shaped from the start, this can often be accounted for by a peculiarity of the ground, a cramped village site or by a special need, for example space for a weaving shop for woollen cloth, the normal domestic function being adequately served by the traditional three main compartments of hall or living-room, kitchen or service room and parlour, arranged in line along the main axis of the building.

But that description takes as its model the larger farmhouse and stresses its basic simplicity. The same by no means applies to the great houses of the wealthy or the grander manor houses. As is to be expected, such buildings follow the fashions of their day, taking full advantage of the decorative possibilities offered by the easily worked freestones in their many gabled skyline, their opulently carved chimneys and multi-light stone windows.

At the other end of the scale, small houses for artisans or smallholders were simple with one or perhaps two gable chimneys and plain verges. Yet even they, where sited near a freestone quarry, were often furnished with stone mullioned windows on the ground floor.

Stone[1]
(geology map fig. 1.3)

Building stone is abundant throughout the county, mostly of a quality suitable only for plain walling, and a number of the more easily recog-nised of these are described below, region by region. But first comes the three outstanding and well-known freestones of Somerset, stone that can be worked for all sorts of dressings such as windows and doorways, ashlar masonry, mouldings and fireplaces. Freestone is homogeneous and of fine grain.[2]

By far the best known of these is Bath Stone (Plate 2), a fine-grained creamy white or pale buff oolitic limestone from around the Bath area. The principal quarries in Somerset were south of the city near Monkton Combe, but the main quarries or mines lay north of the city in Wiltshire. The stone gives rise to many pleasant pale-coloured houses in the area, the walls of neatly squared stones, with coped gables and mullioned windows under stone dripstones or hood-moulds. (The city of Bath itself was entirely built of this fine stone which was perfectly suited to cutting the fashionable Georgian-style classical mouldings and details).

Second only in importance to Bath stone is Doulting stone (Plate 2) a coarser-grained, harder oolitic limestone from quarries at Doulting, which lies between Shepton Mallet and Frome in the east of the county. Suitable for cutting window mullions, fireplaces and all sorts of dressings, the stone weathers to a darker grey colour than Bath stone (although buff coloured when quarried) and lends a pleasant if more sombre appearance to the houses. The whole of this part of Somerset from Bruton and Wincanton to Frome has houses of Doulting stone. (Wells Cathedral and Glastonbury Abbey were both largely built of Doulting stone). Plain walling in smaller buildings, as in other freestone areas, is made of rougher stone taken from the less perfect strata and from small local quarries.

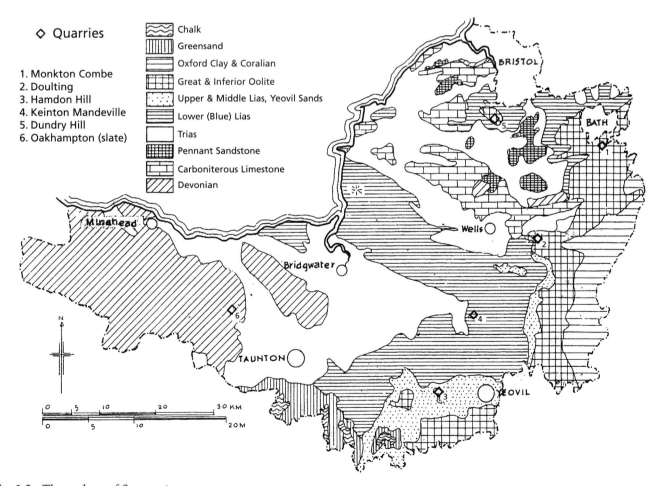

Fig. 1.3 The geology of Somerset.

The third important Somerset freestone comes from the Upper Lias, quarried on Ham Hill or, as on the OS map, Hamdon Hill, which lies midway between Yeovil and Ilminster. This is a conspicuous, outstanding hill where stone has been quarried from Roman times to the present day from within a huge Iron-Age fort. This so called Hamstone richly deserves its high reputation, not only for its ease of working but even more for its incomparable appearance (Plate 2, Plate 3). The stone is a rather sandy-looking limestone, immediately recognisable for its distinctive colour; a light, golden orangy brown that lends such a warm glow to the villages as to give the whole area a comfortable welcoming look, neither so bright as its south Dorset counterpart nor so harsh as the deep reddy-brown of the iron-rich Northamptonshire scarplands. Hamstone window mullions and coped gables are a feature of village houses over a wide area around the hill and within a few miles of the quarries, the stone is used for walling as well, mostly in coursed and squared rubble. (The huge mansion of Montacute House was built entirely of this stone in about 1600 and is of ashlar masonry throughout.) All these features give the buildings within some miles of the quarries that air of quality and prosperity so evident throughout the limestone belt that runs from Dorset to Yorkshire.

Apart from the three outstanding freestones there is an enormous variety of stone used in buildings of all sizes across the county and only a few can be mentioned here.

The most important stone which dominates central Somerset is the Blue Lias (Plate 2, Plate 3), a hard, heavy intractable grey limestone from the Lower Lias which is dug from the ground almost anywhere in a huge arc between the Mendips and the Blackdowns, its most renowned quarry being at Keinton Mandeville, east of Somerton. The stone lies naturally in thin slabs between thicker strata of clays and can be used for walling without further cutting to a useable thickness. It also makes ideal paviors and the ground floor rooms of most farmhouses were floored with these excellent flagstones. The appearance of the Blue Lias buildings is strikingly different from those in the Hamstone area; regularly coursed walls of a cool grey, pleasant in the sunshine but a little cold in overcast weather. No dressings can really be cut from Blue Lias, which is virtually impossible to carve, so windows are of timber except where Hamstone has been imported to make mullions and dripstones, popular in late-medieval times until well into the eighteenth century. The warm brown of the Hamstone contrasts sharply with the grey of the walls. The ancient town of Somerton is entirely built of Blue Lias (Plate 3), the more important of the older buildings with Hamstone dressings.

The southern and eastern parts of South Somerset are underlain by a series of varied limestones which run in an arc from Ilminster via Crewkerne, to Yeovil and Milborne Port, and north to Castle Cary and beyond. Although variable in quality, the stone is always buff or yellow and colours all the villages of the area, contrasting vividly with the grey of the Blue Lias villages further north. The stone quarried from the series includes the Marlstone widely used in Ilminster, the Inferior Oolite seen at Hinton St George, Milborne Port and Castle Cary, and the Forest Marble at Hardington Mandeville.[3]

All around the Quantock Hills and Taunton lies a wide band of red Triassic Sandstone (Plate 3, **Gatehouse, Combe Florey**). This sandstone colours the ploughlands a rich startling red and can yield a dark pinkish sandstone, not used here in such large rectangular blocks as it is in the Midlands, but in smaller more irregular pieces, the buildings seeming even redder for the use of red sand in the mortar joints. Near Taunton itself the stone is surprisingly coloured pale grey, sometimes quite greenish. This is a local anomaly called North Curry Sandstone.[4] The stone is used in some of the larger farmhouses in the area in fairly large rectangular blocks and is even-textured enough to be used for dressings. Quarries were near North

Curry and Norton Fitzwarren, the latter with a medieval church tower built of the stone.

The Quantock Hills themselves are of a much more ancient rock formation, Devonian or Old Red Sandstone, as are the Brendon Hills and Exmoor further west. These Devonian hills provide a variety of building stones; a variable darker red, pink or grey stone which is used in rough knobbly pieces along the north coast, (at **Porlock Weir**, for example) and, more generally, slatey rocks, some used in quite large slabs and some which split naturally into small rough pieces called 'shillet' (Plate 2). This makes for dark grey and dark brownish walls, often so rough as to need rendering in lime mortar, nearly always lime-washed white or buff. Whether built of sandstone or slatey rocks, the white and pale ochre houses are a traditional feature of the Brendon Hills and Exmoor, emphasising the Devon character of the West Somerset landscape and its buildings.

Indeed, here in the extreme west of the county we come to the first notable departure from the plain style of the usual Somerset house (Plate 4). Reinforcing the Devonian flavour of these hilly regions, instead of a central chimney punctuating the ridge, the main stack is sited externally next to the front door. These tall, shouldered lateral stacks are free-standing above the eaves as slender tapering stalks of masonry or brick, their broad bases, especially where there is in addition a protruding oven, crowding against the entrance on one side and constricting the size of the hall window on the other. That this prominent feature became something of an exotic status symbol is hardly in doubt, and houses here and further south in East Devon, were built on this plan at least until the eighteenth century. The lateral stacks are always built in stone up to the eaves level, above that, sometimes in stone but quite often in brick. In some of the older houses the chimneys are rounded, presumably a product of the difficulty of making rectangular corners in rough stone or shillet. It is also possible that these chimneys were deliberately built rounded to make an even greater visual impact; **Bossington**, near the north coast, is a typical example of a village street dominated by its tall lateral stacks (Plate 4).

As well as shillet, true slates occur in the south part of the Brendons, and were quarried at Oakhampton, north of Wiveliscombe and further west at Treborough. These slates are grey with a distinctive silvery sheen of mica, and can still sometimes be seen as roofing and wall cladding. (A famous example is the **'Nunnery' at Dunster**).

Over to the north-east of the county, the Mendip Hills are of Carboniferous Limestone, a hard mauve-grey rock that was not much used as a building stone but can be seen in a few houses of the area, more often in field boundary walls, typically in the village of Priddy. Along the fringes of the limestone hills, the Triassic rocks assume a deeper red and are sometimes in the form of rough conglomorates. Highly coloured stones like these can be seen in nearby villages.

North of the Mendips is a coal-bearing area of confused geology that provides such a variety of different stone as to defy any simple description. One of the few building stones of note is an oolitic freestone from Dundry Hill whose limestone quarries colour the surrounding villages with their mid-greys and provided good freestone for the medieval buildings of Bristol, notably the famous church of St Mary Redcliffe. In the coal-mining area around Radstock and Midsomer Norton the Lower Lias again appears in the form of White Lias, from the very lowest part of the series where the stone is almost pure white.

In the eastern part of Somerset south of Bath and down to Frome along the border with Wiltshire, the Oolite predominates and provides the second important departure from the simple style of most of the county. Here the stone is very much like the Cotswold limestone, but not quite so attractive as that of the true Cotswolds, cooler and less honey-coloured. However, the stone does give rise to very similar architecture, the many-

High Street, Norton St Philip.

High Street, Beckington.

Fig. 1.4   Cotswold style, gabled dormers in North Somerset.

Manor Farmhouse, Long Load.

The Pottery, Muchelney. Note the eyebrows over inserted first-floor windows.

Plate 1   Building styles: the farmhouse.

Hamstone.

Doulting Stone.

Red Triassic Sandstone.

Bath Stone.

Blue Lias.

Devonian Shillet.

Plate 2   Building stones

No.1 The Borough, Montacute; coursed Hamstone rubble.

The Gatehouse, Combe Florey; Triassic rubble.

Market Square, Somerton; Blue Lias limestone.

Plate 3   Contrasting stones.

Porlock Village.

Porlock Weir.

Bossington, a stack with an oven.

Plate 4   Lateral chimney stacks in West Somerset.

gabled style with large gabled dormers, stone-tiled roofs and mullioned windows being strongly reminiscent of South Gloucestershire (fig. 1.4). As in the rest of Somerset, the village houses are built parallel to the street but are provided with one or more wide cross-gables, in fact huge dormer windows, built up in stonework in the same face as the main house, their stone slated roofs often rising to the height of the main ridge. The style is indeed an overspill from the Cotswold tradition which was probably developed to create a large attic space for a weaving loom. (This part of Somerset was famous for its late-medieval and post-medieval woollen cloth production.)

Finally comes Chert, a form of flint, here from the Greensands of the Blackdown Hills whose steep north-facing scarp forms a prominent part of the south-western county boundary with Devon. Chert is paler and less translucent than true flint and is used 'as found', in small irregular pieces laid with a good deal of mortar in plain walling, its whiteish small-sized stones being quite distinctive. Larger pieces can, for expensive work, be split and dressed as small squarish blocks, the shiny pale brown-grey split surface facing outwards, to form a variety of knapped flint walling, seen to perfection in the **Grammar School at Chard** (fig. 1.5).

Fig. 1.5. Knapped Chert.

The geological map (fig. 1.3), shows the broad outline of the formations referred to above with some of the principal quarries indicated. The blanket of alluvium and peat which covers the Levels obscures the underlying geology and their general extent is shown on the topographical map (fig. 1.2). The use of Blue Lias rubble stone from adjoining hills is typical throughout this area.

The building stones referred to above are more concisely shown on the chart (fig. 1.7).

Cob[5]

After stone, Cob is an important traditional walling material. Cob is the west of England name for mass walling in unfired earth. The mix varies according to the nature of the soil but generally is of clay-like earth compacted and liberally mixed with grit, pebbles, straw and dung. The soil is built in layers up to 30cm (12ins) thick, trodden down layer by layer. As each layer has to dry out before the next is laid, the process is a slow one. Where the protective coating is missing, the layers can sometimes be seen, marked by thin courses of straw which was spread to help the drying process and to keep off the rain. Cob walls are thicker than stonework, 70 to 90cm (2ft 8ins to 3ft) and sometimes as much as a metre at the foot. They are always built to taper slightly, thinner at the top, the difference showing up as a pronounced batter or outward slope on the inside, the outer face being kept vertical or nearly so (fig. 1.6).

When the walls are finished they are given a coat of plaster and/or limewash as a protection. Indeed, cob walling must be kept dry or it will soon disintegrate, so it is always built on a plinth of stone, a foot or two high, and the roofing thatch is built with a generous overhang to throw the drips clear of the footings.

Cob buildings have a distinctive character; a certain indeterminacy of outline, walls not quite straight, corners tending to be rounded. Walls are rendered or limewashed, doorways and windows are of wood. Chimneys are of stone or brick, more often than not limewashed with the rest of the building. Cob walls are often replaced with stone, particularly on the front walls but this is not always apparent when rendered. (**Higher Somerhill Farmhouse, Brushford, Dulverton**, a small medieval open hall house, fig. 1.6).

Houses built of cob, or revealing even a fragment of former cob construction, lie south and west of a line drawn from around the Parrett estuary to Wincanton; north and east of the line there are virtually none. The villages of Stocklinch and Barrington are particularly rich in cob buildings.

Fig. 1.6 Higher Somerhill Farmhouse, Brushford, Dulverton.
(CLARE AUSTIN)

Building Stones of Somerset

Name (Geological Formation)	Colour and Type	Location and Notes	Principal Quarries u = universal locally
CHERT (Greensand)	Horny white & yellow, a form of flint	Blackdown hills and immediately north	u
OOLITE (Great and Inferior Oolite)	Variable grey-yellow to a buff limestone	East and south Somerset and east of Crewkerne (similar to Cotswold stone)	u
BATH STONE (Oolite)	Pale fine-grained cream limestone, freestone	North and south of Bath and throughout the city	Box (Wilts.) Monkton Combe (Som.)
DOULTING Stone (Oolite)	Darker grey, grainy limestone, freestone.	Used over a wide area around Doulting; Wells Cathedral and Glastonbury Abbey	Doulting, SW of Frome
DUNDRY Stone (Oolite)	Mid-grey limestone, freestone	Small area south of Bristol	Dundry Hill
HAMSTONE (Upper Lias)	Golden brown limestone, freestone	Hamdon Hill near Yeovil used for miles around	Hamdon Hill
BLUE LIAS (Lower Lias)	Cool grey intractable limestone, coursed	Occurs from Brent Knoll to the Blackdown Hills	Keinton Mandeville and u
WHITE LIAS (Upper Trias or Rhaetic)	Almost pure white	Near Radstock and west of Bath	u
NEW RED SANDSTONE (Trias)	Soft variable red or greenish-grey sandstone	From all around Quantock Hills, Taunton and Mendips	u
OLD RED SANDSTONE (Devonian)	Darker red and pink sandstone	Quantocks, Brendons and Exmoor.	u
SHILLET (Devonian)	Small pieces of grey brown slatey rock	Brendon Hills and Exmoor	u
SLATE (Devonian)	Grey with silvery sheen	Brendon Hills, north of Wiveliscombe	Oakhampton Treborough

Fig. 1.7   The chief building stones in Somerset.

Brick

For a short time in the late-seventeenth century brick became a prestigious building material in Somerset, as it did in some other stone counties, and one can occasionally see rich landowners' farmhouses, even in the Hamstone area, faced with red brick even though they have stone back and sides.

Brick as a walling material has to take third place after stone and cob since it did not come on the scene until the mid-seventeenth century and in any case had a limited geographical range until far later. The industry was centred at Bridgwater owing largely to the town's excellent communications by water, up the River Parrett and its tributaries and along the coast. Bridgwater has abundant supplies of clay nearby and no easy access to building stone, hence in earlier times, cob was used a good deal in this area.

The earliest wholly-brick building in Somerset is generally believed to be **Gray's Almshouses, Taunton** (1635). This imposing two-storey building, with a long row of huge chimney stacks, was built in the Jacobean tradition with stone mullioned windows and stone moulded entrance doorways. Other large buildings, such as the Stable Block at Barrington Court followed (built in 1674 along more Classical lines). Although there were some smaller brick buildings erected during the latter years of the century it was not until the eighteenth century that bricks were produced in any quantity (see **Ashford Farmhouse, Ilton**, fig. 1.8).

Prior to the factory-made bricks from the brickyards which came into use late in the seventeenth century, bricks were made 'on site', or as near as possible to where they were to be used. Such sites were temporary, the bricks being fired in clamps (not unlike clamps made for roots or potatoes), but by the end of the eighteenth century the permanent brickyards were using properly built kilns, including many yards in Bridgwater and a few in other towns such as Wellington, Taunton and Bishop's Hull[5].

By the nineteenth century, good canals, far better roads and later, railways, permitted widespread expansion in the use of bricks. But at least until the First World War (and with the exception of the Bridgwater area itself) the great majority of rural Somerset houses were still built in stone.

Fig. 1.8 Ashford Farmhouse, Ilton. Note the fashionable brick built façades that date from c.1700.

(G. ROBERTS)

Timber

Oak and elm: these are the two timbers used in Somerset houses, either severally or together. For example, some jointed crucks have oak posts and elm principal rafters (see Chapter 3).

Timber for building in rural houses is confined almost completely in its use to roof and floor structures, framed cross walls, screens and partitions within the stone buildings (see Chapter 4), although a few remnants of timber framing in former external walls have been found in Taunton Vale (see Chapter 3). Much more in evidence are the many jettied timber fronts to town houses (Plate 15).

Thatch

During medieval times and at least until the eighteenth century all rural houses were either thatched (the vast majority) or stone tiled. Much thatch remains to be seen in the farmhouses and smaller dwellings of the countryside. In the towns thatch and stone tiles were used traditionally, but thatch has naturally been replaced by fire-proof slate or clay tiles.

The material used was either wheat straw or water reed, the latter longer lasting and of better quality. The thatch was originally supported on wattle, later on lathing, and in many medieval examples the underside of the thatch can be seen to be heavily smoke-blackened from the open fire. It is remarkable that the original fourteenth- and fifteenth-century thatch should have lasted so well, although, of course, the upper layers will have been renewed many times during the last five or six centuries.

Stone Tiles

Stone Tiles were an expensive alternative to thatch and are generally found only in relatively high status buildings in the Upper Lias and more particularly the Oolite areas. The 'pendle', the stratum from which the tiles are made, does not occur in Somerset rocks anything like so bountifully as it does in Gloucestershire and further north along the limestone escarpment. However, stone tiles can still be seen in some of the grander houses and, near the quarries, in more modest buildings too, such as in the village of Montacute next to Ham Hill and in the Oolite country further north, for example in Norton St Philip or Beckington.

Stone tiles are laid in diminishing courses from large stones at the eaves to very small stones at the ridge, a universal feature of limestone roofs wherever they occur. In some villages near the quarries, roofs can be seen with only a few courses of stone tiles above the eaves, the rest of the roof being built with other materials. These few courses presumably formed a damp-proofing for the top of the wall under original thatch. In Montacute there are several houses with many more courses of stone tiles reaching about halfway up the roof slope so, as this would make fixing the thatch extremely difficult, it is assumed that such roofs were originally wholly of stone (Plate 3). Away from the limestone quarries, stone was a prestigious roofing material that could only be afforded on high status buildings erected by the church or other wealthy landowners. The medieval housing project at Mells, erected by Abbot Selwood c.1460, was entirely roofed in stone tiles, although the houses themselves are not large.

Clay Tiles

Clay pantiles have a wide distribution over most of central Somerset and were very often used as a fireproof alternative to the traditional universal use of thatch. The industry at Bridgwater came into its own in the late-eighteenth century and from then on most farm buildings and many houses in Somerset were roofed or re-roofed in red pantiles.

Bridgwater produced clay tiles in great quantities, and the chief product was the pantile and its variants. Pantiles proper are 'S' shaped and are made to overlap at the sides as well as at the top. They are light in weight, quick to lay and fix and, above all they are fireproof when compared with thatch. Huge numbers of farm buildings were erected during the nineteenth century with pantiled roofs and present a delightfully colourful picture, especially when their rich red colour is in contrast with the cool grey of the Blue Lias. The clay, moreover, seems to have a great attraction for lichens which splash the red tiles with orange and grey. Other sorts of tiles were produced including Single Roman, Double Roman and Triple Angular (fig. 1.9). These tiles were used on houses all over the county during the nineteenth century when many thatched houses were re-roofed and many new houses were given clay roofs from the start.

Pantiles   Single Romans   Double Romans

Fig. 1.9 Pantiles, single Romans and double Romans.

Notes
1 For general reference: Hardy, P. *Geology of Somerset*, 1999, Ex Libris Press and Prudden, H. *Geology of Landscape of Taunton Deane*, 2001, published by Taunton Deane Borough Council.
2 Clifton-Taylor, A. *A Pattern of English Building*, 1987, Faber.
3 Personal communication, Hugh Prudden. See also his *Somerset Building Stones, a Guide*, SANHS Proc. 146, 2002.
4 See note[1], Prudden, H. (for Taunton Deane area).
5 Williams, E.H.D., *The Building Materials of Somerset's Vernacular Houses*, SANHS Proc. vol 135, 1991.

TWO

Archeological and Historical Influences

S omerset is a rural county represented by a varied farming landscape of considerable antiquity illustrated here, briefly, by references to some ancient sites that have farming and building associations. The more recent subject of the archeology of landscape helps our understanding of traditional houses set in their different forms of settlement. But our architectural interests in the domestic buildings must not stray too deeply into the large quantities of historical and archeological information which has become available in recent years, so this is a short chapter describing some of the highlights of the prehistoric and early-medieval periods.[1]

From the Neolithic period there are already indications of farming groups of people, clearing the woodlands and maintaining the trees, cultivating cereal crops and animal pastures. In the central Wetlands or Levels, people raised timber walkways across the peat moors between the Polden Hills and the island of Wedmore.[2] Using stone tools they constructed the earliest surviving structure, the Sweet Track, extending from Shapwick to Westhay, the timbers being dated by dendrochronology to 3806BC. Later tracks, some made of hurdles, were laid directly on the ground, providing routes for men and animals across the impassable marshes and access for fishing and hunting. Both Neolithic and Bronze Age people were skilled woodworkers, constructing timber post-built buildings.

In the early Iron Age, some 3,000 years later, a very different type of settlement existed in the water-logged marshes near Glastonbury and Meare (c.300BC). The sites were described as Lake Villages; at Glastonbury the settlement was on an island site with a palisaded enclosure and many round houses of timber and thatch. The occupants farmed on the nearby raised ground while making and marketing woven cloth, metal, glassware and pottery, all of a high quality. This was a very sophisticated community living on a highly unusual site, and making use of the rivers to the coast for trading with the Continent. The two Meare settlements were sited on the edge of the Meare Pool, a large inland lake, some miles west of Glastonbury.[2,3]

In the late Iron Age (c.50BC) the three dominant Celtic tribes occupying Somerset re-fortified the earlier hill-forts of South Cadbury, Ham Hill, Norton Fitzwarren and Brent Knoll. These sites could be used for defence and were probably also centres of trade and administration. Cadbury Castle itself was conquered by the Romans and enlarged in the post-Roman period, AD400–600, with a new rampart and a rectangular hall and associated smaller buildings.[4] The hall was a rectangular aisled structure, having irregular widely spaced wall posts, in the tradition of other excavated halls of the sixth century AD found outside Somerset. At that date Cadbury is considered by some to have had possible associations with Arthur, as a military leader, and has been suggested as one of several contenders for the site of Camelot.

The well-established Iron Age tribal system of the pre-Roman period and the powerful influence of the Roman occupation combined the two strong cultures, Celtic and Roman, making it difficult to identify the greatest influence. In Somerset the introduction of the Roman military road, the Fosse Way, constructed in AD49, linked the Midlands and the North with Exeter and the Dorset coast. The important town of Ilchester marks the intersection of the Fosse Way with another road leading to Dorchester in the south and to the port at Combwich on the Parrett estuary in the west (fig. 2.1). Ilchester was a new centre of activity, at first a fort and later a Roman town. Around it was a concentration of Roman villas and farms, which extended north into the hills round Somerton, along the Yeo valley to the Yeovil area and the Fosse Way towards the south-west. In the north the major Roman town of Bath was also surrounded with villas, while another group was centred on the coastal plain between the Mendip Hills and the Bristol Channel where the sea-marshes round Banwell had been drained by the Romans for their villa estates sited behind the sea wall.[5]

Villas and their estates were the homes of the aristocrats, both Roman and the Romano-British, but the inspiration for their villa buildings came from Rome. Villa plans are complicated, representing a series of rooms of different functions within the same building or group of buildings.[6] This was a new concept in British domestic planning and it is not seen again until the arrival of the high status medieval courtyard houses. The Anglo-Saxons preferred to build houses with separate functions under separate roofs.

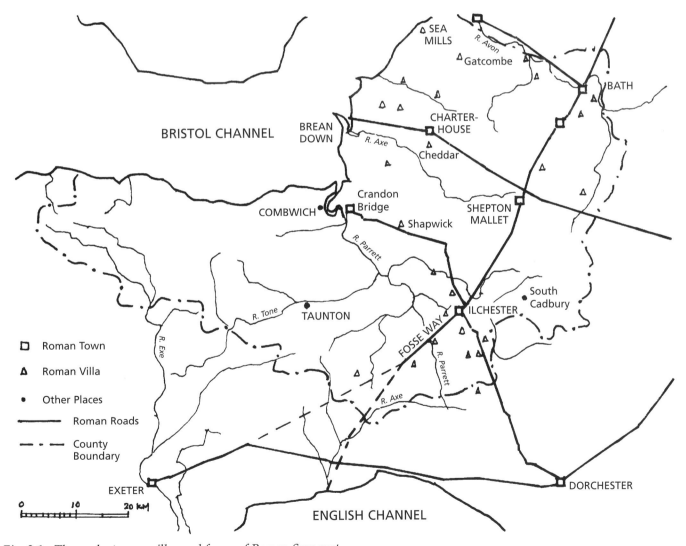

Fig. 2.1 The roads, towns, villas and farms of Roman Somerset.
(PETER LEACH, 2001)

More significant to the development of the Somerset traditional house plan are the Roman groups of small farmhouses. These excavated buildings were found near villas sites in the Ilchester and North Somerset areas.[7] The small buildings were family units of the fourth centuries AD, and marked the change from the prehistoric circular domestic houses found in most pre-Roman settlements to the rectangular form. The two or three-room houses were divided by a cross wall, the entrance being into the dominant heated room, the hall, while the smaller end room, or rooms, were for sleeping and storage. A group of houses and barns of the second and fourth centuries was excavated at Catsgore, Somerton. Built of Blue Lias stone with thatched roofs, the houses measured approximately 12m x 6m (40ft x 20ft) (fig. 2.2). Nearby at Bradley Hill, Ilchester there are two similar Lias stone houses and an attached barn of the fourth century. The windows had the refinement of Hamstone arches and the floor was made of hexagonal tiles. The farm was associated with many bones of both cattle and sheep implying a pastoral basis, with some enclosed fields on the hill. In North Somerset at Gatcombe another farm complex next to a former villa had three farms grouped beside a road, the main produce being cattle. It is clear that these farm groups were considered as the forerunners of the much later Saxon and medieval hamlets and farmhouses of Somerset.

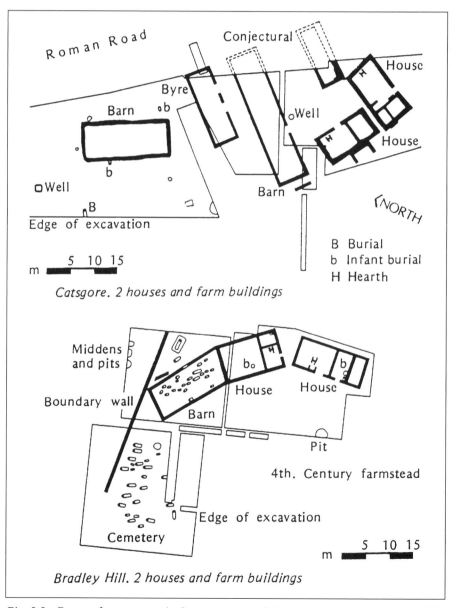

Fig. 2.2 *Roman farm groups in Somerset.*   (M.A. ASTON & I. BURROW, 1982)

Cheddar Palaces

Somerset was one of the four shires comprising the Kingdom of West Saxons (Wessex). From the seventh century onwards, there was a slow spread west-wards of Anglo-Saxon culture, so some evidence of new styles of domestic buildings in the West might be expected, but little has been found of the smaller houses on farms and villages, and society may by then have reverted to the pre-Roman Iron Age pattern. But in the higher status houses, like the **royal palaces at Cheddar**[8], excavations have shown that there were no less than seven different palaces spanning over four centuries, from the ninth to the twelfth, for both Saxon and Norman Kings visiting their Somerset estates. Although their timber-framed structures cannot be fully understood, they represented a very varied range of building techniques, at first using earth-fast posts and later a horizontal foundation.

Of the Cheddar group, the oldest is a royal ceremonial hall called the Long Hall (fig. 2.3). This was a timber structure of the ninth century with a very unusual plan – long and thin (24m x 6m) with slightly bowed side walls and opposed central entrances but no cross walls. The spacing of the wall posts is very close and some of these posts are paired, the inner ones raked. It has been suggested that this curious feature was the framing for an upper hall or gallery.[8] The long proportions of the hall are exceptional. In the tenth century the palace was rebuilt on a nearby site three times over. These West Halls were built with less exaggerated dimensions (approxi-mately 18m x 8m) with seven bays between the external wall posts. There were no 'aisle-posts' to help support the wider roof span of the vast timber-framed East Hall 1, which was built in the twelfth century in line with the last of the West Halls, its large size (33m x 16m) was at least helped by two rows of aisle-posts. Two more East Halls were built, the first aisled but the second, built by King John and described as his 'hunting lodge', although still large was built in stone, and was later divided into three units with a central large hall. These halls were used for large numbers of people following the early royal examples at Yeavering, Yorkshire (c.AD600), where the large aisled hall (31m x 17m) is accompanied by smaller single buildings used as bowers and storage rooms, all in line with the main aisled hall. This is a recognised form of Saxon planning, seen particularly in the Northumbrian monastic groups.[9]

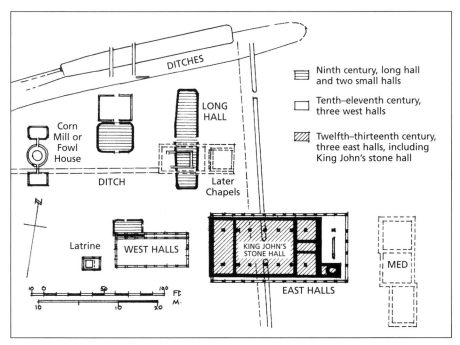

Fig. 2.3 Cheddar Palaces. (P. RAHTZ, *1964, 1979*)

In Somerset, the few Saxon halls which have been excavated at Cadbury Castle and Cheddar illustrate the tradition of the Open Halls, with their wide spanning roofs, seen later in the larger medieval Somerset houses (see Chapter 5).

The West Saxon and Norman royal palaces at Cheddar and the surrounding estate on the Mendip hills was only part of the scattered estates owned by the Crown in Somerset. Even larger were the holdings of the Church, which owned more than one third of the county in 1086.[10] Both the Bishop of Wells and the Bishop of Winchester, the latter with rich estates based on Taunton Castle, together owned much of the best agricultural land. But it was the monastic organisations who were even more powerful, Glastonbury Abbey in particular (fig. 2.4). They not only ran their estates and lives of their tenants with great efficiency, they also drained the Levels and re-directing the rivers to gain more agricultural land for summer pasture. But from our point of view they were also the inspired builders of many of the surviving domestic houses of the fourteenth and fifteenth centuries. These included Ecclesiastical Palaces, manor houses, grange farmhouses and tenants' cottages together with their plots of land in the villages and in the open fields.

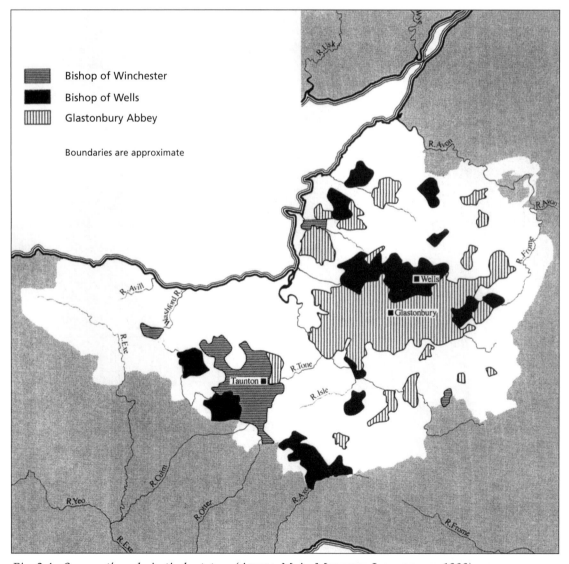

Fig. 2.4   Somerset's ecclesiastical estates. (ASTON, M.A., MEDIEVAL LANDSCAPE, 1988).

Settlements

The County is divided, East-West, by the low-lying areas of the River Parrett and its tributaries. To the West the poor soils of Exmoor, Brendons and Quantock Hills produce pastures and moorlands, where the farmsteads are isolated or grouped in small hamlets in the sheltered valleys. In contrast the central fertile farmlands of Taunton Vale and the more open country of South and East Somerset produced larger settlements and nucleated villages often with former medieval Open Fields. A similar settlement pattern occurs in the North-East of the county which is a mixed area of hill farming, quarrying and mining industries with market gardening supporting the many towns including Bath and Bristol, while the Eastern border with Wiltshire and Dorset combined farming with a cottage industry of cloth-making. In the central Levels area, because of the nature of the drainage, the settlements either lie on the small islands of higher land, or tend to straggle along the rivers and roads.

In the West of the county there are signs that the countryside was already organised with small farms and hamlets before the Anglo-Saxons came here in the seventh century. Unfortunately there is less chance of identifying a former site on the pastures of the western hills than on arable fields in the rich farmland of East Somerset. To get over this, some research by Professor MA Aston was done in the 1980's to find the sites and date the deserted farms on Exmoor and the Brendon Hills, by relating the surnames of the occupiers of the farms listed in the Lay Subsidy List of 1327 to the names of fields and farms found in later documents or maps. This resulted in locating some deserted or ruined sites, providing valuable information about the farm-steads in the fourteenth century.[11]

A recent study of Saxon place-names has also proved helpful, looking for habitation names like 'wick, cote, ton, worth or huish'.[12] If these names are compared to more recent field names shown on estate maps, then a possible site can be found. Some previously unknown sites have been recognised by this method in Shapwick parish with great success.[12, 14]

A study of the deserted villages of the Mudfords near Yeovil shows a very dense scatter of small hamlets, now mostly deserted, but indicating the high level of settlement in the richer farming localities.[13] These deserted units were either abandoned or replaced by larger villages, probably helped by the growth of the cloth weaving trade – a flourishing cottage industry of the south-east of Somerset, producing at first, woollen cloth, later fine linen and sail-cloth. Martock is a typical example of a composite village, formed of several different named smaller units; Bower Hinton, Newton, Hurst and the main village of Martock with its large church, manor-houses and many large farmhouses. There are other composite villages in the area, Queen Camel, Long Sutton, Barrington and Merriott and others.

There are also some examples of Planned Villages in the adjoining area as the composite ones. These are likely to be of the early medieval period, with regular rectilinear layouts of lanes and plots, the scattered houses lying parallel with the streets. Shapwick Parish has been exhaustively researched and a tenth century origin established, being one of many Polden estates owned by Glastonbury Abbey from the eighth century.[14] Shapwick village has an unusual ladder-like arrangement of roads, with the rectangular house plots mostly facing the cross lanes, with wider frontages than depth. The houses as we see them today are in the main detached, lying parallel with the roads. Other planned villages are recog-nised; Hinton St George, Long Load, Wearne and possibly Compton Dundon in the south-east and Bicknoller in Taunton Vale. These villages have the more usual medieval plan with narrow frontages and deep plots, reaching to the back lanes.[1, 13] Open Fields are often associated with planned villages and in Shapwick both the village and open fields were established at the outset.[14]

Notes

1 For general reference:
   Adkins, L. & R., *A Field Guide to Somerset Archeology*, Dovecote Press, 1992.
   Aston, M. & Burrow, I., *The Archeology of Somerset*, SCC, 1982.
   Aston, M. *Aspects of the Medieval Landscape of Somerset*, SCC, 1988.
   Bush, R., *Somerset, the Complete Guide*, Dovecote Press, 1994.
   Costen, M., *The Origins of Somerset*, Manchester University Press, 1992.
   Dunning, R., *The History of Somerset*, Phillimore, 1983.
   Leach, P., *Roman Somerset*, Dovecote Press, 2001.

2 Coles, J.M. & Coles, B.J., *The Prehistory of the Somerset Levels*, Somerset Levels Project, 1989.

3 Lake Villages Museum at The Tribunal, High Street, Glastonbury.

4 Alcock, Leslie, *By South Cadbury... is that Camelot*, Thames & Hudson, 1972.

5 Leech, R.H. & Leach, P. in Aston, M., *The Archaeology of Somerset*, SCC, 1982.

6 Quiney, A., *Traditional Buildings of England*, Thames & Hudson, 1990.

7 Leach, P., *Roman Somerset*, Dovecote Press, 2001.

8 Rahtz, P., *The Saxon & Medieval Palaces at Cheddar*, BAR no. 65, 1979 and *An Interim Report* in SANHS Proc. vol 108, 1964.

9 Barley, M. *Houses and History*, Faber & Faber, 1986.

10 Aston, M. ed., *Aspects of Medieval Landscape of Somerset*, Chapter 3, part 2 by J. Bettey, 1988.

11 Aston, M., *Deserted Farmsteads on Exmoor*, SANHS Proc., vol 127, 1983.

12 Costen, M., *The Origins of Somerset*, Manchester University Press, 1992.

13 Aston, M., *Aspects of the Medieval Landscape in Somerset*, SCC, 1988.

14 Aston, M., Hall, T.A. and Costen, M., ed; *The Shapwick Project*, p.27, 8th Report, University of Bristol, 1993.

THREE

Rural Houses: Farmhouses, Cottages and Village Houses

The vernacular buildings of Somerset, in particular the traditional rural houses, cottages and smaller manor houses, exhibit the regional style of the stone buildings of the south-west of England.[1] We shall be looking at the character of different types of buildings, starting in this chapter with the largest group, the small rural houses (farmhouses and cottages) and tracing their form and development through the medieval and post-medieval periods.

Medieval Houses

Some small domestic buildings standing today survive from the fourteenth and fifteenth centuries, and a few even exhibit features from the thirteenth century. These medieval examples are either isolated farmhouses or detached village houses, built by secular or ecclesiastical landlords, well-to-do farmers or gentry owners. It is normally the higher quality medieval buildings which have survived, while the early labourer's cottages are hard to find, probably having suffered neglect as well as being less well built. Somerset's medieval houses were built of stone or cob, some with cruck trusses embedded in their walls.[2] Many of our earliest tree-ring dated houses have cruck frames. Crucks can also be combined with timber-framed external walls, (the latter is seen more generally in the West Midlands, the Welsh borders and Southern England) but this type of walling is rare in the South West, except in the decorative façades of some fifteenth- and sixteenth-century town houses (see Chapter 6).

Descriptions of the various types of building materials have been given in Chapter 1, so it is sufficient to say here that the vast majority of houses both large and small, were built of stone, less often in cob. In the south and west of the county, where much of the cob buildings are found, the cob was often replaced by stone, particularly on the front wall. In the eighteenth century brick became fashionable in the farmhouses and was used generally in the nineteenth century in areas without stone.

Fig. 3.1 Forsters, Shapwick, a fifteenth-century hall house.

Late-medieval rural houses in Somerset, had long and low proportions, the early ones being of only one or one and a half storeys with the main room, the hall, open to the roof, its timbers and the underside of the thatch becoming heavily smoke blackened from the central open hearth. This hearth would have been the only means of cooking, heating and general lighting. The external appearance has changed very little except for the later addition of dormer windows and chimneys. At one end there was sometimes an upper chamber or 'solar' within the roof space, lit by a small window in the end wall. Such a house, with its 'Open Hall' is **Forsters at Shapwick** (fig. 3.1).

Traditionally, in a farming community, roofs were all thatched, as only the richer owners could afford stone tiles, and pantiles were not introduced until the eighteenth century. To begin with there were no chimneys or dormer windows to break the simple line of the roofs, which were often hipped or half-hipped at the ends giving these modest buildings their low and crouching appearance. The half-hip was preferred to the gable because of the inherent instability of a full gable with an unbraced triangle of masonry or cob above the eaves level. When later on, chimneys were built into the end walls, the thick stack gave ample buttressing to the gable at that end.

Somerset village houses were usually built lying parallel with the street, mostly free-standing and less often in groups like terraces, where the houses have individual designs or periods of build. Except for some hall windows, medieval windows were small, their frames made of timber with internal shutters instead of glass which was a very rare commodity at that time. In the better built houses, wherever freestone was available, stone mullions and surrounds with arched heads were used, occasionally embellished with trefoils or cinquefoils. More lavish decoration such as tracery was confined to special buildings, such as the **Priest's House, Muchelney**, built sometime in the fourteenth century, the traceried windows probably added later when the Abbey was dismantled (Plate 5).

Doorways were located on the long sides of the houses and very rarely at the ends, their broad and squat frames made of heavy oak and the door-head often cut in the form of a low arch. Some of the better built houses, especially those near to quarries, had the distinction of stone arched and moulded doorways, but in the earlier domestic buildings such sophisticated details are rare. Arched door-heads, whether in stone or timber, followed the well-established arch-forms of their century, **Priest's House at Farleigh Hungerford** (Plate 6) being a late-fourteenth century building. A more ornate example, at **Wick Farmhouse, Norton St Philip** (its roof timbers tree-ring dated by dendrochronology d.1372) was a grange farm of the nearby Hinton Priory built of the local Oolite rubble and heavy stone tiles, with a splendid contemporary two-centred arched and moulded stone doorway (Plate 6).

Research within the county has found only occasional examples of timber-framed external walling, usually in the wealthier rural houses. In the Taunton Deane estates of the Bishops of Winchester there are several large farms, such as **Higher Broughton Farmhouse, Stoke St Mary**, where a late-thirteenth century wall post has mortices for external timber framing, now rebuilt in stone (fig. 5.2). Other remnants of internal timber framing can be seen in the Taunton area.[3] The nearby Poundisford Farmhouse at Pitminster, formerly had timber-framed walls with curved braces buried internally now, and there are similar traces of timber in two other houses in Trull, both with a two-room plan. It is possible that these Somerset houses, associated with owners such as the Bishops of Winchester who were familiar with timber structures in Hampshire, were constructed with timber framing as a matter of course.

Another example in the north of the county, **Lodge Farmhouse, Norton St Philip**, had a first floor timber-framed gable wall, with a mullioned window and associated roof structure, d.1491. This was part of a small two-room house, later extended in stone and owned by the Hungerford family of Farleigh Hungerford Castle. It is thought to have been a small Keeper's Lodge in the park there, next to a stone-built Falconry, in the fifteenth century.

However, compared to the large numbers of stone houses, timber buildings were indeed rare, so until further research can produce more examples we prefer to think of the typical medieval small rural house as built of stone or cob in this county, but with timber-framed internal cross walls.

Post-Medieval Houses

In the post-medieval period, the sixteenth and seventeenth centuries, higher standards of comfort and space were required and medieval 'Open Hall' houses were adapted by the addition of fireplaces and chimneys, thus doing away with smokey open roofs and making it possible to add a chamber over the hall. By about the mid-sixteenth century, new farmhouses were built with two full storeys from the start with smaller and lower halls which nevertheless continued to function as the centre of the house. The flat ceilings in the hall, sometimes with decorative moulded beams and joists, replaced the open-roof timbers which continued to be exposed in the chambers above. By c.1600, the superior rooms had larger windows and stone fireplaces, the walls were covered with panelling, and flat ceilings were often decorated with patterned plasterwork in elaborate designs. All this combined to give a rich and impressive interior to all but the smallest farmhouse. For this was the period of Elizabethan and Jacobean wealth and love of decoration (see Chapter 4).

Post-medieval farmhouses were still generally built of stone and were longer and taller than before, the extensive thatched, or later pantiled, roofs often formed a 'cat-slide' down to the low eaves of a continuous outshot or extension at the back of the house, such as that adjoining the yard at Hamlyn's Farmhouse, Long Load (fig. 3.5). The gable ends were quite distinctive with two-light mullioned windows serving the ground and first floors and possibly an attic above. The tall gables were protected by stone copings, corbelled out at the eaves, with the chimneys dominating the elevation (Plate 7). Smaller cottages were also built of two full storeys but with only one heated room, the living-room/kitchen.

The presence of good local freestone (dressed stone) such as Hamstone, Doulting and Bath stone, made it possible for builders within a few miles of the quarries to include such high-quality features as mullioned windows and stone doorways such as Gatehouse, Baltonsborough (Plate 7). Further away from the freestone quarries, particularly in the west of the county and on the Somerset Levels, the walls were of local rubble-stone and the doors and window frames of timber.

After the Dissolution the former monastic landowners were often replaced by newly rich middle-class men; lawyers, yeoman farmers, merchants and lesser gentry folk wishing to build opulently for themselves and to erect practical houses for their tenants. New Renaissance ideas were emerging, in parallel with the increased wealth of the period. Thus the larger houses followed the styles of the Elizabethan and Stuart courtiers living in the area, with much use of stone in mullioned and transomed windows, two-storey porches with round arched front doorways and sometimes, elaborate chimneys, such as at **Manor Farmhouse, Middle Chinnock** and **Higher Rocke's Farmhouse, Butleigh** (Plate 7).

Whereas stone was still the most usual building material, from the early-eighteenth century onwards the new brick and tile industry at Bridgwater supplied bricks for fashionable façades. An early example was **Ashford Farmhouse, Ilton**, which was rebuilt in 1703, which still retains stone mullioned windows and a high stone plinth below the elegant arcaded brick walls (fig. 1.8). (This decorative brick arched feature is also seen in other local houses, so was probably a local builder's speciality.) Brick farmhouses are quite a rarity in the county and are no older than the late-seventeenth or early-eighteenth centuries, and from the beginning of the nineteenth century a good many farmhouses had their thatch replaced with pantiles also from Bridgwater. Pantiles of many interlocking designs can still be seen on some

BASIC MEDIEVAL PLANS from which post-medieval plans derive

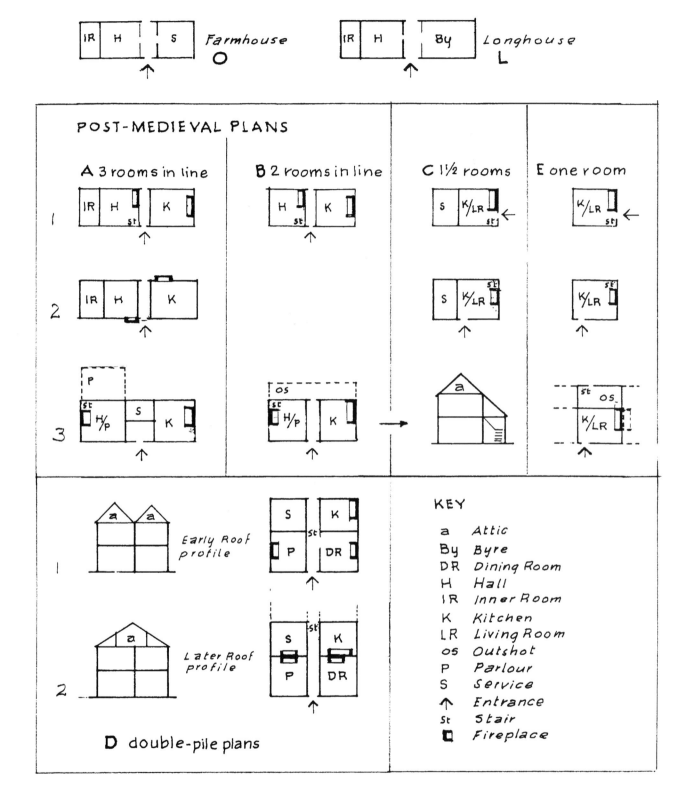

Fig. 3.2 *A diagram of typical ground-floor plans.*

South Cadbury Manor Farm, 'Cary stone' with grey lichen.

Above and right:
The Priest's House, Muchelney (National Trust). (PHOTO: G. ROBERTS)

Plate 5   Village houses in South Somerset.

Wick Farmhouse, Norton St Philip, d.1372. (J. McCann)

Priest's House within the walls of Farleigh Hungerford Castle.

Plate 6   Medieval houses in North Somerset, oolithic limestone walls and roof tiles.

Manor Farmhouse, Middle Chinnock. Note the seventeenth-century turrets.

Left:
Higher Rocke's Farmhouse, Butleigh, with a seventeenth-century two-storey porch.

Below:
Gatehouse, Baltonsborough, a medieval and seventeenth-century property.

Plate 7   Post-medieval additions, to earlier houses.

Symes Farmhouse, North Perrott. Note the eighteenth-century casement windows.

Queen's Arms, Kale Street, Batcombe, with transomed 'cross windows'.

Manor Farmhouse, Stratton-on-the-Fosse, has a seventeenth-century garden front.

Plate 8   The transition from the seventeenth to the eighteenth centuries.

cottages and farmhouses, replacing the original thatch, the discrepancy in the thickness of the two materials showing in the chimney weathering and gable copings which are left standing unnaturally high above the thinner tiles.

Chimneys in Somerset houses were built of stone originally, but most of them have now been rebuilt in brick above the roof line, although the houses themselves are all in stone. Evidently rough stonework could not stand the extreme conditions of heat from the smoke combined with exposure to the weather. Chimneys in the higher status houses were more often built, or rebuilt, in well-cut ashlar freestone (Plate 7).

In the eighteenth and nineteenth centuries another entirely new approach to design began to be fashionable. The symmetry and elegance of the classical style of Italy, France and the Netherlands had spread to the English country districts as well as the towns, and even the smaller houses and cottages presented a symmetrical front (**Symes Farmhouse, North Perrott**, Plate 8). This house still has the traditional casement windows, although with more generous proportions. Indeed, most smaller houses now have central entrances. The better class houses were designed with tall mullioned and transomed windows (later sashes) to suit the ceiling heights of the late Stuart and Georgian periods when the façade was an important feature, even in small houses such as the **Queen's Arms, Batcombe** (Plate 8). Inside, there was a change to smaller entrance halls or wide passages leading to rooms on either side, often with a balustraded staircase at the back of the hall. All the rooms were well lit with the tall windows giving a formality to the rooms, after the more irregular arrangements of the fifteenth and sixteenth centuries. **Manor Farmhouse, Stratton-on-the-Fosse**,[4] an estate of the Duchy of Cornwall since the fourteenth century and tenanted by the Long family of Trowbridge in the seventeenth century, was altered in this way. The fine house (Plate 8) has some ovolo moulded mullioned windows on the back range suggesting the remains of an earlier build, but the main front of the house introduces sash windows (two panes wide) and the central front door has a shell-hood with a coat of arms above, achieving an elegant 'Queen Anne' style façade.

HOUSE PLANS

Fig. 3.2 shows the development of plans in the area. This diagram should be read in two directions; horizontally for the size of the house (numbers of rooms) and vertically for the different positions of fireplaces, staircases and entrances.

In the past house builders were extremely conservative, keeping to traditional room layouts which varied only gradually over the centuries. This slow development of plan arrangement is recognisable throughout the whole country, with only minor local variations in the position of wings, entrances and chimneys. Farmhouses followed the examples of the lord's manor house, with the largest room, the hall, used by everyone, while the family and service rooms were smaller.

Medieval rural houses had their rooms arranged in a single line, usually two or three rooms along the front, originally allowing ventilation on both sides of the house, and shutters could be regulated as required against the weather. The width of the house from front to back was limited by an economic span of the roof structure. If the frontage of the houses was restricted, say in a village street, then additional rooms could be added as a single storey outshot or wing at the back. This arrangement of 'rooms in-line' did not change until the late-seventeenth century, when the 'double-pile plan', two-rooms deep was introduced. Town houses, however, were often restricted to narrow deep plots (Chapter 6).

The size of the house was obviously governed by the needs and social standing of the family for which it was built. These conditions did not change very much between generations, particularly in a stable agricultural community such as Somerset which enjoyed the long-term security of

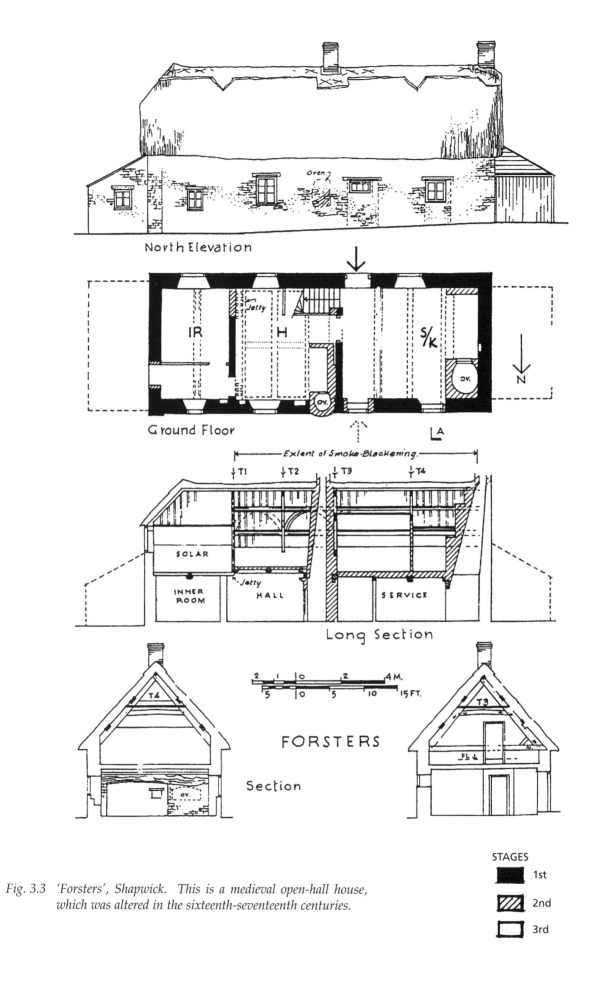

North Elevation

Ground Floor

IR H S/K OV. N

Extent of Smoke-Blackening.

T1 T2 T3 T4

SOLAR

INNER ROOM Jetty HALL SERVICE

Long Section

T4 OV.

FORSTERS

Section

T3

2 1 0 2 4M.
5 0 5 10 15FT.

STAGES
1st
2nd
3rd

Fig. 3.3 'Forsters', Shapwick. This is a medieval open-hall house, which was altered in the sixteenth-seventeenth centuries.

Copyhold and three-life leaseholds from the medieval period to the end of the eighteenth century. Indeed, in Dinnington, this system persisted until the early-twentieth century.[5]

Medieval Plans

In the west of England most farmhouses were long rectangular structures based on the traditional three-room plan arrangement, called here 'the farmhouse plan'; three rooms along the front of the house, sometimes called the tripartite plan (fig. 3.2, plan O). A good example is **Forsters at Shapwic**k, on the Polden Hills, a typical village farmhouse of the early-fifteenth century (fig. 3.3). A wide cross-passage divided the 'high end' (the family living quarters) from the 'low end' (service rooms or kitchen). The high end comprised a central hall and a smaller, often unheated inner room beyond it. This arrangement is described as the Open Hall plan, the hall originally with a central open hearth and the heavy roof timbers exposed and blackened by smoke. Sometimes there was an upper chamber or solar over the service end or, more often, over the inner room, where the first floor joists of the solar floor could be projected out over the ground floor partition into the open hall in the form of a jetty. This not only increased the size of the solar, but provided a distinctive feature, the overhang at the upper end of the Hall, Forsters, Shapwick (fig. 3.3).

Some early houses in the south and west of the area were built without first floor rooms, having only low partitions between the ground floor rooms, the open roof exposed to view throughout the length of the house. The arrangement occurs in Devon, and at **Lancin Farm, Wambrook**, on the Somerset side of the county border, where the former open hall had ground-floor partitions at a lower height than the later inserted floors (fig. 4.19).

In the medieval Hall House the hall was for family use, both for eating and sometimes for cooking in the smaller houses. It was a general living space, a place to receive visitors and discuss business and farming matters, it being the only heated space in the smaller houses. It would be furnished with a large table, benches and one or more chairs, according to the wealth of the family. The inner room was for private use, either for sleeping or storage – both these functions would move upstairs when chimneys were introduced and first-floor chambers were built. In the larger high status houses the service end of the three-room plan was divided into a buttery (for drink) and pantry (for food), while the kitchen with its large fireplace was either part of the service end or sometimes detached from the house, for fire protection. In fact, few examples of detached kitchens have survived in the smaller rural houses.

A version of the three-room plan, the Longhouse (fig. 3.2 plan L, and fig. 3.14), was used in a different way in the uplands of the west and north of England and Wales where a harsher climate and a pastoral tradition of farming dominated in the medieval period. The longhouse is a traditional three-room farmhouse where the animals were housed in a 'byre' in the long low end while the family lived in the upper end only – both humans and animals entering by the cross passage, which was wider than usual to accommodate the cattle passing into the byre. The longhouse can still be seen in parts of Devon, especially on Dartmoor,[6] but no unaltered longhouses have been found in Somerset today. Some features of the longhouse plans can occasionally be detected in farmhouses that have long since ceased to be used for animals. Distinguishing features are a sloping site for the byre drainage, a longer than usual low end below the cross passage which may also be at a lower level and sometimes with a stone dividing wall extending up to the roof on the hall side of the passage. Occasionally there are signs of a former byre's central drain, the outlet showing on the outside of the low end gable wall. Because in a longhouse, the family rooms were restricted to a hall and inner room, the presence of a service room or kitchen in an added wing at the high end, may also be an indication of earlier longhouse use, there being no

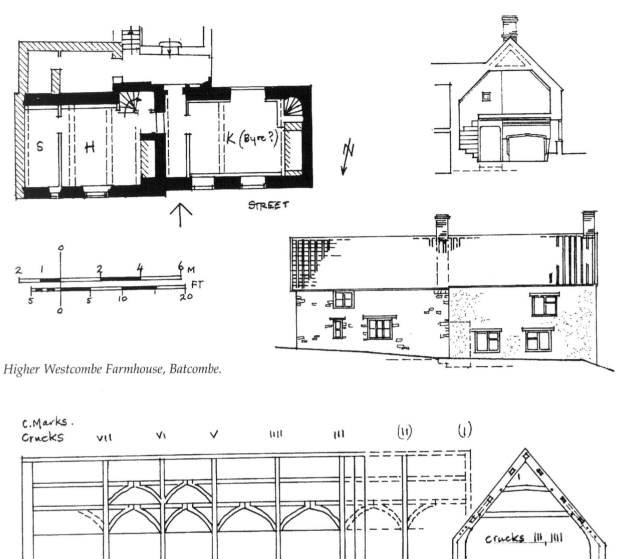

Higher Westcombe Farmhouse, Batcombe.

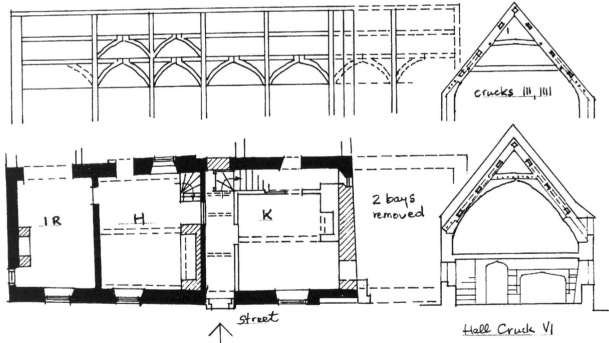

Nos 47 and 49 Goose Street, Beckington, d.1391.

Fig. 3.4   Houses with long low-ends; they had possible trade use.

low end available. A small post-medieval farmhouse, **Higher Westcombe Farm**, on the edge of **Batcombe** village (fig. 3.4) has some of these features, combined with a stone wall between the hall and cross passage. (For further examples of possible former longhouses see Roof Structures, later in this chapter, and fig. 3.14).

In the cloth-producing parts of the county, such as in the Shepton Mallet area and in north-east border towns including Beckington and Rode, the woollen cloth industry was traditionally a 'cottage industry', the areas producing a high quality 'broadcloth', as wide as 1.5m (60ins) and the looms were particularly large. As the service ends of the houses were extra long, they may have been used for trade purposes and weaving centres in the late-medieval period. (Perhaps one could call them 'industrial longhouses'?). This contrasts with the later flax weaving areas in South Somerset where sail-cloth was only 60cm (24ins) wide and was woven on narrow looms more suitable for a cottage industry. So, in the north we think that **47 and 49 Goose Street, Beckington** (fig. 3.4) may have been a woollen clothier's house and workshop but this is not confirmed by documentation. The cruck trusses in the former long service end were tree-ring dated d.1391 and the carpenter's marks imply that two bays are missing at the low end.

Although the three-room plans are the most common surviving medieval house type, occasionally the medieval two-room plan can be found, either with or without a cross passage between the two rooms (fig. 3.2, plan B and C). The larger room would have been an open hall with a central hearth, while the smaller room was used for sleeping or storage – a fairly basic arrangement. Some research has been done in the county to identify these rare two-room houses, which will have been greatly altered since the Middle Ages. In a comparison of about 100 surveyed medieval houses, only 18 were originally built with the two-room plan. Of these 18 houses, 11 had open halls, and 6 were tree-ring dated to the late-thirteenth and fourteenth centuries. So the majority of our surveyed medieval houses had the larger three-room plan.

Several houses in the village of Batcombe near Bruton were owned by named clothmakers in the post-medieval period. The Ashe family are known to have lived at **Lower Alham Farm, Batcombe**, (fig. 3.5) sited in the fold of the hills beside a stream serving several former fulling mills.[7] James Ashe was a famous seventeenth-century clothier, living at Lower Alham where he may have used a large unheated wing at the rear for a workshop for his weavers and for the storage of wool and cloth. He upgraded the living quarters in the mid-seventeenth century, adding an open-well staircase and large mullioned and transomed ovolo moulded windows, both fashionable features. Nearby at **Laburnham Cottage, Westcombe**, the George family, clothiers and dyers, lived in a small house of some quality, with a long service end which may have been a workshop and storage area. George George, in his will of 1539 left his furnaces and vats to his sons. These men were building up prosperous businesses, alongside their village houses, and in the case of James Ashe, he went on to found a much larger business at Freshford to extend his successful 'Spanish Cloth' industry.[8]

Fig. 3.6 The flax industry at Stoneways, West Chinnock.

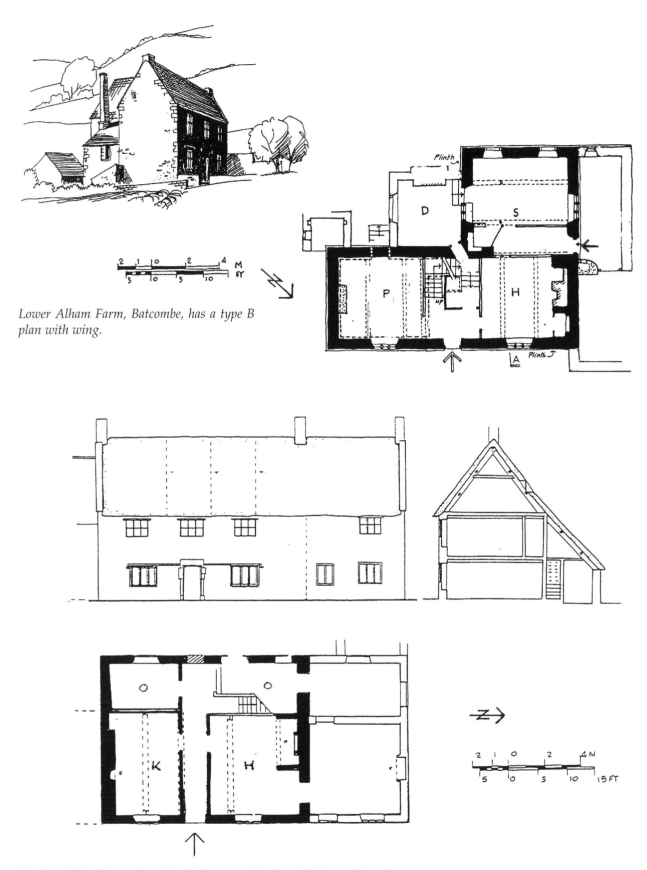

Lower Alham Farm, Batcombe, has a type B plan with wing.

Hamlyn's Farmhouse, Long Load, has a type B plan with integral outshot.

Fig. 3.5   Post-medieval farmhouses, with two-room plans.

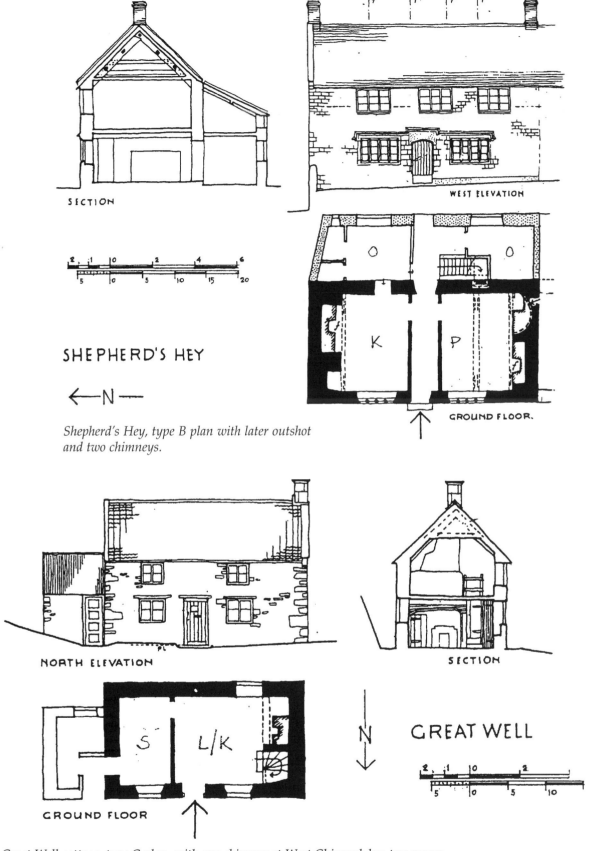

SECTION

WEST ELEVATION

GROUND FLOOR.

SHEPHERD'S HEY

←—N—

Shepherd's Hey, type B plan with later outshot and two chimneys.

NORTH ELEVATION

SECTION

GREAT WELL

GROUND FLOOR

Great Well cottage, type C plan, with one chimney at West Chinnock has two rooms.

Fig. 3.7   West Chinnock Cottages with two rooms.

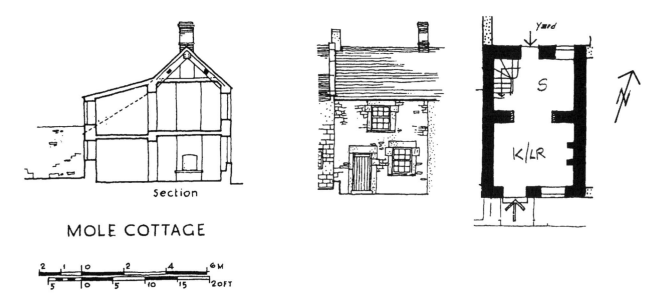

Section

MOLE COTTAGE

Mole Cottage, Batcombe, a nineteenth-century terrace.

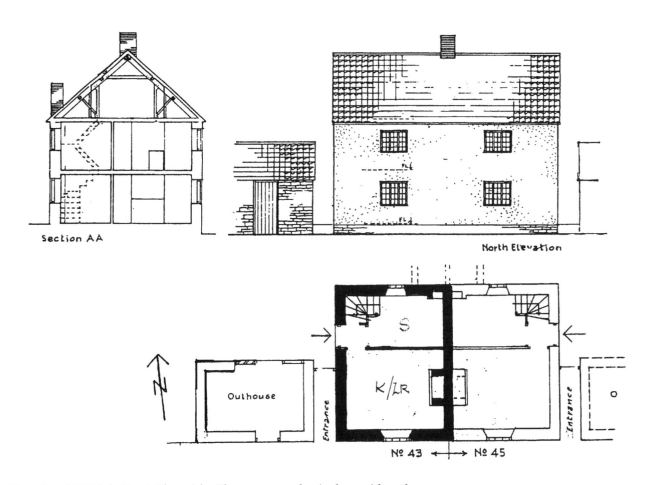

Section AA

North Elevation

Nos 43 and 45 High Street, Shapwick. There are several pairs here with outhouses.

Fig. 3.8   One-room plans, type E3, suitable for terraces and pairs.

Post-Medieval Plans
(fig. 3.2)

Returning to the general run of domestic houses of the sixteenth and seventeenth centuries; without altering the basic arrangement of the three-room plan, chimneys and fireplaces were introduced, either as additions to existing houses or as built-in features of newly erected ones. This made it possible to floor over the hall to give extra bedchambers. **Forsters at Shapwick**, built in the fifteenth century, illustrates this phase, with fireplaces and first floors added in the sixteenth and seventeenth centuries (fig. 3.3). The first stage towards a built-in fireplace was often in the form of a large smoke-bay (fig. 4.16). Where stone fireplaces were installed from the first, they were built in prescribed positions in the South West; the hall fireplace, almost invariably backed onto the cross passage and the larger kitchen fireplace was built on the low-end gable wall, the fireplace often with a newel staircase beside it in the thickness of the chimney breast (fig. 3.4).

However, in the west of the county, towards the Devon border, the external lateral chimney stacks are a notable feature on the front of the houses (fig. 3.2, type A2) and are seen in the houses at **Bossington and Porlock** (Plate 4), projecting forwards, often with a bulging oven attached, and capped by a tall 'stalked' chimney stack. In larger houses lateral stacks sometimes occur on the back wall of halls and were a recognised status feature.

Post-medieval requirements demanded more space in the home and a higher degree of comfort. This resulted in improved kitchens, although the hall was still being used as a general space and the inner room was still reserved for the family, either as a bedroom or a parlour. Upstairs some of the chambers or attics were often used for farm storage purposes as well as for sleeping. The rooms were arranged without corridors, one room opening into the next giving little privacy.

Another three-room plan, the Central Service Plan (fig. 3.2, type A3) was introduced in the seventeenth and eighteenth centuries having the main rooms at each end of the house, a central entrance and behind it a small unheated service room, sometimes used as a dairy in this county of many dairy farms. It is, however, more usual to find a dairy with cheeseroom above, in an added wing. That said, the central entrance plan is a late development when the priority for symmetrical front entrances overtook the long tradition of off-centre cross passage.

In other parts of England, particularly the south-eastern counties and the Midlands, it is quite common to find a three-room plan with an entrance lobby next to a pair of back-to-back fireplaces built in place of a cross passage. The Lobby Entrance Plan (not illustrated) is very compact, with its characteristic single central stack often seen in Kent and Sussex. In Somerset this type of plan is rarely found and where it occurs the fireplaces are likely to have been added into a former cross passage.

From the sixteenth or seventeenth century onwards, partly in response to the desire for symmetry, smaller houses were built with two-room plans (fig. 3.2, B) having a central entrance passage and two heated rooms, a parlour and a kitchen, with gable chimneys at either end. If a third room was required a wing or outshot under a lean-to roof would be added at the back (**Shepherd's Hey, West Chinnock**, fig. 3.7). This plan was particularly suited to village sites, where the length of frontage was often restricted for economic reasons. Here the newel stair is in the traditional place, next to the fireplace but was more usually placed at the back of the entrance passage. **Hamlyn's Farmhouse, Long Load** (fig. 3.5) is one of many seventeenth-century farmhouses in the area having an integral outshot running all along the back of the two-room house, to provide plenty of service space. The wall between the front part of the house and the outshot was often timber-framed. In the prosperous farming area around Martock in South Somerset some of the houses have tall covered wagon entrances between the house and the barn,

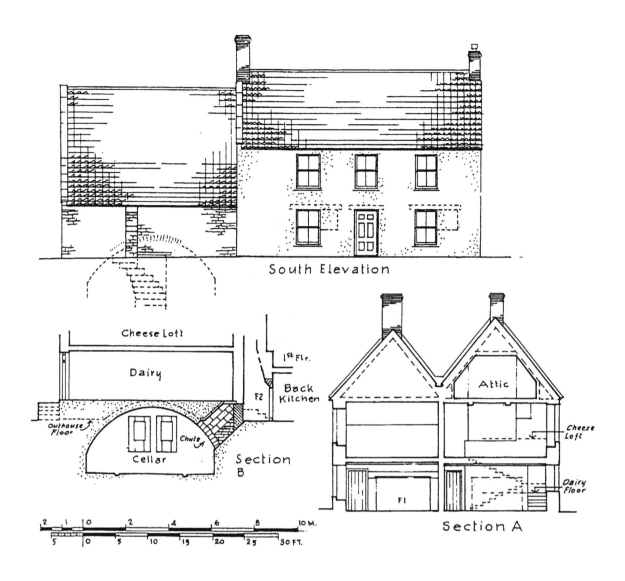

South Elevation

Cheese Loft

Dairy

1st Flr.

F2

Back Kitchen

Outhouse Floor

Chute

Cellar

Section B

Attic

Cheese Loft

Dairy Floor

F1

Section A

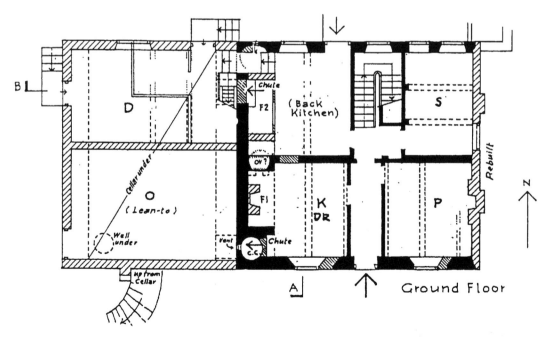

Ground Floor

Fig. 3.10 New Farmhouse, Shapwick, a double-pile house plan, type D1.

leading through to the yard. Such houses can be seen lining the streets in Long Load.

Smaller two-room houses (type C) had only one chimney and one heated room, the kitchen-cum-living-room next to a small service room, the entrance being either into a lobby beside the gable fireplace or, more often, directly into one of the two rooms (fig. 3.2, C). The smaller room was used for storage with the bedrooms upstairs approached by a winding stair next to the stack. These small houses usually of the late-seventeenth century onwards, are quite common in villages. The very small **Great Well Cottage at West Chinnock** – it faced the village well (fig. 3.7) – is a pleasing eighteenth-century example and is so small that one ascends the newel staircase next to the stack with some difficulty.

Single-cell plans (type E) are very rare survivors in Somerset, one exception being a small seventeenth-century cottage in Haselbury Plucknett, which has a single room with a porch at the back and a chamber above.[9] In villages, however, houses with a one-room frontage, but two rooms deep, are well suited for pairs of cottages or terraces, such as were often built in the eighteenth and nineteenth centuries (fig. 3.2, E). The front room was the living-room with the kitchen at the back. **Mole Cottage, Batcombe,** (fig. 3.8) is a very small house, and is part of a stone terrace built in 1827 perhaps for the silk weavers working for the factory opposite. In the nineteenth century pairs of artisans' cottages in **High Lane, Shapwick** (fig. 3.8) were built on the 'waste' (common land) along the roadside. This is a group of eight small semi-detached cottages with their entrances at the side, opposite a separate outhouse, one for each household – a very neat design for a country lane.

In the seventeenth and eighteenth centuries it became fashionable in the larger houses to build a double-pile plan (fig. 3.2, type D). This symmetrical plan had two rooms along the front, probably a parlour and dining-room, and two at the back, the kitchen and other service rooms, making a deep and approximately square plan, where at least three rooms were heated. The entrance and stair hall was central and the roof space was used for attic bedrooms and storage. Early double-pile houses have their front and rear ranges separately roofed with a valley gutter in between (**New Farmhouse, Shapwick**, fig. 3.10). This good-quality house was built for a gentleman in the early-eighteenth century, with an elegant Georgian staircase and thin panelled doors (the house was named 'New Farm' in a 1795 Estate Survey). A large service wing was introduced for farm use in the nineteenth century. In the fully developed late-eighteenth and nineteenth century forms, the whole double-pile house was roofed under one wide span (fig. 3.2, type D, sections) thus avoiding the awkward guttering between the parallel roofs. The plan was very suited to large farmhouses, where extra wings at the back would accommodate many servants and farmworkers, or dairies with cheeserooms above.

Fig.3.9 Balster's Barn, West Chinnock, a former jointed-cruck barn.

ROOF STRUCTURES

The comparatively new science of dendrochronology is now used for dating timber structures. This is a scientific study based on the analysis of the irregular patterns made by the way the annual tree-rings are spaced (good years and bad years) compared with similar patterns in living trees and other examples where the date of the structure is known. Very many examples throughout the whole country have been examined in this way to form a basis for comparison. Oak is the only timber with an established database so far, which means that many houses cannot be tree-ring dated because, at least in Somerset and Devon, their roofs are so often made of elm or fast-grown oak with too few rings.

Tree-ring dates refer to felling dates of the trees and not actual building dates, but in the great majority of cases the roof timbers were used green rather than seasoned and therefore it can be assumed that the building was

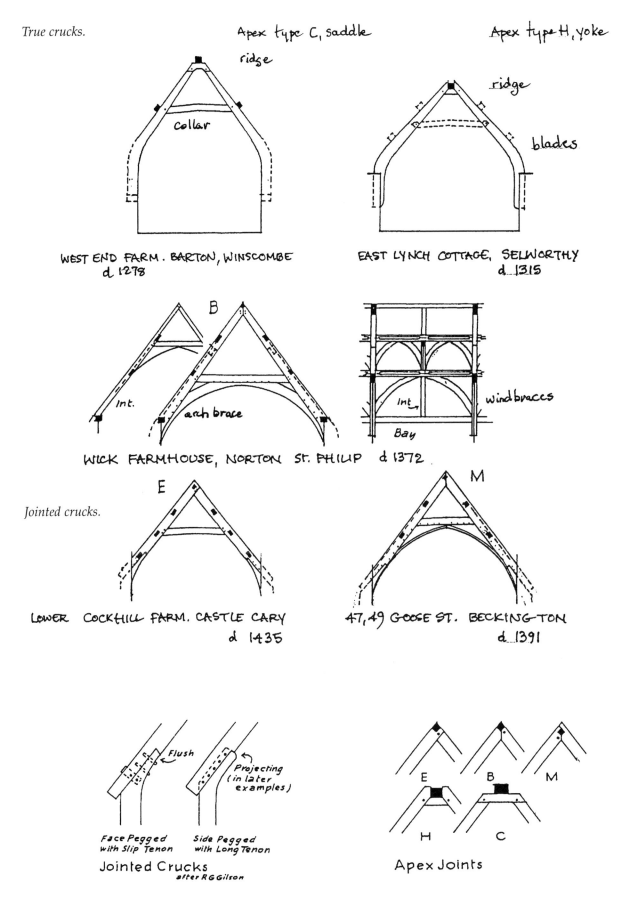

True crucks.

Apex type C, saddle
ridge
collar

WEST END FARM. BARTON, WINSCOMBE
d 1278

Apex type H, yoke
ridge
blades

EAST LYNCH COTTAGE, SELWORTHY
d 1315

B
Int.
arch brace

Int.
Bay
windbraces

WICK FARMHOUSE, NORTON ST. PHILIP d 1372

Jointed crucks.

E

LOWER COCKHILL FARM. CASTLE CARY
d 1435

M

47,49 GOOSE ST. BECKINGTON
d 1391

Flush
Projecting
(in later
examples)

Face Pegged
with Slip Tenon
Side Pegged
with Long Tenon

Jointed Crucks
after R G Gilson

E   B   M
H   C

Apex Joints

Fig. 3.11 Comparison of cruck trusses, apex joints and jointed crucks.

erected within a year or two of the felling date. Where sapwood is absent in the sample, a range of felling dates are given. In this text, dates prefixed 'd' are established by tree-ring analysis, those prefixed 'c' are estimated dates based on stylistic comparisons of types of building. In recent dendrochronological investigations in Somerset some 40 or so roofs have been successfully tree-ring dated, which helps to confirm a chronological order for the different designs of roof discussed.[10]

Medieval Period

No domestic roof structure from before the late thirteenth century has so far been dated by dendrochronology in the county. There is archeological evidence for post holes in the ground in timber structures at the Saxon royal palaces at Cheddar and elsewhere, while the nave roof at Wells Cathedral has been tree-ring dated to d.1213.[11] That roof is a 'common rafter roof', a form of early roof without trusses. The type occurs particularly in the south and east counties of England. However, apart from some church roofs, the type is not seen in domestic structures in Somerset, except in one isolated example, **Lodge Farmhouse, Durston**.[12] Instead, we find a strong tradition of cruck trusses, where the roof is divided into bays longitudinally by the substantial cruck trusses, in contrast to common rafter roofs, with no bays.

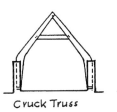 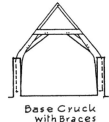 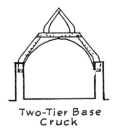 

Fig. 3.12 Typical profiles of Somerset roofs.

Cruck Truss   Base Cruck with Braces   Two-Tier Base Cruck   Arch-Braced Collar Truss

Cruck Roof Construction
(figs 3.11, 3.12)

Somerset shares with its neighbour Devon a particularly good medieval tradition of roof construction, Devon having some splendid rich decorative examples. Both counties use cruck trusses and decorative arch-braced roofs over their open halls, together with exposed timber-framed cross walls and stone external walls. Their design is fairly consistent, the elbow shape of the cruck blades allowing some scope for headroom when first-floor rooms were added later. Our dated examples include true and jointed crucks in smaller houses (described in this chapter) and the more elaborate base crucks in the wider spanning high status houses (see figs 5.3, 5.4 and 5.7 for distribution maps and a list of dated cruck roofs).

The origin of crucks is a matter of some speculation. Examples seen in France, the Netherlands and Germany are small in number compared with English and Welsh examples and are often later in date. It is possible that influences could have travelled both ways between these countries and England, but with the large numbers of crucks surviving here and also mentioned in documents, it seems that the design is more likely to have originated in the west and central regions of England.[13]

The West Country crucks are not like the more primitive-looking crucks seen in the West Midlands and Northern England (the blades shaped in one continuous curves from base to apex). Somerset cruck roofs have low eaves with the roof trusses in the form of pairs of cruck blades, elbowed at eaves level and forming an unobstructed arch shape over the open halls (figs 3.12, 3.13). Crucks were very suited to this purpose, having no horizontal tie-beams at eaves level to obstruct the open space. Two cruck blades, joined by

Lower Cockhill Farmhouse, Castle Cary, a fifteenth-century jointed cruck hall.

Manor House, Curry Mallet. This former hall or barn displays true crucks.

Fig. 3.13   Two Medieval Open Halls with cruck trusses.

a high collar, were embedded in stone or cob walls, the crucks extending from near ground level to the apex, with a heavy ridge and horizontal side purlins supporting the common rafters. Thus the cruck blades carry the roof load directly to ground level. Two-bay halls often had a central arch-braced cruck truss to strengthen the roof, together with windbraces in the slope of the roof to give longitudinal bracing and a decorative arch across the hall (see the roof at Wick Farmhouse, Norton St Philip, d.1372 (fig. 3.11). For wider spanning base crucks see figs 5.3, 5.4.

Early true crucks have occasionally survived in small farmhouses in the region, our two tree-ring dated examples both coming from the hilly areas of the county (figs 3.11, 3.14). **West End Farmhouse, Barton at Winscombe**[14] is dated to d.1278 and is the earliest cruck found so far in Somerset. This farmhouse is sited on the north-west edge of the Mendip Hills. Two true crucks (c1, c2 – see fig. 3.14), the blades made of squarish timbers extending down to within a metre of the ground floor, have cambered collars and an early form of saddle apex (joint type C)[13] carrying a heavy square-set ridge and former single purlins pegged to the back of the crucks (fig. 3.11). The saddle apex over the open hall had the refinement of an arch-shape cut out of it and the two trusses and the ridge are all smoke-blackened. These timbers are the only survivors of the thirteenth-century roof structure. The span of the roof was only about 5.2m, a small span showing its modest beginnings, and was probably a three rooms-in-line grange farm of the Dean and Chapter of Wells, who owned the Barton estate in the early-thirteenth century.[14]

The other early cruck farmhouse, sited at the opposite end of the county on the northern side of the Exmoor hills is **East Lynch Cottage at Selworthy**[15] which dated to d.1315 (figs 3.11, 3.14). Its modest proportions are similar to the Mendip house and it has plain curved cruck blades springing from the side walls just above ground level, up to the apex and another early yoked apex (type H) – the type often seen in the nearby early farmhouses of Devon and West Somerset. The farmhouse, built against the slope of the hill, has remained small, with the exposed cruck (c3 – see fig. 3.14) now visible in the low-end barn. There were two single hip crucks in the gable ends supporting the ridge, but the low-end cruck has gone (a former peg hole can be seen in the ridge) giving the typical hipped shape of medieval farmhouses in the area (fig. 3.14). Its early ownership is not known.

Because of the known dates and similarity of both plans and cruck structures it is worthwhile comparing these two thirteenth- and fourteenth-century open hall houses with three fifteenth-century examples from the western hills at Chipstable, Skilgate and Otterford (fig. 3.14). In the case of the two fourteenth-century examples there are only 36 years between the tree-ring dates, the next three houses being from the fifteenth century. Remarkably, since one is just below the Mendip Hills, the others in the Exmoor and Blackdown areas, all five houses have very similar dimensions – the internal span is about 5.4m, the bay size between crucks about 3.5m, and all the houses originally had four bays in length. All five houses are built along the contours, sloping towards the low ends and built into the steep hill behind, presumably for protection from bad weather. The first two houses had open smoke-blackened cruck frames, without any signs of a cross wall to divide the houses when they were first built. We can conclude therefore that there were originally only low partitions between the rooms. At East Lynch Cottage the fourteenth-century ridge was heavily blackened as well as the two surviving crucks. It is possible, though not certain, that these houses were former longhouses and East Lynch Cottage still has its low-end barn.

One of the many ways of identifying former longhouses is to study the relationship of the cross walls between the inserted hall fireplace, the cross passage and the byre when the medieval house was upgraded in later centuries (figs 3.2, 3.14). Earlier we noted that in a longhouse the wide cross passage is also the entry for the cattle into the byre, so the dividing cross wall

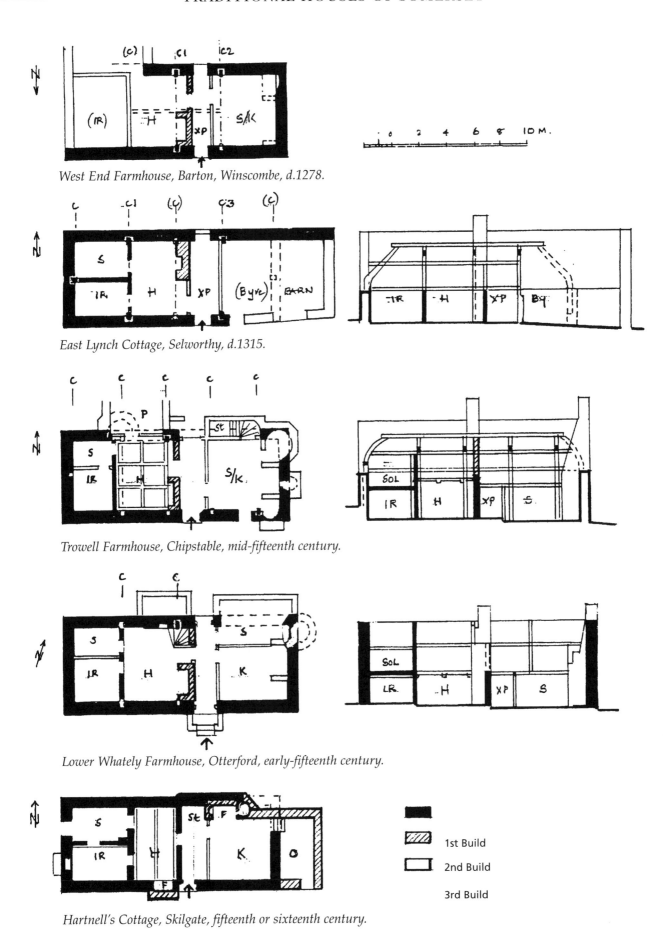

West End Farmhouse, Barton, Winscombe, d.1278.

East Lynch Cottage, Selworthy, d.1315.

Trowell Farmhouse, Chipstable, mid-fifteenth century.

Lower Whately Farmhouse, Otterford, early-fifteenth century.

1st Build
2nd Build
3rd Build

Hartnell's Cottage, Skilgate, fifteenth or sixteenth century.

Fig. 3.14   West Somerset farmhouses, possible former longhouses.

would be on the hall side of the passage between the humans and animals. The much more common three-room farmhouse plan is thought to have been founded on the superior manor-house plan, where the cross passage was traditionally part of the hall, with only a screen between them. The closed partition would be at the service-room side of the passage (think of the screens passages in any of the well-known medieval open halls, such as at Lytes Cary, near Somerton). Returning to the two ancient buildings we are comparing, West End Farmhouse and East Lynch Cottage (figs 3.11, 3.14), both houses originally had low partitions; later they both had fireplaces and stone cross walls added on the hall side of the passage. This would have made the two houses more likely to have been derived from a longhouse, with a byre or agricultural third room at the low end, suited to their age and locations.

The comparison shows that four of these five houses have similar roof forms, the fifth with a modern roof (fig. 3.14). **Trowell Farmhouse at Chipstable** is a well-sited farm perched on a remote steep hillside in the Brendons. The farmhouse has a smoke-blackened jointed cruck roof and an end hip cruck, but the roof could not be dated by dendrochronology. R. Gilson and E.H.D. Williams considered it to have a fifteenth-century date on the basis of the jointing of the crucks. The house was upgraded to a high standard by the Abbot of Muchelney in the 1500s with a high-end solar, a parlour wing and a low-end kitchen with a large fireplace, corn drying kiln and curing chamber (fig. 3.14).

Lower Whately Farmhouse at Otterford (fig. 3.14) is on the Blackdown Hills close to the Devon border. The house has a smoke-blackened cruck-framed roof with an open cruck truss over the former two-bay hall. Like Trowell Farmhouse it had a solar at the high end, the room below being divided into a small inner room and service room, there being no service room in the low end of a longhouse. In the late sixteenth century a hall fire-place and stone cross wall were inserted between the hall and the passage, thus sealing the hall from the suggested byre. The cruck has an early yoked apex (like East Lynch Farm) so this house could also be of the fourteenth or fifteenth century. Both Trowell Farmhouse and Lower Whately Farmhouse had substantial inserted cross walls between hall and passage and can therefore be considered, along with other features, as potential former longhouses.

A third house, **Hartnell's Cottage at Skilgate** (fig. 3.14), a late-medieval building, also has a divided inner room and a long low end, running down the slope, but in this example the hall is particularly small, necessitating the inserted fireplace to be positioned outside the house on the front wall next to the entrance doorway. (Skilgate is within the area of lateral stacks). Unfortunately the roof has been replaced so we cannot be sure of its original date, although the hall beams are of the early-sixteenth century.

Examples of tree-ring dated true crucks extend from the late-thirteenth century to the end of the fourteenth century in our Somerset examples (fig. 5.7). After that date, jointed crucks were more commonly used in the county, although we would expect on further sampling to show an overlap in dates. Jointed crucks are formed of a separate post and principal rafter, jointed at the elbow (fig. 3.11) and, in our sampled roofs, the type enjoyed a longer date range than the true crucks, from the late-fourteenth century to the mid-sixteenth century. This change to jointed crucks made in two pieces may indicate a depletion in suitable oak and elm trees at that time in Somerset.

Two forms of joint are most commonly found, the earlier and rarer type, connects the post to the principal rafter with 'face-pegs' and 'slip-tenons' taken right through the cruck. The more common 'side-pegged' joint has a stronger long mortice-and-tenon joint (fig. 3.11). Unfortunately not enough examples have been tree-ring dated to show a decisive development as many of the crucks had principal rafters made of elm with fast-growing oak posts, neither suitable for dendrochronology.

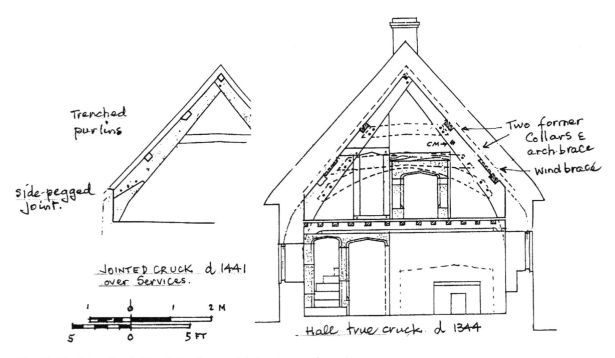

No. 21 Woolston Road, North Cadbury, with two types of crucks.

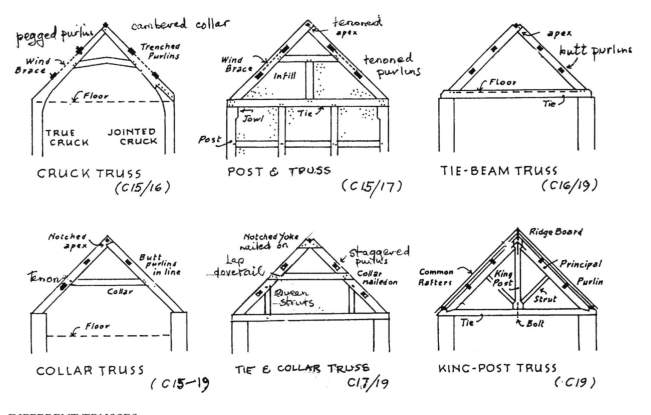

DIFFERENT TRUSSES

Fig. 3.15   Comparative Somerset roof trusses (see 5.3, 5.4 for base crucks).

A medieval village house, **No. 21 Woolston Road, North Cadbury** (fig. 3.15) had both types of cruck trusses with different dates, both being smoke-blackened. It had a true cruck over the hall, was arch-braced and windbraced, dated d.1344, and the side-pegged jointed cruck over the service room dated d.1441, presumably a replacement. Surprisingly the true cruck had mortices for two collars and arch-braces. The higher collar was perhaps introduced when a chamber was added over the hall. The fine stone-built house has a thatched roof, stone mullioned windows and arched stone door-ways of the late-sixteenth century, a typical date when fireplaces and framed ceilings were often added to the formerly open hall. The inserted stone features in the hall show the classic arrangement of a large open fireplace (now blocked) next to a stone arched door to the cross passage, and a smaller arched doorway leading to a newel staircase winding above the door.

Another high quality roof with true cruck trusses and two tiers of arched windbraces is seen at **Wick Farm, Norton St Philip**,[16] in the north of the county (fig. 3.11). The smoke-blackened roof was tree-ring dated d.1372. The house was a grange farmhouse of the Carthusian priory of Hinton Charterhouse, in an area where many cruck roofs are found, both true and jointed, usually with a type M apex (fig. 3.11). Wick Farm has true crucks, while Nos 47 and 49 Goose Street, Beckington (fig. 3.4) has later jointed crucks dated d.1391. It has a solar over the inner room, a wide arch-braced cruck over the hall and four jointed crucks with two collars each, over the service end. The roof was formerly two bays longer, judging by the missing carpenters marks I and II.

Cruck trusses were rarely built after the beginning of the sixteenth century, except possibly in some barns with wide spans. Late-medieval cruck trusses are often combined with post and truss frames, the latter forming cross partitions in rural houses, particularly in South Somerset (fig. 3.15). These structures also rely for their stability on having their timber trusses rooted into stone or cob walls down to a stone plinth. The corner posts have jowled heads to receive the tie-beam and principal rafter and vertical studs were pegged and tenoned into horizontals rails supporting hazel wattle-and-daub infill; this type of infill is usually medieval, later followed by horizontal rod and daub in the post-medieval period (fig. 3.16). The proportions of the infill panels in partitions is a guide to date, with wide panels being earlier than the narrower rod and daub panels.

In a pioneering study of late-medieval houses in Stocklinch village, C. Austin and R. Hall[17] recorded seven medieval cruck-framed houses with post and truss cross partitions and unusual timber gable-end walls. The jowled posts of the end walls were embedded in the walls up to eaves height; above, the gable truss frame was exposed under a wide overhanging verge of thatch, with vertical studs filled with wattle and daub. The smoke-bays in several of the houses are described in Chapter 4 (fig. 4.17).

Elsewhere in the south of the county, there are occasional examples of these unusual gables combined with half-hips in thatched roofs. The roofs have special hip trusses, with scalloped-shaped intermediate trusses combined with post and truss gables, cut off at collar height to accommodate the half-hips, (see **Gifford's Farmhouse, Langford, Norton Fitzwarren**, fig. 3.17). Another earlier and simpler way to form a hip was to build a single axial end- cruck supporting the ridge, a feature also occasionally seen also in South Somerset and Devon.[18]

By the early-fifteenth century cruck trusses were giving way to straight principal rafter trusses resting on the top of the stone walls. Low purlins connect the principal rafters only just above eaves level instead of wall-plates that are not much used in Somerset. Many of these straight principal roofs have closely spaced lighter intermediate trusses with elaborate arch-braces and tiers of windbraces in patterns. These roofs are often seen in late-medieval farmhouses, where the windbraces were used for bracing the roof as well as decorative features in the rooms below (figs 5.5, 5.6).

Partitions, wattle-and-daub, dating from medieval times and into the sixteenth century.

Rod-and-daub, seventeenth to nineteenth centuries.

An external wall during repair work, also with cruck posts.

External cob walls on a stone plinth (note the cruck post on the right).

Fig. 3.16   Internal plastered partitions and external cob walls.

Post-Medieval Roofs

After the early-sixteenth century roof trusses were more simply framed without crucks. The tie-and-collar truss with vertical 'queen struts' was introduced to provide an attic space when more bedrooms and storage were required, particularly in the larger farmhouses (fig. 3.15). Smaller houses may continue to have collar trusses only, their collars often being halved and dovetailed to the principals instead of morticed and tenoned. King-post roofs are a nineteenth-century feature in Somerset, occasionally seen in barns and houses with wide spans (fig. 3.15).

Purlin positions and apex joints changed with the date, the earliest medieval purlins being pegged into the top of the principal rafter or trenched into it (fig. 3.15). More refined work had tenoned purlins into the principal rafters. In post-medieval roofs, purlins were scarfed together through the principal and finally they were staggered and tusk-tenoned, all helping to give a sequence of roof types.

However, roofs themselves cannot always be a guide to dating a house, as replacements after fire damage or improvements of attic spaces very often occurred from the seventeenth century onwards. In our village studies we found that in the estate village of Shapwick, of the 18 surveyed houses (dating from before 1700) only eight retained their original roofs. This is an unusually low proportion of survival, due to the major rebuilding of the estate houses in the late-eighteenth century.[19]

The next chapter describes the more decorative features in these rural houses: doors, windows, fireplaces, staircases and floor beams and other internal features.

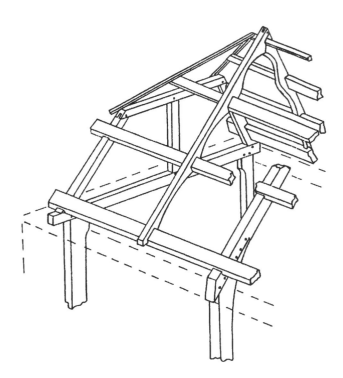

Fig. 3.17   Roof trusses with a half-hip roof: Gifford's Farmhouse, Langford, Norton Fitzwarren. (R. GILSON)

Notes

1 The houses described here have been surveyed by the Somerset Vernacular Building Research Group, R.G. Gilson, the late E.H.D. Williams, Mark McDermott and Susan Shaw. Copies of the surveys are deposited in the Somerset Record Office, Taunton.

2 Williams, E.H.D., *The Building Materials of Somerset's Vernacular Buildings*, SANHS Proc. 135, 1991.

3 Williams, E.H.D., *Vernacular Architecture Notes*, SANHS Proc. 134, 1990.

4 Dallimore, J., SVBRG survey of Manor Farmhouse, Stratton-on-the-Fosse, SRO, 1993.

5 Information from R. Gilson.

6 Beacham, P., ed., *Devon Building*, Devon C.C., 1990.

7 Information from D. Sage, Batcombe.

8 *Somerset Villages. The Vernacular Buildings of Batcombe*, SVBRG, 1988.

9 *Somerset Villages. The Vernacular Buildings of Haselbury Plucknett*, SVBRG, 1994.

10 Somerset Dendrochronology Project, instigated by the Somerset Vernacular Building Research Group, with the dendrochronologists, Dan Miles and Mick Worthington of the Oxford Dendrochronology Laboratory. The results were published in the *Vernacular Architecture Journal*, vols 28 to 30, 1997-99.

11 Tree-ring dating carried out by Dan Miles.

12 Gilson, R.G., *Three Somerset Manor Houses*, SANHS Proc. 129, 1985.

13 Alcock, N.W., *Cruck Construction*, CBA Research Report no. 42, 1981.

14 West End Farmhouse surveyed and researched by R.G. Gilson (1979) and Susan Shaw (1997), SRO.

15 East Lynch Cottage, Selworthy, surveyed by R.G. Gilson (1981) and the National Trust (1991), SRO.

16 Wick Farm, Norton St Philip, surveyed by R.G. Gilson and E.H.D. Williams, 1981, SRO.

17 Austin, C. and Hall, R., *The Medieval Houses of Stocklynch*, SANHS Proc. 116, 1972.

18 Gilson, R.G. and Williams, E.H.D., Half-hipped Roofs in Pre-seventeenth Century Somerset Buildings, *Vernacular Architecture Journal*, vol. 16, (1985).

19 SVBRG, *Somerset Villages, The Vernacular Buildings of Shapwick*, 1996.

FOUR

Features and Decorations

There is a great variety of design in arch-forms, mouldings and decorative carvings to be seen in domestic buildings and each feature can be arranged in chronological sequence to give an approximate date to the original building phase or later alterations. Not all house builders were able to afford such decoration, but it is surprising to find quite modest houses with an arch-shaped lintel over the entrance door or some mouldings round the fireplace inside.

Fig. 4.1   A seventeenth-century interior with decorative plasterwork, Prior's Farmhouse, Stringston. (PHOTO: G. ROBERTS)

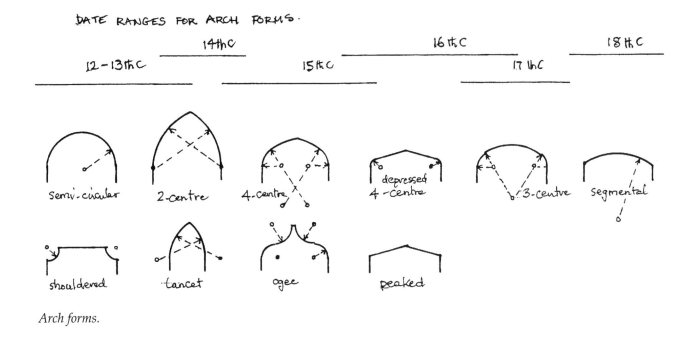

Arch forms.

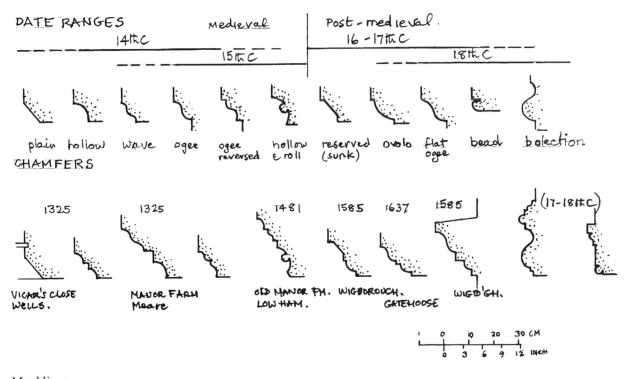

Mouldings.

Fig. 4.2 Arch forms and mouldings, giving a range of dates.

Dating

As well as the stylistic way of dating, there are two more positive methods to give an actual date for a house or feature; either by studying datestones on individual houses, or by the modern method of dating timbers by dendrochronology.

Datestones are found infrequently built into external walls or forming part of internal decorations such as plasterwork plaques. These are precise dates giving either the original building phase or later alterations. But datestones in themselves are not reliable evidence on their own as they can be re-set or even added for a family event such as a marriage, when the initials of husband and wife are recorded with a date. The datestones are also restricted to certain periods, in the case of recorded houses in Somerset, between the 1530s and 1890s, the largest numbers being of the seventeenth century when Renaissance display required such decorative statements. The earlier medieval equivalent of the datestone, the coat-of-arms, requires a considerable knowledge of both heraldry and local families for identification.

The second way of dating positively is the comparatively modern scientific study of dendrochronology (fig. 5.7). This method is more precise and is a very expert and expensive process. The phases of building can be readily given, provided there are suitable oak samples available. So far the tree-ring examples obtained in Somerset are mainly of medieval roofs and this gives a reliable date for some of the earlier structures.

Arch Forms
(fig. 4.2)

Our descriptions start with arch forms as these are seen most obviously in entrance doorways and windows, features which are often updated in the latest fashionable style. Fig. 4.2 starts with the Norman semicircular arch, which hardly survives in domestic work, the exception being the twelfth century **Saltford Manor, near Bath** (fig. 5.1).

The medieval two-centred arch appears first in the form of the 'lancet' window of the thirteenth century, followed by the more generous two-centred form of the fourteenth century, typically at Manor Farmhouse, Meare (figs 4.3, 4.4). Next came the four-centred arch of the fifteenth and sixteenth centuries, not so exaggerated in height as the two-centred one and most familiar to us as the 'Tudor Arch' associated with the new wealth of the sixteenth century. Tudor buildings still mostly used the 'gothic' or medieval style of decoration (Brympton d'Evercy, Plate 10).

In the late-sixteenth and seventeenth centuries the arches became more flattened with the 'depressed four-centred arch' and the square-headed opening becoming popular. Some slightly more exotic forms of arch are shown in the lower row in fig. 4.2, but these are only occasionally found in Somerset houses. The so-called shouldered arch is not really an arch. It comprises two corbels and a flat lintel, and derives from some medieval stone buildings. It is occasionally seen in heavy timber doorways of the late-medieval period. The ogee arch was used in the fourteenth and early-fifteenth century in traceried windows (No. 1 The Borough at Montacute, fig. 4.9). The peaked head was very popular in the seventeenth century on timber internal doorways.

Mouldings

Mouldings occur around windows, fireplaces and doorways and on internal beams. Fig. 4.2 illustrates the various types of mouldings, from the plain and hollow chamfers to combinations of different shaped mouldings. They are usually made of stone in Somerset, while medieval timber doorways still survive in areas without access to dressed stone.

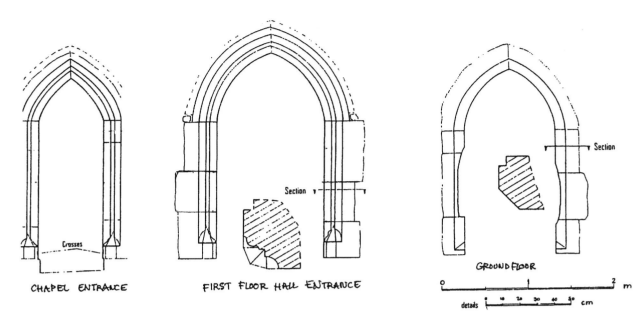

Manor Farmhouse, Meare, dated 1325, has stone two-centred arches.

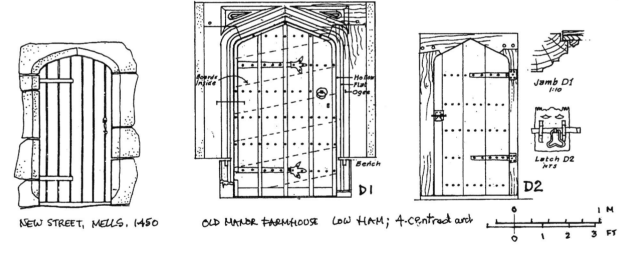

New Street, Mells, dated 1450 and Old Manor Farmhouse, Low Ham both have four-centred arches.

Fig. 4.3   Medieval doorways of the fourteenth and fifteenth centuries.

There are five main chamfers: the plain diagonal chamfer, the hollow, the ogee (2 forms), the later ovolo and the bead mouldings (fig. 4.2). Both the plain and the hollow chamfers were used in medieval and post-medieval examples in the more utilitarian positions in the house. Meanwhile entrance doors and hall fireplaces have more decorative mouldings, particularly in fourteenth and fifteenth-century doorways – as at **Manor Farm, Meare**, d.1325 (fig. 4.3) and the floor beams at **Old Manor Farm, Low Ham**, d.1481, (fig. 4.19) where the latter has a small roll moulding inside a wide hollow which is a very recognisable feature of fifteenth-century work. Two other medieval mouldings are illustrated, but are not so common – the wave and the double ogee, both used in door frames in the fourteenth and fifteenth centuries.

In the post-medieval period, the fashionable ovolo moulding helps to give a more generous look to manor house and farmhouse stone mullioned windows of the Elizabethan and Stuart periods (North Cadbury Court, fig. 4.10). A more unusual high status moulding, the reserved or sunk chamfer, had a shorter life span from the mid-sixteenth to the early-seventeenth century. It is mostly used sporadically in small manor houses and farmhouses in South Somerset – particularly the Shepton Mallet area, where the local quarry at Doulting may have been the source of the design which is also used in the nearby smaller village houses in Batcombe and West Pennard. **The Manor Farmhouse, Coxbridge**, has a dated façade, 1577, where all the main mullioned and transomed windows have the reserved chamfer, while a later wing uses the ovolo moulding. (This is an early date for the reserved chamfer in the county).

In the late-seventeenth and eighteenth centuries the ogee or scroll moulding was enlarged and flattened to become the main moulding of the classical cornice, the 'cyma' a typical feature of the Georgian house. Another fashionable moulding of a similar date was the bolection, a bulgy moulding used in fireplaces, architraves and panelling. At the same time bead moulding was introduced round openings, often forming part of typical eighteenth-century architrave (fig. 4.2).

DOORWAYS

A few houses of the fourteenth century have been recorded in the county and these have high status and ecclesiastical backgrounds such as the Abbot's **Manor Farm, Meare**,[1] where the first-floor beams have been tree-ring dated to d.1325. This house provides a splendid group of stone doorways with broad two-centred arches, moulded in the main rooms (first-floor hall and chapel), while the less important rooms have wide plain chamfers and diagonal stops (fig. 4.3). The consistency of these doorways and tall traceried windows which occur throughout the building confirms the early-fourteenth century date of the whole of the surviving house.

Smaller domestic examples of similar two-centred arched and moulded entrance doorways can be found in the fourteenth-century Priest's House, at Muchelney and at **Wick Farmhouse, Norton St Philip** (fig. 4.4). This latter house has been tree-ring dated to d.1371. Both examples have hood mouldings (or dripstones) over the arches which may have previously terminated in carved heads (now removed).

In the fifteenth century many town and village houses had stone doorways still with full four-centred arches. They were plain chamfered and had the more usual step and run-out stops (fig. 4.3). Examples of these features can be seen at **New Street, Mells**,[2] the planned street built by Abbot Selwood c.1450. Unusually, in this stony county, the Old Manor Farmhouse, Low Ham, has a timber moulded entrance doorway with carved spandrels. Here the arch-braced roof over the Great Chamber and the framed ceiling to the hall have been dated d.1481 (fig. 4.3).

Wick Farmhouse, Norton St Philip. d.1371 (roof).

Manor Farmhouse, Meare, d.1325 (floor).

Tickenham Court, the hall service doors, d.1471–76 (roof).

The Fish House, Meare, fourteenth century.

Fig. 4.4 Stone medieval doorways dating from the fourteenth and fifteenth centuries.

Gatehouse, Baltonsborough.

Higher Rocke's Farmhouse, Butleigh.

Barrow Court, Barrow Gurney.

Norton Court, Norton Fitzwarren.

Fig. 4.5 Elizabethan and Jacobean doorways, probably all seventeenth century.

Stone Plaque
over porch cornice

Gatehouse, Baltonsborough, datestone 1637.
(L. CLAPP)

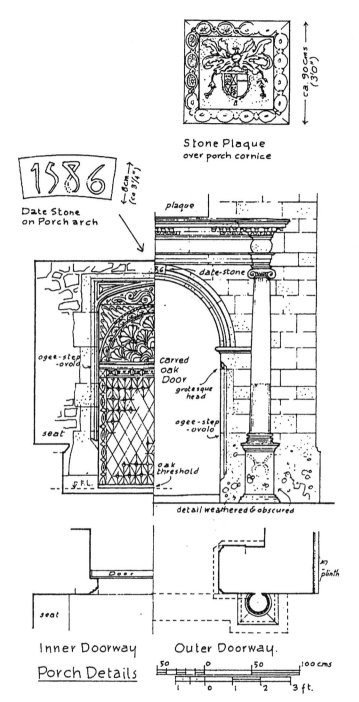

1586

Date Stone
on Porch arch

plaque

date-stone

ogee-step
-ovolo

Carved
Oak
Door

grotesque
head

ogee-step
-ovolo

seat

oak
threshold

J.F.L.

detail weathered & obscured

Door

plinth

seat

Inner Doorway   Outer Doorway.

Porch Details

50   0   50   100 cms
1   0   1   2   3 ft.

Bishop's Hull Manor House, Taunton.

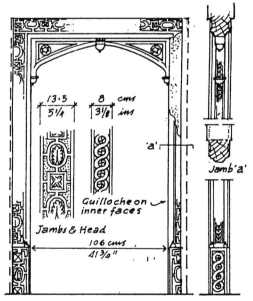

13·5   8   cms
5¼   3⅛   ins

'a'

Guilloche on
inner faces

Jamb 'a'

Jambs & Head
106 cms
41¾"

New Farmhouse, Shapwick, c.1600, with
timber internal doorway.

Fig. 4.6   Doorways: decorative styles of the late-sixteenth and early-seventeenth centuries.

Other mid-fifteenth century examples of four-centred arches can be seen at **Tickenham Court** where the arches on the service doorways to the screens passage are heavily moulded and have diagonal stops (fig. 4.4). A pair of service doors is found at the **Fish House, Meare**, an early-fourteenth century building, again with four-centred arches with diagonal stops. These doorways suggest a fifteenth-century addition to the earlier structure (fig. 4.4).

In the late-sixteenth or early-seventeenth century, examples of doorways and other decorative features show the overriding influence of the Renaissance in following the new classical trends. Up to this time decoration in traditional houses was based on gothic ornament, but a few local grandees were experimenting with ideas that they introduced into Tudor court circles, the courtiers and officials having travelled on the Continent. They were experimenting in such houses as Lacock Abbey and Longleat (both in Wiltshire) from where the masons and carpenters may have helped to spread these new designs.

Manor House, Bishop's Hull, Taunton, with a datestone of 1586 over the porch doorway, is an E-plan house of great interest (fig. 4.6). The storeyed porch has a sophisticated doorway with a semicircular arch, Ionic columns and an entablature, while the main entrance arch is four-centred and elaborately carved in the Elizabethan style (fig. 4.6). Another decorative carving in the form of an arched timber doorway is seen in **New Farmhouse, Shapwick**, (fig. 4.6) where the four-centred archway has carved spandrels, and guilloche patterns with linked ovals and squares on the frame, all well-known Elizabethan motifs. **Gatehouse, Baltonsborough**, has two porches, one with Ionic columns and a steeply pitched pediment (fig. 4.5). The other with a datestone 1637 (fig. 4.6) has a lively rendering of classical mouldings. With all these experimental examples the most pleasing is at **Higher Rocke's Farmhouse, Butleigh** (fig. 4.5) where the simple semicircular arch has an ovolo moulding and a flat surround, the only decorations being a fluted keystone and a pretty raised carving forming a capital to the pilasters.

Two other doorways which illustrate a contrast of styles, typical of the seventeenth century is **Norton Court, Norton Fitzwarren** (fig. 4.5), with a fully four-centred arch and carved leaf decoration in the spandrels, the ovolo mouldings combined with hollows, and a deep plain hood mould overall. This is a typical doorway of the turn of the century found in many Somerset houses. The other example at **Barrow Court, Barrow Gurney** (fig. 4.5) has a depressed four-centred doorway with a refined broken pedimented doorhead, which suggests the skills of a well-known mason from the Bristol area. (Pevsner dates this doorway at c.1630–40).[3]

These last entrance doorways are mostly from high status houses, but the stone doorways of the simpler arched sort are seen all over Somerset and, where stone is not available, some village houses have robust timber two-centred or shouldered arches.

WINDOWS

The different shapes of window mullions are shown in fig. 4.7. In early work the commonest is the hollow chamfer, shown here in the fifteenth century at **New Street, Mells**, with trefoil cusping and at **Weaver's Cottage, Batcombe**, a sixteenth-century example with arch-heads (fig. 4.7). Medieval mullioned windows had arched and cusped heads from the thirteenth to the early-sixteenth centuries and were probably the most decorative features of the exteriors of both small houses and manor houses. Very large examples, such as the first-floor hall at **Manor Farmhouse, Meare** (d.1325) have very tall windows in the gable walls, with similar lower ones on the sides (fig. 4.8). These windows have beautiful external two-centred arched heads over a quatrefoil with two cinquefoil lights, and an elegant inner cinquefoil arch. The windows below, at ground-floor level are not nearly so elegant and may have been added as part of the sixteenth-century alterations.

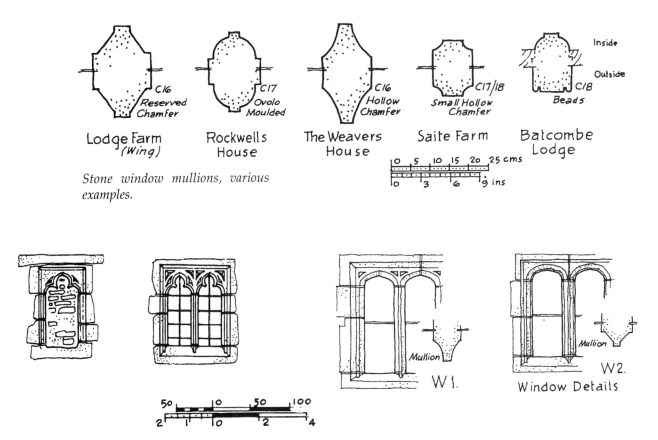

Stone window mullions, various examples.

New Street, Mells, fifteenth century.

Weaver's Cottage, Batcombe, sixteenth or seventeenth century.

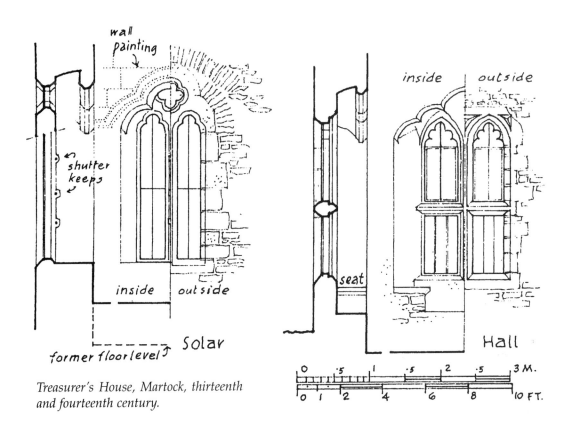

Treasurer's House, Martock, thirteenth and fourteenth century.

Fig. 4.7 Stone windows and mullions.

Clockwise, starting right:
Solar window at Treasurer's House, Martock, thirteenth century. (G. ROBERTS)

Manor Farm, Meare; the first-floor hall window, early-fourteenth century.

Hall window with seat, Treasurer's House, fourteenth century.

Fig. 4.8   Medieval window tracery.

Grammar School, Martock, fifteenth-century four-centred arches.

The Borough, Montacute, medieval cusped arches.

Poundisford Park, Pitminster, depressed four-centred arches, sixteenth century. (R. TUCKER)

Lower Alham Farm, Batcombe, seventeenth century, mullioned and transomed windows.

Manor Farmhouse, South Cadbury, square-headed windows, datestone 1687.

Fig. 4.9 The small domestic mullioned window.

Another superior ecclesiastical house, **Treasurer's House, Martock** (figs 4.7, 4.8) has early windows; in the thirteenth-century solar there is a plate tracery tall window with trefoil heads and again in the inner arch, the window is surrounded by red painted masonry joints. The hall was built slightly later – the early-fourteenth century windows with cinquefoils, are repeated in the inner arches over the window bays with seats and shelves in the recess.

In the late-fifteenth and sixteenth centuries domestic windows were usually under square heads, and these often had arched sub-lights in better class work, some still cusped. **No. 1 The Borough, Montacute** (fig. 4.9) has two differently designed cusped windows of the fourteenth and fifteenth centuries, while the moulded doorway has a four-centred arch suggesting the fifteenth century. It is possible that the windows were retrieved from the post-Dissolution Montacute Priory, where the monks had been responsible for planning the medieval market square in the twelfth century. Two other arched windows, one at the **Grammar School, in Martock** (fig. 4.9) shows the change from the four-centred arch, to the later depressed four-centred arch, illustrated here from Poundisford Park, Pitminster (fig. 4.9) and built prior to the 1570s.

Finally, the square-headed mullioned windows (without arches) were commonly used in groups of two to six lights in a horizontal row in farm-houses of the late-fifteenth, sixteenth and seventeenth centuries. The example at **South Cadbury Manor Farm** (fig. 4.9) has a convincing datestone of 1687, nicely carved with volutes. Another window with both mullions and transoms and chubby ovolo mouldings is found at **Lower Alham Farm, Batcombe** (fig. 4.9) where a seventeenth-century façade was added by James Aishe, a Batcombe clothier (fig. 3.10).

Towards the end of the sixteenth century the hall range at North Cadbury Court was rebuilt in the opulent Elizabethan Renaissance manner (d.1589) (fig. 4.10). The north façade has some remarkable decorations of the refined classical sort on the oriel bay and the porch, using the ovolo moulding for its enormous many-light windows. The two-tier oriel bay has the windows subdivided both horizontally and vertically in groups of 18 and 12 lights. The bays have Ionic and Corinthian pilasters at the corners with cornices decorated with Elizabethan lozenges and Tudor roses. Both the porch and oriel bays are capped with elaborate crestings, with scroll brackets and central shell capping. These decorative features are reminiscent of the crestings at Longleat, Wiltshire, built in the 1570s.

Fig. 4.10
North Cadbury Court, rebuilt in 1589. The porch and oriel bay with decorations is reminiscent of Longleat in Wiltshire.

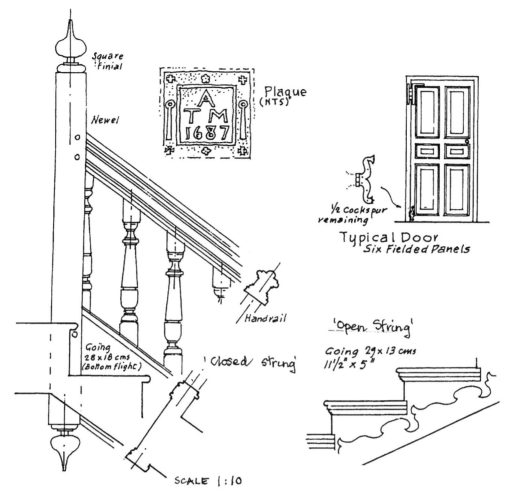

Plox House, Bruton.

New Farmhouse, Shapwick, late-seventeenth or eighteenth century.

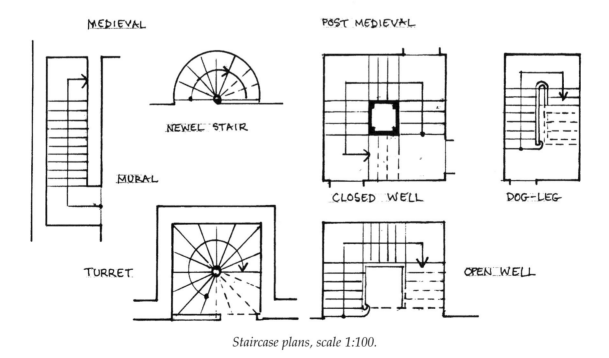

Staircase plans, scale 1:100.

Fig. 4.11 Staircase details and plans.

Longleat represents an early example of the change from traditional gothic decoration to the newly introduced classical features. These were first instigated by Edward Seymour, Duke of Somerset and Lord Protector of England, when he built the earlier part of Somerset House in London. At Longleat a French mason, Alan Maynard was experimenting with classical design for the bay windows and it is very possible that he and his co-designer Robert Smythson could have designed the bays at North Cadbury Court.[4]

STAIRCASES
(fig. 4.11)

In medieval farmhouses a steep ladder stair led to the solar chamber but these rarely survive. After the open halls were floored over in the fifteenth and sixteenth centuries a more centrally placed stair would be needed. This was the 'newel stair', built into a curved recess, next to the doorway from the cross passage into the hall (fig. 4.11). The staircase is made of either timber, with an oak newel post supporting solid-baulk timber treads, or in stone with the newel post made in sections as part of the tread (such as at **Lytes Cary Manor**, fig. 4.12). **Manor Farmhouse at Middle Chinnock** (c.1600) has a timber newel stair in a square turret (fig. 4.12). Both these materials were commonly used in cottage and farmhouse staircases throughout the medieval and post-medieval periods in both the hall and kitchen gable wall.

In the fifteenth and sixteenth centuries, when first-floor chambers were in general use, another version of the newel staircase, the 'turret stair' was introduced (fig. 4.11), usually positioned on the back wall of the hall in the form of a semicircle or half octagon in plan. In the north of the county many turret stairs were used in the fifteenth century, such as at New Street, Mells (fig. 6.12). There is also a very fine example at the George Inn, Norton St Philip (fig. 5.13). More rural stair turrets are a feature of the Somerset-Devon border area, built into the hillside and made of cob and rubble (Lancin Farmhouse, Wambrook).

By the late-sixteenth century the staircase adopted in the larger houses was the 'well stair'. Early examples such as at **Wigborough Manor, South Petherton**, d.1585 (fig. 4.11) had four flights of stairs and quarter landings round a solid 'well' made of timber framing and plaster, the staircase giving access to mezzanine closets and garderobes on the way up to the attic. A grander stone staircase at Montacute House is of a similar late-sixteenth century date, but follows the influence of the French chateaux staircases with a solid stone well, arches over the landings and niches with seats on the way up to the Long Gallery. Both these houses, within a few miles of each other, are struggling with the changes in style in their semi-classical decorations; a style which had not yet fully developed.

In the seventeenth century 'well staircases', however, are usually more often 'open' with handsome carved and turned balusters and newel posts with knobs and pendants for each flight. A rather experimental balustrade is found in **Gray's Almshouses, Taunton**, c.1635 (fig. 4.13) and a more mature example occurs at **Plox House, Bruton**, datestone 1687. Here the fine stair leading up to the attics has a hinged dog-gate on the landing (fig. 4.13). Another type of seventeenth-century balustrade is sometimes used on the upper flights of open stairs. These are called 'splat' or 'shadow balusters' and are cut out of a single board, with a rather pleasing design at **West Farmhouse, Ashwick** (fig. 4.13).

Many later stairs are in the form of two parallel flights in a 'dog-leg stair', which takes up less room than a well stair and the design is virtually universal throughout the eighteenth and nineteenth centuries. (fig. 4.11).

Manor Farmhouse, Middle Chinnock: the attic and first-floor landing (left) *and a seventeenth-century newel staircase in a turret.*

Lytes Cary Manor, a fifteenth-century stone newel staircase.

Fig.4.12   Newel and turret staircases.

Plox House, Bruton, 1687. This stair has a dog-gate on the half-landing.

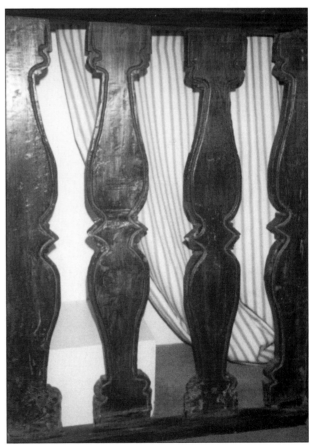

Gray's Almshouses, Taunton, c.1635.　　　　*West Farmhouse, Ashwick; with 'splat' balusters.*

Fig. 4.13　Seventeenth-century staircase balustrades.

FIREPLACES

The addition of chimney stacks and wall fireplaces into the main rooms of the smaller houses in place of an open hearth, probably took place generally in the sixteenth or early-seventeenth centuries and can only be dated by the style of decorations and arch-forms. The following examples are taken from a large number in the county, most of them undated.

In the high status lay and ecclesiastical houses a few rare examples of the hooded medieval fireplaces survive, such as the first-floor hall fireplace in the **Manor Farmhouse, Meare** (fig. 5.9). This rare early-fourteenth century fireplace has a tapering stone hood, supported on brackets with elegantly carved and moulded candle brackets on each side. This unusual hood is designed on plan on the basis of a half octagon, with the angle projecting centrally, forming a bent shaped lintel, jointed by joggled joints to the corbelled brackets. These brackets have chamfers which terminate in carved trefoils (repeated on the plainer ground-floor fireplace).

The Abbot's Parlour, Muchelney Abbey, c.1500, contains a well-known example of a square-headed lintel carved with large quatrefoils and an over-mantel surmounted by crouching lions (not illustrated). **Perriams at Butleigh**, a fifteenth-century village house (figs 4.14, 4.15) has a fireplace design seen sporadically through North and South Somerset, with a depressed four-centred lintel under a mantelshelf which extends over circular moulded candle brackets resting on half-columns. Another such fireplace is seen at The Tribunal, Glastonbury.

Another late-fifteenth century fireplace at **Laburnham Cottage, Westcombe**, (fig. 4.14) has a wide depressed four-centred arched lintel (moulded hollow-step-ogee) with diagonal stops but no corner columns. These wide openings are often combined with relieving arches in the wall above. The inserted hall fireplace at **Forsters, Shapwick** (fig. 4.15), which was described in Chapter 3, is a good early example of a square-headed stone fireplace with a mantelshelf, moulded with the typical fifteenth-century scooped hollow moulding with an inset roll. The free end of the mantelshelf has an inverted pyramid stop beneath it while the jamb mouldings are stopped at the foot with a cushion stop, unusual in small domestic houses. The fireplace may have been originally made for a larger house.

At **Shapwick House** (fig. 4.15) the first-floor hall fireplace has rather a flat depressed arch with carved spandrels above the fireplace installed during the seventeenth-century conversion. The frame is moulded, hollow-step-ogee, terminating in a scroll stop. This combination of mouldings is typical of the post-medieval period. (For the phases of build at Shapwick House see fig. 5.10).

Kitchen fireplaces are much less decorative than in the hall and mostly take the form of large timber lintels (or bressumers) over stone jambs, with only a small plain chamfer on each side. Some manor houses of the 1600s have massive stone arched kitchen fireplaces, such as the manor house in **Creech St Michael** (fig. 4.14). At Shapwick House the detached late-medieval kitchen, d.1428, was replaced in the early-seventeenth century by a kitchen in the west wing (fig. 4.15). A large flat three-centred arched lintel (now in four pieces) has wide plain chamfers and a relieving arch above. One of the stones has carefully inscribed 'witch marks,' often a seventeenth-century feature, when superstition was at its height. The marks were thought to protect the household from evil influences coming down the chimney. In this case, there are six-pointed stars, a four-pointed Christian symbol and other recognised patterns, probably introduced by the servants.

Our last seventeenth-century example is the **Old Brewery House, Bruton** (fig. 4.15) where the parlour panelling incorporates a timber carved over-mantel with a typical Jacobean mini-arcade. Below, the stone fireplace has a depressed arch and classical mouldings to the mantelshelf, with a large ogee moulding to the shelf, all representing the change of style.

Seymour's Court, Beckington, c.1600.

Above left: *Manor Farm, Coxbridge, West Pennard, 1586.*
Above right: *Dodington Hall, Holford, 1581.*

Laburnham Cottage, Westcombe.

The kitchen fireplace in a manor house in Creech St Michael.

Left: *Perriams, Butleigh, fifteenth century.*

Fig. 4.14 Fireplace designs, fifteenth to late-seventeenth centuries.

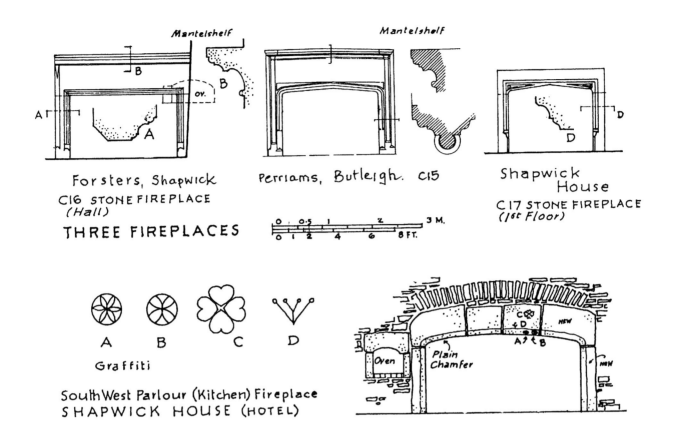

Mantelshelf

B

OV.

A

A

Forsters, Shapwick
C16 STONE FIREPLACE
(Hall)

THREE FIREPLACES

Mantelshelf

Perriams, Butleigh. C15

0 0·5 1   2   3 M.
0 1 2   4   6   8 FT.

Shapwick House

D

D

C17 STONE FIREPLACE
(1st Floor)

A   B   C   D

Graffiti

SouthWest Parlour (Kitchen) Fireplace
SHAPWICK HOUSE (HOTEL)

C
D
N&W

A B
Plain Chamfer
Oven
N&W

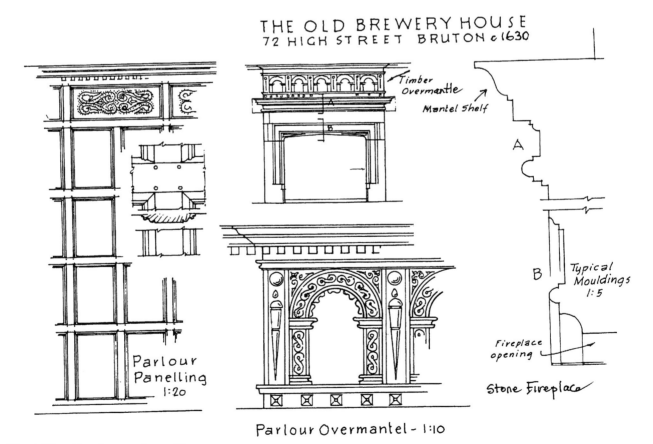

THE OLD BREWERY HOUSE
72 HIGH STREET BRUTON c1630

Timber Overmantle
Mantel Shelf

A

B   Typical Mouldings 1:5

Fireplace opening

Parlour Panelling 1:20

Parlour Overmantel - 1:10

Stone Fireplace

Fig. 4.15   Fireplaces and panelling.

The inventiveness of house owners at the end of the sixteenth century is demonstrated by the examples shown (fig. 4.14). They have similar design ideas expressed in different forms, and these ideas probably derived from foreign pattern books, mostly from Flanders and Germany. Fireplaces have the usual classical mouldings flanked by classical pilasters; seen in a rather fussy Elizabethan design at **Manor Farm, Coxbridge, West Pennard**, with a datestone of 1586 on the façade. At **Seymour's Court, Beckington** (fig. 4.14) there are some elegant Ionic pilasters next to a depressed four-centred arch, reflecting a mixture of the styles. Finally, there is an elaborately carved and rather eccentric fireplace at **Dodington Hall, Holford** c.1581. On each side stand supporting creatures carved in the round like Greek caryatids under Ionic capitals (fig. 4.14).

SMOKE-BAYS AND SMOKE-HOODS

The smoke-bay was devised in the medieval period to confine the smoke from the open hearth. It can be regarded as a transitional stage between the open hearth and the fully developed fireplace and chimney.

The normal spacing between medieval roof trusses (the bay) was about 3.5m (11ft 6ins) with a far narrower bay of about 1.5m (5ft 0ins) forming the smoke-bay as part of the roof structure, usually the last bay against the low-end gable wall. The front frame was supported on a heavy beam spanning the width of the house. This feature is often the only evidence of a previous smoke-bay.

A study of late-medieval houses in **Stocklinch** near Barrington was carried out by two pioneering researchers in the county, Clare Austin and the late Sir Robert Hall.[5] 'Mannings', the house illustrated here (fig. 4.16) shows a three-bay structure with a smaller bay for the smoke-bay against the gable wall, the jointed cruck and post and truss frames being bedded into the cob walls, with the end frame exposed externally in the gable above the cob wall. This unusual feature can still be seen in the area, with its projecting bonnet of thatch protecting the vulnerable cob wall below. The house was in a dilapidated condition at the time of the survey and showed vertical studs and wattle-and-daub infill between the tie and collar of the truss, but without obvious framing in the top triangle, which may represent a former smoke vent in the end wall (fig. 4.16).

Another superior medieval house in the same area, **Hayes End Manor, South Petherton**,[7] has massive timber-framed trusses combined with crucks and two large smoke-bays. The kitchen smoke-bay was added in the sixteenth century and, surprisingly, the whole of the front wall of the bay was canted about 6 degrees from the vertical towards the chimney. It also shows two notches in the principal rafters, possibly for the base of a chimney (in stone slabs?).

An alternative form of flue was the smoke-hood, also seen at Stocklinch. The hoods are timber-framed and smaller, therefore easier to add to an existing house, which suited the sixteenth- and seventeenth-century owners, introducing more than one hearth to the house. The walls around the hearth were likely to be of stone on the ground floor, with a timber beam and corner post supporting a sloping timber hood, back to the chimney (fig. 4.16). These Stocklinch hoods were of the late-sixteenth or seventeenth century, a feature which is often recognised by the sloping sides of the hoods seen in many farmhouses in South Somerset. The flues are mostly rebuilt in stone or brick.

CURING CHAMBERS, KILNS AND OVENS

In Somerset, as in other pastoral farming counties, a key requirement was the preservation of meat. This was achieved by smoking the joints of meat or sides of bacon in a special curing chamber adjoining the farmhouse kitchen fireplace (Flaxpool Cottage, Crowcombe, fig. 4.17). Before proper fireplaces

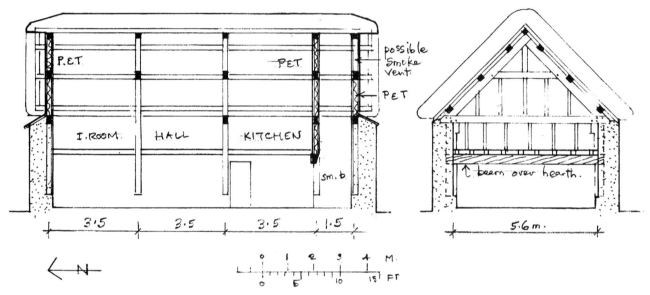

Mannings, Stocklinch. Note the unusual gables, cob walls and the post-and-truss frames.

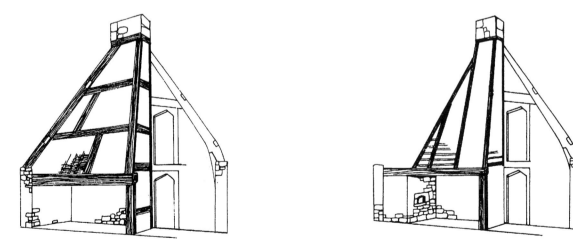

Wattle-and-daub smoke hood and rod-and daub smoke hood.

Fig. 4.16   Late-medieval houses in Stocklinch, smoke bays and hoods (C. AUSTIN, R. HALL)

were built, the smoking was done by hanging the meat in the smoke-bay, but this was not very satisfactory as the smoke was variable and sometimes the heat was too great.

The chambers we see today were probably built from the sixteenth century onwards and are only datable from the style of the timber bressumer above the fireplace. A massive curing chamber is found at **Ford Cottage, Seven Ash, West Bagborough** (fig. 4.17). There is usually a small opening at hearth level, leading to a circular chamber approximately 1 metre in diameter, often with a circular ledge at about 1 metre height. The circular chamber continues up and curves back to the main flue quite high up under the roof slope. Early examples had return openings for the smoke within the hearth area itself and this low doorway beside the fire would show heavy blackening (**Flaxpool Cottage, Crowcombe** fig. 4.17). A loading door for the meat was usually at ground-floor level next to the fireplace, though it has been found on the first floor in the chamber above. The reason for the circular ledge is not clear, but it may have helped the draught and supported a metal grid to prevent the meat falling on the smouldering wood below.

When curing chambers fell out of use they were often replaced by bread ovens, small domed stone or brick chambers with the loading door raised 80–100cm above the hearth, to allow burning faggots to be loaded into the oven, although these sticks were removed before baking. There is no flue to the oven. Larger ovens are often nicely made in dressed stone or brick, such as at **Lenny Barn at Over Stratton** (fig. 4.18). Small ovens could be built on the back wall of the fireplace or under the newel stair, a very common arrangement in the eighteenth and nineteenth centuries. A stone slab would be used to close the oven but this was improved, with the addition of hinged cast-iron doors of interesting designs, or even with a built-in pottery 'cloam' oven, coming from Devon and made in Barnstable at that time.

In the wetter parts of the county, particularly in the west, 'corn drying kilns', chambers for drying the grain, were built beside the fireplace, in a chamber which often projected beyond the house walls.[5] At **Lower Wedcombe Farm, Brompton Ralph**, there is a fine complex of kiln, ovens and newel staircase, all built at the gable end of a two-room cruck-built house of c.1400, the kiln and ovens probably built c.1600. The kiln has a domed roof and a former high-level vent to the stack, the grain being loaded from a doorway and storeroom beyond the kiln structure (fig. 4.17).

Fig. 4.18   A Hamstone oven, c.1700, Lenny Barn, Over Stratton.

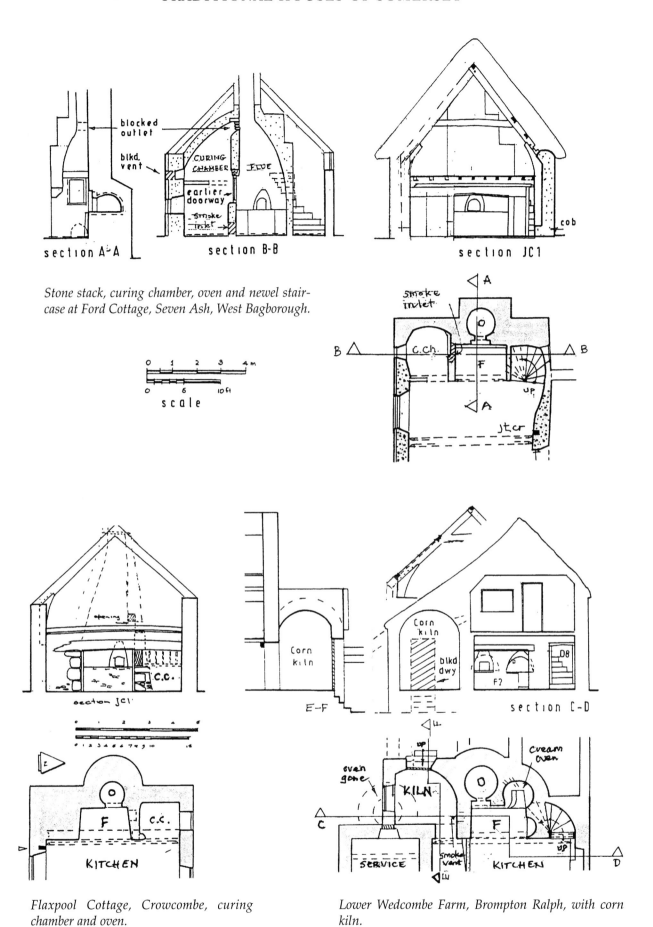

Stone stack, curing chamber, oven and newel staircase at Ford Cottage, Seven Ash, West Bagborough.

Flaxpool Cottage, Crowcombe, curing chamber and oven.

Lower Wedcombe Farm, Brompton Ralph, with corn kiln.

Fig. 4.17 Smoke bays, curing chambers and corn kilns.

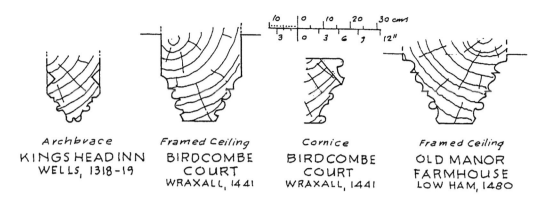

Archbrace
KINGS HEAD INN
WELLS, 1318-19

Framed Ceiling
BIRDCOMBE
COURT
WRAXALL, 1441

Cornice
BIRDCOMBE
COURT
WRAXALL, 1441

Framed Ceiling
OLD MANOR
FARMHOUSE
LOW HAM, 1480

Medieval beams King's Head Inn, Wells, tree-ring dated, d.1318-9; Birdcombe Court, Wraxall, d.1441; Old Manor Farm, Low Ham, d.1480.

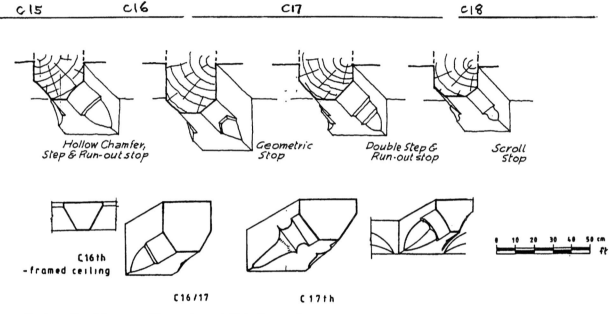

C15   C16   C17   C18

Hollow Chamfer,
Step & Run-out stop

Geometric
Stop

Double Step &
Run-out stop

Scroll
Stop

C16th
-framed ceiling

C16/17

C17th

Post-medieval beams at Batcombe and Chiselborough.

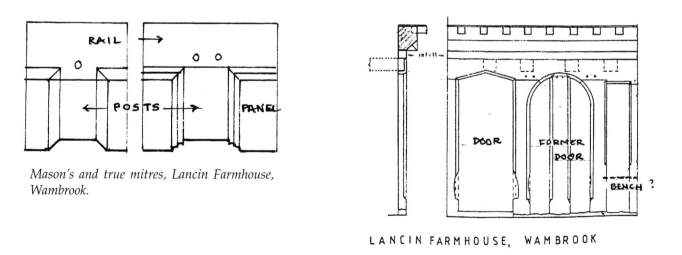

RAIL

POSTS

PANEL

Mason's and true mitres, Lancin Farmhouse, Wambrook.

DOOR

FORMER
DOOR

BENCH ?

LANCIN FARMHOUSE, WAMBROOK

Fig. 4.19 Beams, mouldings, stops and post-and-panel partitions.

Muchelney Abbey, sixteenth century.

Lottisham Manor; moulded framed ceilings.

Trowell Farmhouse, Chipstable, linen-fold panels.

Yarde Farm, Staplegrove.

Decorative stops to door frames.

Fig. 4.20   Timber details, from the late-fifteenth to seventeenth centuries.

FLOOR BEAMS

Timber floor beams are one of the best features for dating purposes. The open halls were floored over with oak or elm beams and almost squarish floor joists, set flat and tenoned into the main beams. If the span was large the beams were massive and carpenters thinned them down by carving plain chamfers along their edges, varying in width – the wider the chamfer the earlier the date (anything from 20cm to 3cm in the eighteenth century). The early plain chamfers in the fifteenth and sixteenth centuries were usually slightly hollowed (**Laburnham Cottage, Batcombe**, fig. 4.19). The mouldings along the edges of the beams were finishing with various decorative 'stops'. These can give a useful date range, seen here with illustrated examples from Somerset houses, the most common being the 'step and run-out' and the later 'scroll-stop', although there are many more decorative stops seen locally (fig. 4.19).

Some medieval beams have elaborate mouldings, with rolls, hollows and 'cavettoes' (the last a very deep hollow). **Birdcombe Court, Wraxall**, had a wing added in d.1441, while its arch-braced roof and first-floor moulded beams are contemporary (both have been tree-ring dated (fig. 4.19). The construction of the wing floor is unusual, having a flush finish made up of alternate floor boards rebated into the top surface of the joists (fig. 4.19).

Another way to make the hall ceiling more decorative was to form a 'framed ceiling' with a grid of main beams and sub-beams making six, nine or twelve large panels in a room (fig. 4.20). The really ostentatious ceilings have their exposed floor joists laid in different directions in the panels, while the deeply moulded beams, sometimes have decorative leaf carvings or bosses at the intersections. These ceilings are mostly of the late-fifteenth or early-sixteenth centuries. Many small houses have simpler framed ceilings with deep plain chamfers of the seventeenth century. At the same time these heavy displays of dark timber began to be succeeded by flat plaster ceilings, decorated in low relief in the better class houses described at the end of the chapter.

PARTITIONS

Most internal cross walls in Somerset were built of timber framing from the medieval period onwards. This took two forms: framed partitions and post and panel partitions. The former consisted of posts, head and cill beams with a mid-rail, the wide panels between filled with wattle and daub. In the seventeenth century the infill changed to rod and daub, in more vertical panels (fig. 3.16).

Post and panel or (stud and plank) partitions are more decorative and usually include one or two doorways, such as at **Lancin Farmhouse, Wambrook**, (fig. 4.19), an open hall house, where the hall ceiling was added in the sixteenth century at a higher level than the original late-medieval partition. Here the posts are jointed to the head and cill beams with a mortice and tenon joint, while the thinner panels were framed by chamfers cut out of the post, using at first, the mason's mitre and later the 'true mitre' (fig. 4.19). The chamfers sometimes stop about 50cm (20ins) above the floor level, giving evidence for an earlier bench seat along the partition, a feature found quite often.

An unusually rich post and panel partition was added c.1500 to a remote medieval farmhouse, **Trowell Farmhouse, Chipstable** (fig. 4.20). These panels had tall linenfold carvings and the posts were deeply moulded next to a four-centred arched doorway of the early Tudor style. The farm was owned by Muchelney Abbey.

WALL PANELLING

This feature was an expensive luxury which could be afforded only by the more well-to-do owners. It is a light form of timber wall cladding where a timber lining was fixed to the wall behind, or occasionally forming a screen.

Above: *Manor Farm, Forton, Chard, seventeenth-century painting on sloping ceiling.*

Left: *Manor Farm, Charlton Mackrell, eighteenth-century panelling.*

Below: *Priory House, Bruton, an added eighteenth-century over-mantel.*

Fig. 4.21   Painted panels, seventeenth and eighteenth centuries.

Panelling was introduced in the sixteenth and seventeenth centuries, presumably as a display feature to be added to existing walls and took the place of wall hangings, painted cloths or tapestries. The framing had four or six small panels in the height of the room with a cornice above and often a frieze of wider panels, carved in a decorative way below the cornice (**Old Brewery House, Bruton**, fig. 4.15). Over the stone fireplace the panelled over-mantel of timber here consists of a typical Jacobean decorative arcade with carved carrot-shaped motifs between the arches. The panelling in the 1630s has 'true mitres' to the mouldings which surrounds each panel (fig. 4.19).

In the mid-seventeenth and eighteenth centuries a more classical style was adopted. The panel proportions were more generous with a cornice and a larger panel above a 'dado' rail over a smaller panel below (fig. 4.21). The panels were either flat or raised using 'fielded' panels, giving the walls a pleasing richness. Later the panels were framed with the fashionable project-ing 'bolection' moulding of c 1670. (fig. 4.2). This moulding, often used in fireplace surrounds, did not last long into the eighteenth century while fielded panels continued in many Georgian houses.

Painted Wall Decoration

Medieval wall paintings are rare and are painted directly on to the wall surfaces, such as the magnificent solar painting, recently restored by the National Trust at the Treasurer's House, Martock (see Chapter 5). There are many other examples of high quality paintings, but we illustrate a modest farmhouse with religious texts painted on the soffit of the ceiling at **Manor Farmhouse, Forton** (fig. 4.21) painted in muted colours. This is seventeenth-century work, while **Manor Farmhouse at Charlton Mackrell** (fig. 4.21) has an early-eighteenth century panelled dining-room added to an earlier house. The very elegant panel paintings show idyllic country scenes so typical of the period. At **Priory House, Bruton**, in an eighteenth-century conversion of a fifteenth-century town house, there is a romantic scene painted in the Dutch style, the painting including Glastonbury Tor and the Levels (fig. 4.21). However these painted scenes are not common and it is the art of decorative plasterwork which dominated the Somerset houses in the 1600s that occurs in many farmhouses and manor houses.

Fig. 4.22   Plasterwork: four fleurs de lis from the heraldic type to the floral flourish popular in the eighteenth century. From left to right: Lytes Cary, c.1530; Orchard Wyndham, c.1540; Forsters, Shapwick 1712; Beckington Abbey c.1620.

Orchard Wyndham c.1540.

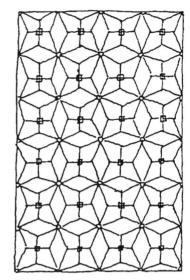

Lytes Cary, c.1530.

Hall ceiling at Poundisford Park, Pitminster c 1570.

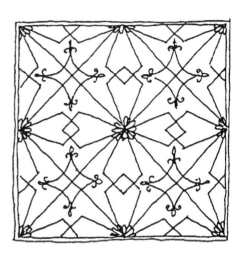

Poundisford Lodge, Pitminster.

Hall ceiling at Nettlecombe Court, c 1600.

No. 18 Fore Street, Taunton.

Fig. 4.23   Dense-packed ceiling patterns of the sixteenth century, to the later
pendants and enriched double ribs of the seventeenth century.

Decorative Plasterwork

Somerset is particularly rich in internal plasterwork, not only in the manor houses but in many farmhouses, whose adoption of such a telling form of decoration always comes as a delight, as shown in the variety of designs of fleurs-de-lis (fig. 4.22).

By the mid-sixteenth century exposed floor joists and beams formed the normal hall or parlour ceiling and upper chambers were still for the most part open to the roof timbers. However, towards the latter part of the century, flat plaster ceilings were adopted, covering the floor joists between the beams. At this time windows were becoming larger and rooms were better lit, and the flat white ceilings and the cross-light from the windows together presented an irresistible opportunity for decoration. The mouldable nature of plaster provided the means.

At first, ceilings were decorated with a geometric pattern of straight thin ribs, forming squares, octagons and lozenges (the solar at **Orchard Wyndham, Williton**, c.1550, fig. 4.23). The early patterns of straight ribs followed timber prototypes in Tudor palaces, and in the Orchard Wyndham ceiling were combined with fleurs-de-lis and coats of arms. These designs were followed by more open patterns with curves and leaf shapes, all made of narrow ribs.

The curvilinear designs in the larger houses derived from late-medieval fan-vaulting, where the ribs fanned out and gathered together again to sweep down to stone pendants, such as those in Henry VII's Chapel at Westminster Abbey. Their domestic plasterwork derivatives however, were, of course, far simpler and smaller but nevertheless formed focal points in the design. For example, those in the ceiling of the hall at **Poundisford Park, Pitminster**, were dated c.1570, from one of the pendants having the initials of a second marriage. The Jacobean ceiling at **Nettlecombe Court** (fig. 4.23) has the more florid character of the 1600s but still retains its pendants.

A very common form of plaster decoration was the small frieze, a narrow strip of plasterwork usually with a repetitive design, moulded in relief and set high up on the walls of the room near the ceiling. Early work on ceilings and friezes was at first confined to the larger houses. The fashion caught on in a surprisingly short time, so that by the end of the sixteenth century many houses of any quality, large or small, were furnished with a decorated ceiling and frieze in the hall and perhaps in the principal chamber too (various friezes, fig. 4.24)

Friezes were cast in short lengths from a wooden carved mould and the design was repeated round the room. Ceiling ribs, however, were run individually by hand onto the flat plaster backing, any decorative motifs taking the form of emblems, such as the Tudor rose, which were moulded on the ground and stuck to the ceiling pattern with plaster. Designs for friezes were complicated; close-packed leafy scrolls, with grotesque monsters or vases and all manner of inventive devices among the foliage, the whole strip of decoration not much more than 6ins/150mm wide. These designs looked for their inspiration to the patterns of classical Rome, but came to us in England via pattern books from Flanders and Germany.

All these early designs have a fresh experimental feel and contain in both ceilings and friezes a new light-hearted element that is enormously attractive. Although these small high-up friezes are hard to see, when looked at in detail they are immensely rewarding – particularly the Peacock Room, Orchard Wyndham c.1600, and at **Whitestaunton Manor** there is a deep frieze of great originality, c.1630 (fig. 4.24).

Parallel with decorated ceilings and friezes, the new chimney-piece with a mantelshelf presented an obvious opportunity for decoration, emphasising the fireplace as the focal point of the room, nearly always the hall. The decorations took the form of elaborate Overmantels (fig. 4.25), incorporating coats of arms in the grander houses, Old Testament stories, strapwork plaques or

The Peacock Room, Orchard Wyndham, a 'grotesque' design c.1600.

Yea Cottage, Cushuish, Cothelstone c.1600.

Court House, Chard 1620.

Whitestaunton Manor, c.1630.

West Coker Manor House, c.1600. Note the strapwork.

The Old Manse, Beckington, dated 1670.

Fig. 4.24 Friezes and overmantels, a variety of imaginative designs.

sometimes, in more modest houses, just the initials of the owner and his wife with perhaps a date (the **Old Manse in Beckington**, fig. 4.24). These simpler devices were common in the farmhouses but the really grand properties had on each side of the mantelpiece, a symbolic figure representing 'Plenty' or 'Wisdom' or other appropriate characters (Gaulden Manor, Tolland). The Tudor Room at Gatehouse, Combe Florey has two truncated effigies (called Terms) each side of the overmantel, on architectural pedestals, dated 1593 (fig. 4.25).

Some of the most appealing overmantels contain popular biblical scenes such as the Garden of Eden, as at **Parsonage Farm, Over Stowey** (fig. 4.25) or, more popular still, 'Abraham and Isaac' shown on a plaque at **Marshwood Farm, Carhampton** (fig. 4.25) where Isaac is kneeling on the sacrificial pyre and both figures are in Jacobean dress, with a little light relief provided by the ram and an angel in the background.

These scenes are often surrounded by 'strapwork' patterns, formed from interwoven flat straps (imitating leather). This robust form of decoration which came to us from Flanders, was typical of Elizabethan and Jacobean work (see **West Coker Manor House,** fig. 4.24).

One exceptional seventeenth-century overmantel is that at **Binham Farmhouse, Old Cleeve** (fig. 4.25) where two female figures frame a scene depicting 'the Triumph of Time' from Petrarch's *I Trionfi*.[8] The panel is large and finely executed; with a winged figure on a chariot drawn by deer (representing the swiftness of time) and supported by both old and young figures.

That such an outpouring of designs, considering that nothing of the sort preceded it, all happened during the last few decades of the sixteenth and the early-seventeenth centuries is truly amazing. All surfaces that could be used were covered with designs, and even the sides of the beams were given floral decorations, a notable example being **Prior's Farmhouse, Stringston** (fig. 4.1). The unsophisticated nature of the plaster decorations of this farmhouse in no way detracts from the rich effect achieved.

By the Jacobean and Stuart period, designs in both ceilings and friezes had moved on. Ceiling ribs became wider, the patterns larger in scale with more open space between the ribs, the panels usually furnished with a floral spray in the corners. The wide ribs were either left plain or enriched with small floral patterns. Friezes had become deeper in great houses such as Montacute, with repetitive patterns or small scenes in panels around the rooms. Overmantels, however, changed rather less and still provided the all-important opportunity for opulent displays of coats of arms and other designs of as showy a nature as possible.

One curious transitional ceiling at **Gaulden Manor, Tolland**, incorporated classical bay-leaf wreaths in large ovals and circles with biblical central figures and an incongruous heavy pendant in the middle (1640). The bay-leaf wreath heralded a complete shift in emphasis towards the classical style of Renaissance design. By the mid-century, after the Civil War, heavy classical designs had completely taken over, with overpowering ceiling wreaths, large cornices and pompous friezes with garlands of flowers and fruit. Supreme examples of the style can be seen at **Dunster Castle**, and **Halswell House, Goathurst** (fig. 4.26) where the plasterwork was added in the 1680s. The feature that caught on at virtually all social levels was the oval ceiling wreath, almost filling the space of the ceiling of the smaller houses (**Stockland Lovell Farmhouse, Fiddington**, fig. 4.26). But even in this sophisticated ceiling design, the plasterer could not resist putting in the odd pagan motif of 'Jack in the green,' often seen in gothic work, while elsewhere in the same ceiling, a classical 'putti' or cherub appears.[9]

Friezes, towards the end of the seventeenth century had practically disappeared and overmantels too were becoming out of fashion, fireplaces being merely surrounded by heavy bolection mouldings.

Only one plasterer has been named in the county, Robert Eaton from Stogursey.[10] He is referred to in a letter from John Frauncis of Combe Florey

Parsonage Farmhouse, Over Stowey: 'Adam and Eve'. *Marshwood Farm, Carhampton: 'Abraham and Isaac'.*

Above left: *Wigborough Manor, South Petherton, a mermaid.*
Above right: *Binham Farm, Old Cleeve, 'The Triumph of Time'.*

Above left: *Gatehouse, Combe Florey, the Tudor Room, 1593.*
Above right: *Montacute House, hall chamber c.1600.*

Fig. 4.25 Overmantels of the sixteenth and seventeenth centuries, with varying degrees of sophistication.

Above left: *Halswell House, Goathurst, a magnificent ceiling, c.1690.*
Above right: *Nettlecombe Court parlour ceiling.*

Above left: *Naturalistic modelling and a grotesque 'green man'.*
Above centre: *Nettlecombe Court, wing ceiling.*
Above right: *Dunster Castle, dining-room, cornice and frieze, c.1681.*

Stockland Lovell Farmhouse, Fiddington, c.1700, parlour.

Fig. 4.26   Classical oval wreaths.

(near Stogursey) in 1599, who was waiting for a builder called Bartlett for his new chimney so that 'Robart Yeaton, the plester man' can carry out the decorative plasterwork there.   The sixteenth-century **Manor House, Combe Florey**, was rebuilt in the eighteenth century, but the earlier Gatehouse survives with a magnificent overmantel in the main chamber, dated 1593 (fig. 4.25). It is reasonable to assume that the craftsman Robert Eaton, who was clearly due to work at the main house, had worked on the overmantel in the Gatehouse six years earlier. The modelling of the Combe Florey plasterwork figures; the chubby faces framed in bonnets, the picture frame round the strapwork cartouche and bulging shields of arms can be compared to other contemporary examples in Somerset such as those in Montacute House. There the overmantel in the hall chamber has a cartouche and flanking Terms which are very similar to those at Combe Florey (fig. 4.25). Other overmantels can also be attributed to Eaton on stylistic grounds.[11]

Notes

1 Dendrochronological dating carried out by English Heritage, following a survey of the manor house by SVBRG, September 2001.
2 Williams, E.H.D., Penoyre, J. and J. and the late Hale, B.C.M., *New Street, Mells* in SANHS Proc. 130, 1985.
3 Pevsner, N., *The Buildings of England, North Somerset and Bristol*, 1958, 1979.
4 Girouard, M., *Robert Smythson and the Elizabethan Country House*, Yale, 1983.
5 Williams, E.H.D., *Curing Chambers and Kilns*, SANHS Proc. 134, 1990.
6 Austen, C. and Hall, Sir R., *The Medieval Houses of Stocklinch*, SANHS Proc. 116, 1972.
7 Gilson, R., survey of Hayes End Farmhouse, South Petherton, SRO Vernacular files.
8 Snodin, M., *Triumph of Time*, one of Four Triumphs confirmed by the Victoria and Albert Museum, London.
9 Gilson, R., survey of Farm Estate, Fiddington. SRO Vernacular files.
10 We are indebted to Robert Dunning, *Victoria County History* editor for this information.
11 Penoyre, J. and J., *Decorative Plasterwork in the Houses of Somerset, 1500–1700*, SCC, 1994.

FIVE

High Status Houses

SECULAR AND ECCLESIASTICAL HOUSES

The larger houses of the countryside are usually thought of as manor houses but this is not necessarily always the case. High Status houses vary in size from the country houses of the aristocracy, bishops or abbots of nearby monastic establishments to the smaller houses of wealthy laymen. Even the quite small houses of village priests were built to a high standard by their ecclesiastical owners. The manor house represented, essentially, the organisational centre of the manor estate as well as being the family residence of the lord, or his representative if he was living elsewhere. It was here that the manorial court was held, where justice was dispensed and property disputes were settled. All these builders could afford standards of luxury, on whatever scale, far and away above the general run of dwellings for the inhabitants of either town or country.

In the context of our study of Somerset houses, the few early-medieval houses that can be identified, have only survived in part, but they are helpful in understanding the sequence of development of the larger domestic buildings. They range from the ground-floor Open Halls or the more rare First Floor Hall houses of the thirteenth to fifteenth centuries, to the inventive Tudor and Elizabethan E-plan and H-plan houses (there are many examples of these in Somerset). Finally to the classical experiments of the late-seventeenth century and the imposed purity of Georgian classicism, in houses generally built after 1700. Our study does not extend beyond that date.

The owners of these larger houses were building to impress and to an extent to compete with their neighbours in comfort, novelty and splendour. The post-medieval owners were often court officials, lawyers and merchants from London or Bristol, who were able to buy the monastic manors after the Dissolution. Somerset was a populous place in the late Middle Ages and by 1515 it had the second highest tax assessment in the country after Middlesex.[14] These builders' advanced architectural ideas were absorbed into the smaller local houses appearing at first as decorative features such as bay windows, porches and arched doorways together with internal improvements in comfort and decoration.

The larger houses described here had both secular and ecclesiastical owners, while the smaller priests' houses are also included for their interesting plans and decorative features.

MEDIEVAL HOUSES AND THEIR ROOF STRUCTURES

Early houses may contain only a surviving hall, solar or chapel, the original building being approximately dated by the survival of its early roof design or by the mouldings of doorways, windows, fireplaces or beamed ceilings,

The tall Norman house from the north. (G .ROBERTS)

First-floor hall window.

Fig. 5.1   Saltford Manor near Bath, a remarkable twelfth-century survival.

all of which can be dated stylistically. Only a few timber roofs and floors have been dated precisely by dendrochronology.

Saltford Manor, near Bath,[1] is a rare survivor of the late-Norman period, built in the mid-twelfth century by the Earls of Gloucester who endowed the nearby Keynsham Abbey (fig. 5.1). The spectacular house is a tall two-storey rectangular block with a high roof (rebuilt in the seventeenth century) and a former first-floor hall with adjoining solar supported on heavy beamed floors over ground-floor services and storage. A remarkable semicircular arched window to the hall has zig-zag decoration over paired lights with a central column between them in the late-Norman manner (fig. 5.1). The house was converted in the seventeenth century to three storeys and the original roof replaced, but Saltford Manor remains a marvellous example of an unchanged single range first-floor hall of the mid-twelfth century. Such halls are seen occasionally throughout the country and in Somerset there are some later monastic grange farms which also had first-floor halls (see below).

Another early form of high status house was the 'aisled hall house,' which was the successor to the medieval aisled buildings of royal castles and palaces, found in the excavations of the twelfth-century royal palaces at Cheddar. The aisled hall (as its name suggests) has two rows of columns or posts forming aisles, as in a church, the posts introduced to help the roof to span across the wide halls of these grand houses. At the Bishop's Palace at Wells the ruins of an aisled hall built by Bishop Burnell in 1275 was an example of such a hall. At present we know of only one surviving candidate for a former aisled hall – it is at **Manor Farmhouse, West Newton** where there are remnants of five aisle posts (two pairs and one in the end wall of the hall) but alas, no original roof over.[3] It is possible that there never were any other aisled halls, there being a strong local tradition of large cruck-framed structures (see the many recorded examples of R. Gilson and the late E.H.D. Williams. [2,3,4]

At the end of the thirteenth century there were some interesting developments in roof structure found in a few Somerset manors and large farmhouses. Some of these houses have recently been tree-ring dated (fig. 5.7) and have a curious hybrid structure which harks back to the fully aisled hall, but without the inconvenience of the aisle posts themselves. Such early buildings were built by wealthy landowners who introduced new methods of construction from other parts of the country, combining them with the local tradition of cruck trusses. True and jointed cruck roofs are described in Chapter 3.

Higher Broughton Farmhouse, Stoke St Mary (fig. 5.2) was a grange farm of the Bishop of Winchester who owned the rich manor of Taunton Deane.[5] The farmhouse exists today, rebuilt in later centuries, but still with parts of its original late-thirteenth century roof over hall and service end. The former open hall had no aisle posts but instead a large arch-braced cruck truss (only one half remains) together with a timber-framed end wall of the hall extending from the ground to the apex of the roof. This closed frame has two tall posts, like aisle posts, supporting a braced tie-beam, the braces forming a characteristic arch shape. The whole structure is called an 'aisled-end truss' and is most striking when seen in a farmhouse of moderate width like Higher Broughton (6.5m span) where aisle posts are not necessary and may only survive here in the service end wall for display as a high status feature. This truss and a surviving service room end cruck have been tree-ring dated to between d.1267 and d.1299, one of the earliest domestic roofs found in Somerset to date. Stokesay Castle in Shropshire, also built in the late-thirteenth century, has probably the best known arch-braced cruck roof in the country spanning a much larger hall without posts and combined with an aisled-end truss in the end wall. Higher Broughton Farm although very much smaller and nothing like so grand, was built at the same time and with a very similar roof form.

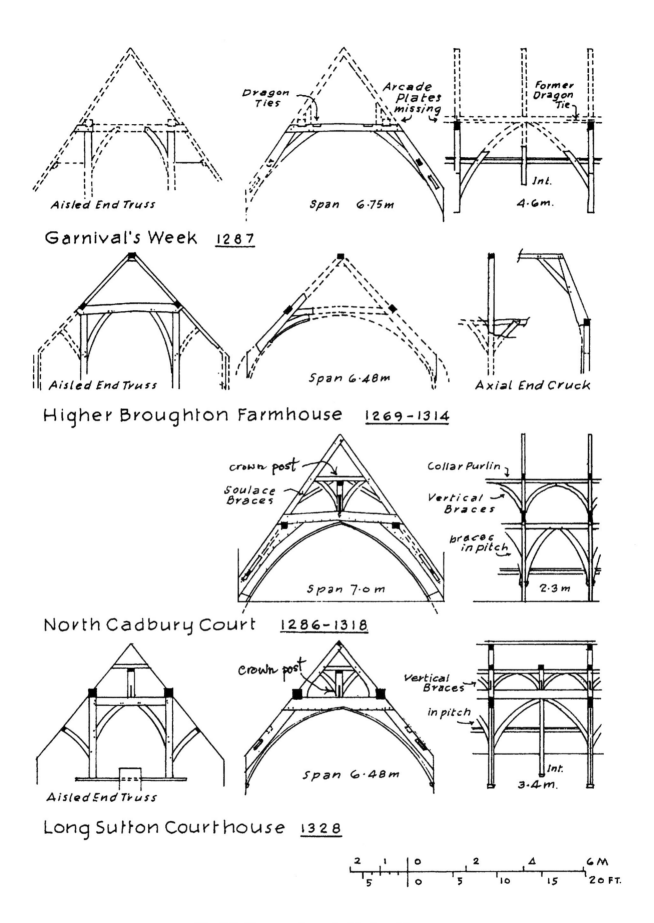

Fig. 5.2   Base crucks and aisled-end trusses.

Garnival's Week, Milverton (fig. 5.2) has had its roof tree-ring dated to d.1287. It also has the remains of an aisled-end truss combined with a base cruck over the hall which has massive windbraces below square-set plates used instead of purlins (the plates are another relic of aisled-hall construction). Base crucks were a form of truss designed to span across wide halls without having to resort to free-standing posts. The arch-braced crucks reached up no higher than the tie-beam with another form of roof above the tie. Garnival's Week had a secular owner, John de Gernevillle, documented in 1327 as having a messuage and land in Milverton.[6]

Bratton Court, Minehead[3] is recorded as having traces of three aisled-end trusses, one at each end of the hall and one in the low-end gable wall. Here a base cruck with intermediate trusses spans over the large two-bay hall, an exceptional survivor from the fourteenth century.

Base-cruck trusses of the early-fourteenth century, have an unusual form of upper roof for our area (fig. 5.2). Such roofs provide longitudinal bracing to the common rafters by adding small crown posts supporting collar purlins, the former braced in four directions. These features are seen more often in the South East and Midlands of England, and are very rare in the South West – so much so that they are regarded here as alien importations.

North Cadbury Court (figs 5.2, 5.3) in the south-east of the county, has a wonderful solar roof tree-ring dated d.1286–1318 with massive base crucks and a crown-post upper roof which included soulace bracing to the common rafters. The crucks were once closely spaced, the arch-braces very heavy and their windbraces finished with a moulded terminal. The roof, being over a first-floor solar rather than a hall, had no aisled-end truss and the base crucks were later repositioned and their arch-braces removed altogether to insert an Elizabethan Long Gallery. The arch-braces were restored in the twentieth century.

Another aisled-end truss can be seen in the **Court House, Long Sutton**,[3] where the upper roof of the base crucks is of hybrid design, with small upper crucks as well as crown posts (figs 5.2, 5.3). Tree-ring dated d.1328, this is a remarkably complete hall house (the roof is still visible, although the hall is now floored over) with a compact two-storey service end and a large porch. The **Tudor Tavern, Taunton**[4] still has its open hall roof on view, a spectacular base-cruck roof combined with crown posts above. This high status town house was built c.1350 (fig. 6.4). Recent tree-ring dating of the roof timbers provided the date d.1323–24 (figs 5.7, 6.4, 6.6).

Base crucks in Somerset are more often built with their upper structure in the form of a second tier of small crucks sitting on the tie-beam (fig. 5.4). Such two-tier crucks, are seen in monastic houses and barns built by Glastonbury Abbey from the late-thirteenth to the late-fourteenth centuries. Both **Doulting Barn**,[3] dated d.1288–90 and **Glastonbury Barn**,[2] d.1334–44, are magnificent examples of the two-tier cruck roof, one of the most decorative of all designs (figs 5.3, 5.7). This two-tier version of a base cruck is virtually confined to Somerset, with only a few examples in Wiltshire and Dorset.

There are some interesting smaller houses, built by the monasteries and cathedrals for their ecclesiastical officials and grange estates. Glastonbury Abbey built two such houses, both now called Bridge Farm; one is at Butleigh only a few miles from Glastonbury, sited beside a stream. The other is nearby at Baltonsborough, where it controlled an important sluice for the monastery, described as 'the house of Oswold Delaburne' in the perambulations of Abbot Bere of 1503. It is also mentioned in an early-thirteenth century document.[7] **Bridge Farmhouse, Baltonsborough**, has been greatly altered but has exceptionally rich cusped two-tier base-cruck roof trusses, smoke blackened and hidden in the roof space (figs 5.4, 5.7). The roof timbers are tree-ring dated to d.1336. **Bridge Farmhouse, Butleigh**[8] is smaller and less ornately roofed, but has survived better, with an open hall (now floored over) with service rooms in the main range and a small two-storey contemporary

Below: *North Cadbury Court, solar; base crucks and crown posts, d.1285–1317.*

Right: *Abbey Barn Glastonbury, a two-tier base cruck roof, d.1334–1344.*

Below: *Court House, Long Sutton; base cruck, aisled-end truss d.1328. (J. McCann)*

Fig. 5.3   Base cruck roofs of the late-thirteenth and fourteenth centuries.

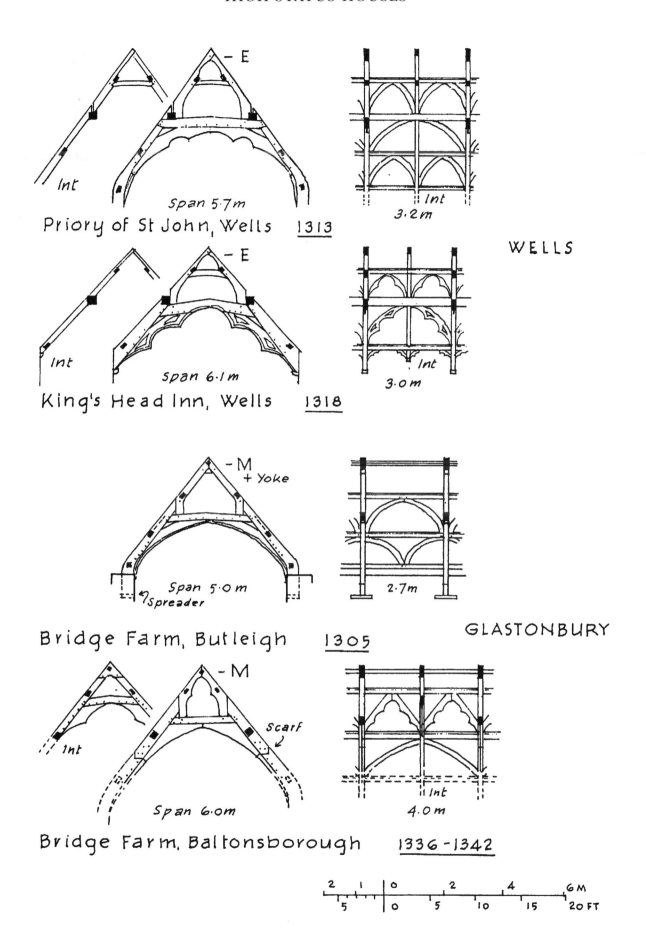

Priory of St John, Wells 1313

King's Head Inn, Wells 1318

WELLS

Bridge Farm, Butleigh 1305

GLASTONBURY

Bridge Farm, Baltonsborough 1336-1342

Fig. 5.4 Two-tier base cruck roofs (letters indicate apex types).

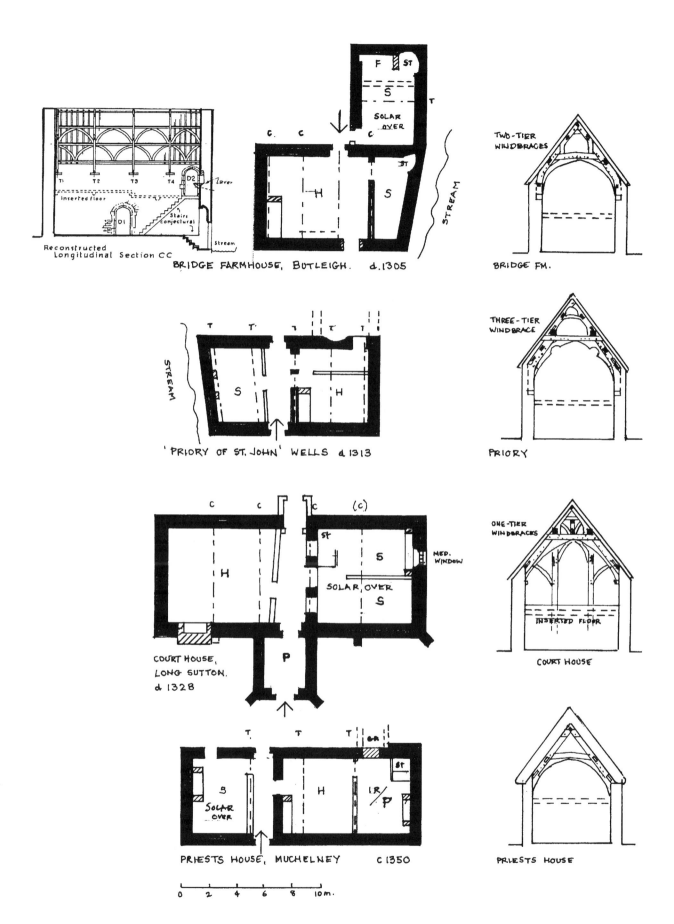

Reconstructed
Longitudinal Section CC

BRIDGE FARMHOUSE, BUTLEIGH.   d.1305

TWO-TIER
WINDBRACES

BRIDGE FM.

'PRIORY OF ST. JOHN' WELLS   d.1313

THREE-TIER
WINDBRACE

PRIORY

COURT HOUSE,
LONG SUTTON.
d.1328

ONE-TIER
WINDBRACES

INSERTED FLOOR

COURT HOUSE

PRIESTS HOUSE, MUCHELNEY   c.1350

PRIESTS HOUSE

0   2   4   6   8   10m.

Fig. 5.5   Fourteenth-century houses with ground-floor halls.
(ORIGINAL SURVEYS BY R. GILSON AND E.H.D. WILLIAMS)

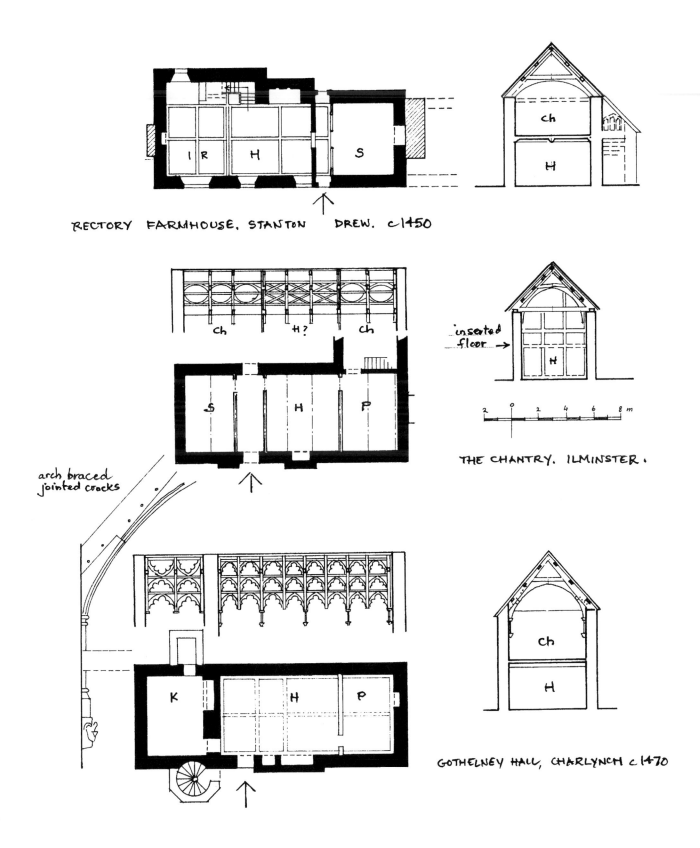

RECTORY FARMHOUSE, STANTON DREW. c1450

THE CHANTRY. ILMINSTER.

arch braced
jointed crocks

GOTHELNEY HALL, CHARLYNCH c1470

Fig. 5.6 *Fifteenth-century houses with ground-floor halls and first-floor chambers open to the roof.* (ORIGINAL SURVEYS BY R. GILSON AND E.H.D. WILLIAMS)

chamber wing (figs 5.4, 5.5, 5.7). The hall roof has raised two-tier base crucks, smoke-blackened and tree-ring dated d.1305. This tree-ring date was repeated in the first-floor beam of the wing which, having a smaller span, has simple arch-braced true crucks instead of two-tier base crucks. One of these true crucks was evidently reused from an earlier building, having a mortice for a former lap joint and a date of d.1263. The main range has a decorative four-bay roof with scallop patterned windbracing and two four-centred arched stone doorways, one at ground level entering from the yard and the other into the first-floor chamber, probably from a straight flight of stairs in the hall. This stair has been removed but there was a short newel stair from the ground floor down to the stream, where there is an external doorway with a two-centred arch. No windows or fireplaces survive from the medieval period although there are indications of a former fifteenth-century lateral stack in the hall; the large kitchen fireplace is an addition. The fourteenth century use of this house is hard to understand, its plan limited to a ground-floor hall open to the smoke-blackened roof with a contemporary solar wing. Although this could have been a grange farm, its simple form seems more suited to a hostelry or guesthouse for the nearby abbey, but in this case no documentary evidence has been found to bear it out.

In contrast, there are two small houses in Wells, each with the same type of roof. The first house, next to the site of the **Priory of St John in Wells**,[2] is similar in plan, structure and date to the Butleigh Bridge Farmhouse (figs 5.4, 5.5). Its proximity to the former Priory of St John suggests it may also have been a guesthouse or even the house of the prior himself. Lying parallel to the street, it has a compact two-room plan with a small but complete roof of two-tier base crucks and intermediates, tree-ring dated d.1313. The decorative roof has arch-braces and three tiers of arched windbracing, all smoke blackened. The little hall had an open hearth, with a rather late inserted fireplace and there was a newel stair in a small wing. The four bays of the roof define the original length of the house, the south end adjoining a stream. Both this house and the next to be described have the very unusual, if not unique feature of carpenters' marks cut in both Roman and Arabic scripts. Arabic numerals in each are confined to one side of the house with Roman on the other, seen mainly on the windbraces.

The second house lies in the High Street of Wells. This is a small town house, now the **King's Head Inn**[4] which has a magnificent two-bay two-tier trussed roof (no visible cruck post) tree-ring dated d.1318 – only five years later than the Priory House base cruck roof, which it so much resembles in design (figs 5.4, 5.7). The hall roof is at right angles to the street, as in most medieval town houses (figs 6.4, 6.5).

Priest's Houses

A well-known village house, owned by the National Trust, **Priest's House in Muchelney**,[9] is thought to have been built in the early-fourteenth century, a date suggested by the style of the two-centred arched doorway and the true-cruck roof over the open hall and solar (fig. 5.5). In the late-fifteenth century when the Abbot of Muchelney was rebuilding his own quarters, the Priest's House may also have been upgraded and given similar traceried windows, a hall fireplace and a framed ceiling in the parlour. The house has the typical three rooms in-line plan of a rural farmhouse, originally with a turret stair and garderobe extension at the back. The smoke-blackened roof has widely spaced true-cruck trusses, the hall cruck arch-braced with one tier of windbraces. The cruck has an early saddle apex of the fourteenth century and the whole roof was of a simpler design suitable for a rural priest and farmer of the glebe lands.

Two priest's houses of the fifteenth century in the north of the county, have similar plan forms but their roofs were no longer crucks. **The Old Vicarage, Congresbury**[10] (not illustrated) and **Rectory Farmhouse, Stanton**

Drew,[11] (fig. 5.6), were both two storeys throughout and built by Bishop Beckington c.1450 from the evidence of heraldic plaques. The Congresbury house is smaller with two rooms and passage, a mural straight staircase and a large porch. The Stanton Drew house has three rooms, with a lateral stack, a straight stair leading to the chambers and to a small upper room. This was either an oratory or a muniment room having a barred three-light arched window facing east (fig. 5.6). Both houses had arch-braced collar trusses open to the first-floor chambers and both houses had ground-floor halls with beamed ceilings, perhaps of secondary importance to the chambers above.

The last example of a priest's house is **The Chantry at Ilminster**,[12] a large two-storey house built c.1460, facing the churchyard, west of the church. It is likely that it was shared between two or three chantry priests. Originally the house was L-shaped with three equal-sized rooms with chambers over and a two-storey service wing (fig. 5.6). The roof is ornate with eight bays in the main range having many arch-braced open trusses and two closed trusses, one on each side of the central hall. This hall roof has two tiers of cusped windbraces, the other rooms with plainer ones. What is odd is the proportion of the hall, rather tall, almost a cube, with an open roof. The end rooms below the passage and the hall both have lateral stacks on the front of the house, and the high-end parlour has an original gable fireplace. The chamber over the parlour is thought to have been an oratory, and had a small window overlooking the chantry in the church.

Opinions differ on whether the hall was originally of one or two storeys. Margaret Wood[10] thought it was always divided into two floors. W.A. Pantin[13] held the view that there might have been a gallery access to the chambers, the roof being visible from the ground-floor hall. E.H.D. Williams and R.G. Gilson were also of the opinion when they surveyed the house, that it was a tall ground-floor hall, as the stud and panel partition between hall and high-end reached right up to the apex of the roof, and had no horizontal cill at the present first-floor level. However, the earlier windows were taller than the level of the present first floor. There is a horizontal rail at a higher level which may represent the original floor level, with a chamber above having its superior roof open to view. Indeed, the late Maurice Barley[14] wrote:

> Out of the 13 stone-built parsonage houses in Somerset, 10 were built on two levels from the start. The first floor rooms were not in any way the more important; it seems that the houses were designed for several men leading more or less independent lives and fluctuating in numbers.

This is quite appropriate for The Chantry at Ilminster, where in 1458 there were no less than four different chantry bequests with named chaplains. The house was probably built by John Wadham (the founder of Wadham College, Oxford) who built the large chantry chapel in the church opposite the house in Ilminster.

A Summary of Tree-Ring Dated Roofs
(fig. 5.7)

A short digression from the chronological description of houses is necessary here to describe the distribution of tree-ring dated cruck roofs in their two main groups: the true and jointed crucks in the smaller houses and the base crucks and two-tier crucks in the high status houses. Both form of crucks have a wide distribution throughout the county, but the special type of base cruck, the two-tier cruck appears as a speciality of the two main ecclesiastical owners, Glastonbury Abbey and Wells Cathedral. They both use this unusual form of base cruck and the examples are grouped around the two centres (fig. 5.7, map). This may suggest that both establishments shared the same craftsmen who were familiar with this uncommon design.

Medieval Somerset Roofs with Tree Ring Dates

Sampling by Daniel Miles, Michael Worthington and Dr Martin Bridge. *entries are by others.

Type	Building	Parish	Felling date	C13	C14	C15	C16
Base Crucks and Aisled-end Trusses	Garnivals Week	Milverton	1287				
	Higher Broughton Fmh	Stoke St Mary	1267 - 1299				
	N. Cadbury Court, wing	North Cadbury	1285 - 1317				
	Court House	Long Sutton	1328				
	Rectory Farm Barn *	Englishcombe	1314 - 1558				
Two Tier Base Crucks	Abbey Farm Barn	Doulting	1288 - 1290				
	Bridge Farmhouse	Butleigh	1305				
	Priory of St John	Wells	1314 -15				
	Kings Head Inn	Wells	1318 - 19				
	Tudor Tavern	Taunton	1323 - 24				
	Abbey Barn	Glastonbury	1334 - 44				
	Bridge Farmhouse	Baltonsborough	1336 - 42				
	Hannam Manor, solar	Cheddar	1341 - 42				
True Crucks	West End Fmho, Barton	Winscombe	1278 - 79				
	Castlebrook Farm Barn	Compton Dundon	1283 - 88				
	East Lynch Cottage	Selworthy	1315				
	Crane Farmhouse	Somerton	1338				
	21 Woolston Road	North Cadbury	1344				
	Wick Farmhouse	Norton St Philip	1371 - 72				
	Yew Tree Farmhouse	Chew Stoke	1386				
Jointed Crucks	47 & 49 Goose Street	Beckington	1391				
	Stockland Lovell Fmh	Fiddington	1404				
	No.2 Lower Cockhill	Castle Cary	1435				
	Lancin Farmhouse *	Wambrook	1533				
Principals with Curved Feet	Birdcombe Court, wing	Wraxall	1441				
	Pilton Manor, dovecote	Pilton	1441 - 46				
	20 Vicars Close	Wells	1466				
	Viaduct View	Pensford	1512				
Arch-braced Collar Trusses	The George Inn	Norton St Philip	1431 - 32				
	Whitestaunton Manor	Whitestaunton	1446 - 78				
	Tickenham Court	Tickenham	1471 - 76				
	Low Ham Manor Fmh	High Ham	1481				
	Shapwick House	Shapwick	1489				
Tie/Collar and Post & Truss	23, 25, High Street	Rode	1429				
	24 High Street	Bruton	1430				
	16, 18, High Street	Bruton	1454				
	31 High Street	Bruton	1453 - 54				
	20 High Street	Bruton	1462				
	43 St Thomas Street	Wells	1462 - 63				
	28 St Thomas St	Wells	1485				
	Lodge Farmhouse	Norton St Philip	1491 - 1523				
	Wigborough Manor	South Petherton.	1585				

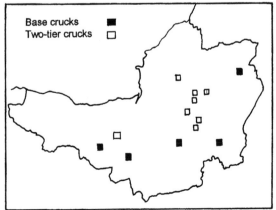

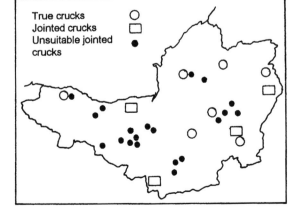

Fig. 5.7   Medieval Somerset roofs, dendrochronology dates and cruck distribution maps.

The other group of the more conventional base crucks (those with different types of upper roofs, see fig. 5.2) are scattered across the rich farming lands in the south of Somerset. Three of these houses were in secular ownership and the fourth, Higher Broughton, Stoke St Mary, was owned by the Bishop of Winchester as part of his large demesne estate in Taunton Vale. It seems probable that the design of this group of roofs was inspired by examples in the South East of England. The second map shows the distribution of the dated houses with the true and jointed crucks found in farmhouses throughout the county. Because of the excessive numbers of roofs, particularly jointed crucks, which have failed to date successfully, we show only six dated examples of true crucks and four of jointed crucks, as described in Chapter 3 (fig. 3.11). The smaller dots on the map are the unsuccessful ones owing to the unsuitability of the timbers, mostly elm or fast-growing oak, again sited on the rich agricultural land.

The chart (fig. 5.7) shows the sequence and various types of Somerset roofs dated by dendrochronology between 1996 and 2002.

Ecclesiastical Manor Houses

Somerset has a few examples of large medieval houses built by bishops and abbots as retreats from their working establishments. The best known belonging to the Bishops of Bath and Wells were at Wookey and Banwell. (Abbots of Glastonbury had favourite houses at Meare, Sharpham and Pilton and some other grange estates near Glastonbury may have been used as residences or retreats.) The earliest bishops' houses, **Banwell Court**[15] and **Court Farmhouse, Wookey**,[16] have been largely rebuilt and only a few original features remain; a fourteenth-century traceried window opening in the solar gable at Banwell and a magnificent thirteenth-century entrance doorway formerly leading to a hall or chapel at Wookey.

At **Martock** the Treasurer of Wells Cathedral owned a large estate and house, now called **Treasurer's House**.[17] Much of the layout and structure survives from this thirteenth- and fourteenth-century building (fig. 5.8). It has a T-shaped plan with a fifteenth-century detached kitchen added to the corner of the solar wing. The wing is the earliest part, having one of the most complete domestic interiors of the thirteenth century; a plate-tracery solar window with trefoil cusping surrounded by exceptional wall paintings with figures and sprigged masonry joints painted in red line. (The house and paintings have recently been restored by the National Trust). The first-floor beams of a passageway in the wing are at a lower level than the wing floor and could show the original floor level, although the thirteenth-century roof has been replaced. At right angles to the wing is the large main hall built in the early-fourteenth century, with cinquefoil cusped inner arches over the windows and inviting stone seats below (fig. 4.7, 4.8). The ground-floor hall is unusual in that it has a two-light traceried window in the end gable wall, and there is no trace of a fireplace, although there must have been one, probably a lateral stack. The magnificent arch-braced roof is considered to be a fifteenth-century replacement (fig. 5.12). Two large two-centred doorways lead from the hall and passage to the yard of the fifteenth-century detached kitchen.

Abbots' houses have suffered from post-medieval alterations a good deal less than houses belonging to bishops. Meare Manor House, now **Manor Farmhouse, Meare**, near Glastonbury is a very complete example of an abbot's country house, built by Abbot Adam of Sodbury (figs 5.9, Plate 9). The tall L-shaped house had an exceptionally large first-floor hall over a retainers' hall and cellar in the main range (the first-floor beams, d.1325). The surviving large hall has tall cinquefoil-headed lights in two-centred arched windows and a rare hooded fireplace with carved foliage to corner candle brackets (fig. 5.9). Only the stub ends of the arch-braced roof trusses remain to indicate a former more steeply pitched roof (probably another decorative two-tier cruck open roof like the other fourteenth-century roofs built by

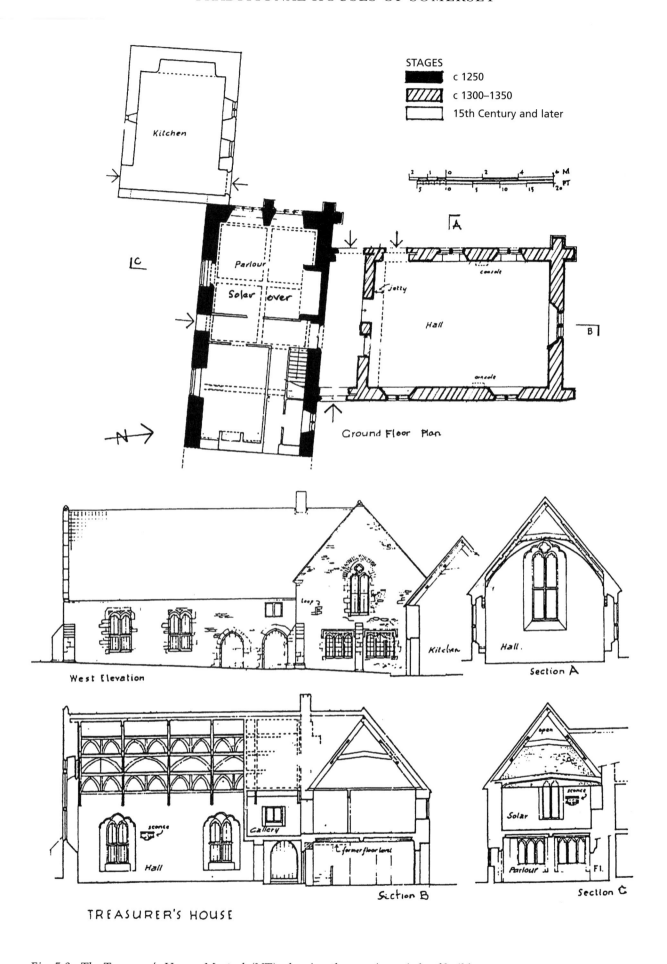

STAGES

■ c 1250
▨ c 1300–1350
□ 15th Century and later

Fig. 5.8 *The Treasurer's House, Martock (NT), showing three main periods of build.*

Glastonbury Abbey). However, the original length of the hall is not easily recognised now and the low dividing screen could have been on either side of the hooded fireplace, with the Abbot's chamber at the south end, its moulded doorway (D3) leading to the chapel in the wing. This would mean that the fireplace could either have been in the hall or in the Abbot's chamber. If the latter, then perhaps the hall had a central hearth or brazier built over the former vaulted cellar below (now demolished). But if the hall included the hooded fireplace, at the Abbot's dais end, then the size of the hall suggests a space suitable for entertaining on a large scale. There was access down to the enclosed yard and possible former detached kitchen. Monastic first-floor halls are rare survivors and their planning is not generally understood, but the sheer size of this hall goes some way to confirm that the former Meare Manor was a summer residence of the Abbots of Glastonbury. In the early-sixteenth century Abbot Bere added extensive residential additions, but these have not survived.

The front wing originally contained a large first-floor chapel, with many arched windows, now blocked (fig. 5.9). Service rooms below became a domestic kitchen in the sixteenth century. An elegant two-storey porch provided access from the adjoining parish church.

The Manor Farmhouse has recently been surveyed[18] and interestingly the house has not much changed since the nineteenth century records made by A. Nesbitt and J.H. Parker.[19] The house was also illustrated by Margaret Wood in 1965.[10]

Shapwick House, Shapwick[20] is a large Glastonbury manor house not far from Meare. The house as it stands today has passed through many changes but retains a fifteenth-century roof, d.1489 (fig. 5.10). Its medieval origins are referred to in a survey of 1327, where it is described as 'a Court'.[21] Evidently the fifteenth-century roof is itself the remains of a later rebuild. The house is very tall, 9m to the eaves, suggesting a large first-floor hall open to the decorative roof as the hall at Meare Manor would have been.

The house was also described in a survey of Abbot Bere in 1515[21]: 'in the demesne there with hall, chamber, storeroom, kitchen, stable, garden and barton inside the moat and an oxhouse outside the moat.' A portion of the moat referred to has been found in a recent archeological dig some 15m north of the house, flanked by a building, probably twelfth century.[22]

The building at the time of the 1515 description was T-shaped, an east–west hall range with an eastern chamber wing, both roofed at the same time (fig. 5.10, development plans). A detached kitchen lay to the west (d.1428). After the Dissolution and various other ownerships, the manor was acquired, in the early-seventeenth century, by rich lawyer Henry Rolle, who was later to become Lord Chief Justice under the Commonwealth. He remodelled the house in the high Jacobean manner (see Collinson's print, fig. 5.10). He inserted a long gallery beneath the hall roof, built a new west wing to balance the east wing with huge mullioned and transomed bay windows to the hall and wings, both back and front. He adapted the ground floor as his 'hall', building many chambers above instead of the original first-floor hall. He died there in 1656.

In the nineteenth century the house was once again modified and given a new symmetrical south front with a central porch. The house is now a hotel.

The extensive medieval roof of Shapwick House is of interest in that it was built, very unusually, with seasoned timbers. It comprises two ranges of arch-braced trusses to the hall and wing, both with two tiers of windbracing and intermediate trusses to give a densely packed appearance. The roof (d.1489) was built a good deal later than was expected based on stylistic grounds. Both roofs were grossly mutilated to receive Henry Rolle's long gallery, but enough remains to bear witness to the former splendour of this Glastonbury Abbey building.[23]

A useful comparison can be made of these three medieval hall houses, all built by ecclesiastical owners. The houses have similar sized halls, although

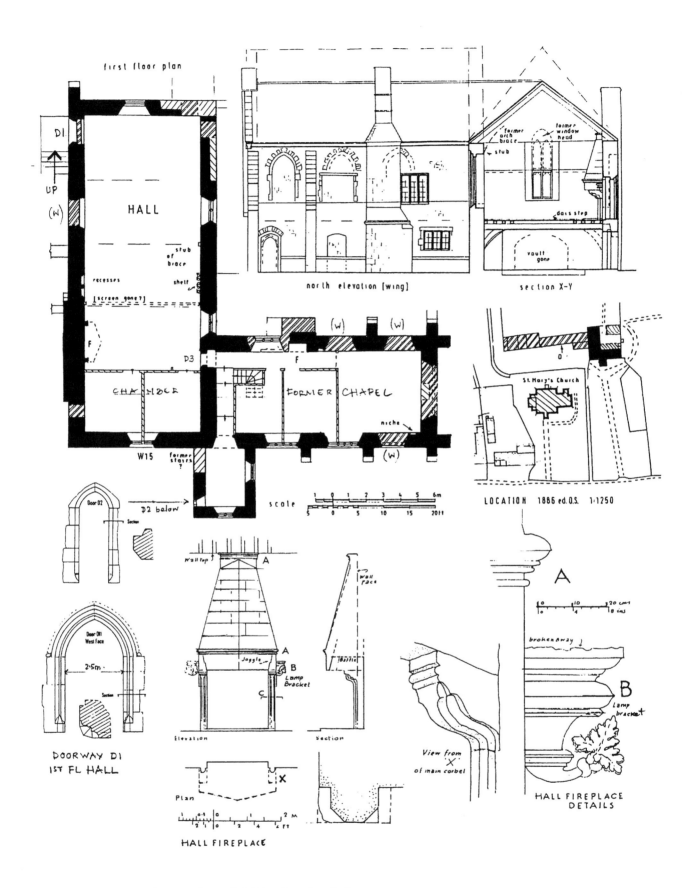

Fig. 5.9   Manor Farmhouse, Meare, d.1325, a first-floor hall.

here Shapwick House (fig. 5.10) is drawn to a smaller scale to fit the page. The internal spans of the halls are: Treasurer's House, 6.6m, Meare Manor, 7.0m and Shapwick House, 6.5m.

One exceptional roof should be mentioned here. **Lodge Farm, Durston**,[24] near Taunton is an interesting house with a traditional three-room plan, a ground-floor hall, cross passage and a solar over the services. There is a large porch with a chapel on the first floor above (Plate 9). The hall would have had a wagon roof like a church; the many common rafters with curved braces are heavily smoke blackened and apparently were never boarded in. The only longitudinal member is a collar purlin instead of the more usual purlins in the roof slope. The house has two-centred traceried windows and the hall is separately roofed from the solar. As discussed above, this is a distinguishing characteristic of fourteenth-century houses, the end of the hall showing as a free-standing gable.

Secular Houses

Turning to secular houses of the grander sort, there are several well-known houses dating from the medieval period. **Clevedon Court in North Somerset** was built by Sir John de Clevedon c.1320, using an earlier hall as a detached kitchen for his fourteenth-century house, with the typical large three-part plan and cross-wings, seen in most houses of the period (not illustrated). A remarkable oriel chamber used as a chapel has large square-headed windows with reticulated tracery, said to be of the early fourteenth century when that type of tracery was built. (It appears in a seventeenth-century painting of Clevedon Court). No early roof survives to our knowledge.

The fifteenth century brings another blossoming of decorative roof types, the arch-braced collar roof, used in many of Somerset's greatest houses – a good example is the hall of **Treasurer's House, Martock** (fig. 5.12). In the north of the county, **Birdcombe Court, Wraxall**,[25] has a fifteenth-century wing added to a fourteenth-century hall range (fig. 5.11). The arch-braced roof formerly open to the wing chambers and the heavily framed ceiling of the parlour below, are both tree-ring dated d.1441, giving a precise date for the cusped windbracing and associated beam mouldings. Cusping is also associated with fourteenth-century roofs. The principals of this roof have short curved feet, representing the last phase of the cruck roofs, overlapping the introduction of the straight principal rafter roof (fig. 5.11).

Also in North Somerset, **Tickenham Court** (d.1471) has a splendid open hall and solars with roofs of the arch-braced collar type, and in the south of the county **Lytes Cary** near Somerton (c.1453) and **Cothay Manor, Stawley** (c.1480) have beautiful roofs still open to view. But there are many others which are hidden in attics such as at **Fairfield, Stogursey** (fig. 5.12) with carved gothic arches on the solar trusses, and **Whitestaunton Manor**[26] near Chard (figs 5.11, 5.12) where the hall roof is heavily cusped and moulded (d.1446–78). This roof has 'false' hammer beams, with heavy moulded arch-braces, the truss once supported on former carved brackets. At Whitestaunton, in the sixteenth century a hall chamber was inserted and wings were added to make a U-shaped plan, absorbing a previously detached medieval kitchen.

In the west of Somerset there is a courtyard house, **Orchard Wyndham, Williton**[15], which spans the centuries from the early-fifteenth to the late-seventeenth. Here the house has probably acquired its courtyard form by accretion rather than as an original concept. The manor belonged to the Orchard family, followed by the Sydenhams and later the Wyndhams who have made it their family home to this day. The earlier roofs are cruck framed. The existing hall is tall and open to a decorative timber roof of c.1500, formerly with cusped windbraces. The remains of an earlier hall (or kitchen) has a large true-cruck roof.

Collin Son's print c1790.

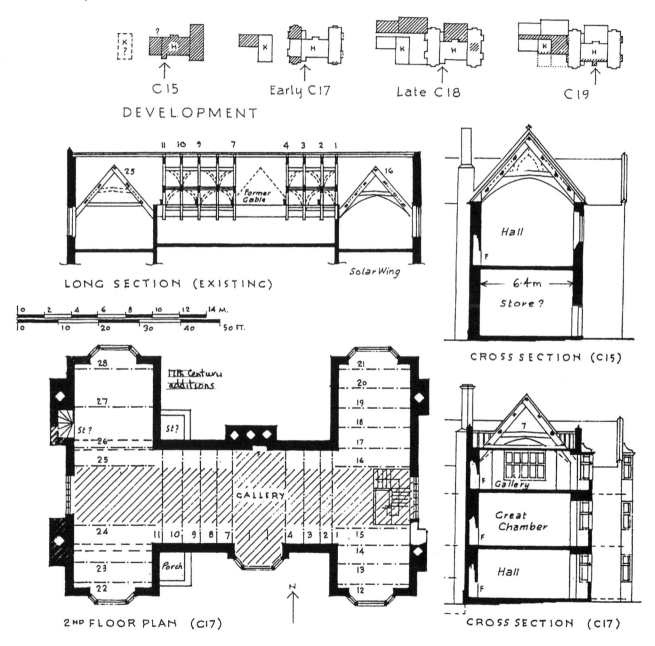

Fig. 5.10 *Shapwick House (Hotel). Development, medieval roof and plan of the Long Gallery, in the early-seventeenth century.*

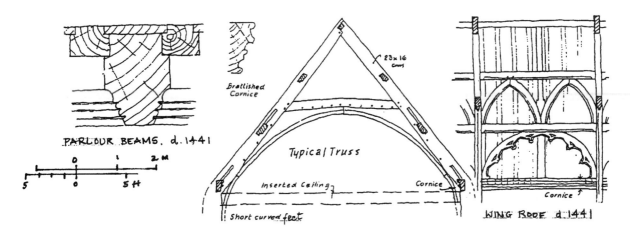

Birdcombe Court, Wraxall, the wing, d.1441.

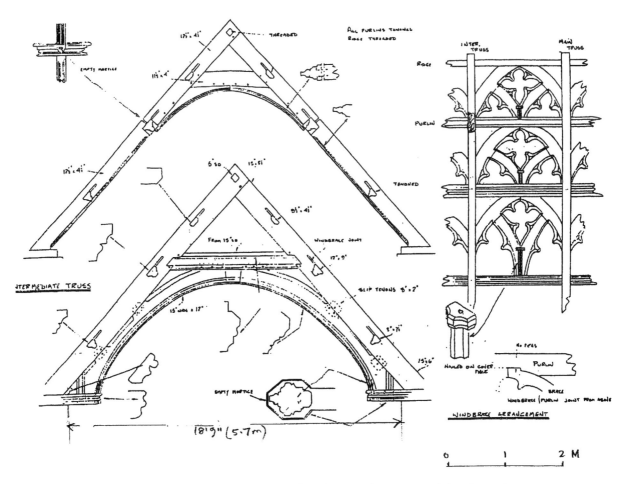

Whitestaunton Manor, hall roof d.1446–78, with unusual 'false hammer beam trusses'. (R. GILSON)

Fig. 5.11   Fifteenth-century roofs, arch braced and heavily cusped.

The Treasurer's House, Martock, hall roof.

Fairfield House, carved cusping on arch-braces.

Whitestaunton Manor, hall roof.

Fig. 5.12   Decorative arch-braced roofs of the fifteenth century.

The plans of these secular houses are all in the late-medieval tradition of having large ground-floor halls with two-storey cross-wings. By the fifteenth century there was a tendency for the grouped mullioned windows to be made larger and taller, terminating in the splendid displays of the Elizabethan and Jacobean periods, as seen in the rebuilt hall range at **North Cadbury Court** (d.1589, Plate 10). But some owners of smaller manor houses were building in a refreshingly new way, with smaller squarish halls and flat beamed ceilings rather than leaving their roof structures open to view from the ground. The halls had large chambers above, these rooms still with open roofs.

A remarkable early example is **Gothelney Manor, Charlynch**,[15, 27] built in the mid-fifteenth century by a well-to-do lawyer (fig. 5.6). The 'Great Chamber' as it became known in the Elizabethan period, has a particularly ornate arch-braced roof, with three tiers of cusped windbraces supported by arch-braced jointed crucks bracketed on carved posts and corbelled heads. This Great Chamber or upper hall (now an attic) was combined with a tall flat-ceiled hall below with painted moulded beams. Nearby, another fifteenth-century house, also built by a lawyer, **Blackmore Farm at Cannington**, has the same arrangement of two halls, the upper one with an open roof and a large chapel in a wing. Unusually the chapel has an upper-floor gallery with a view of the altar below.

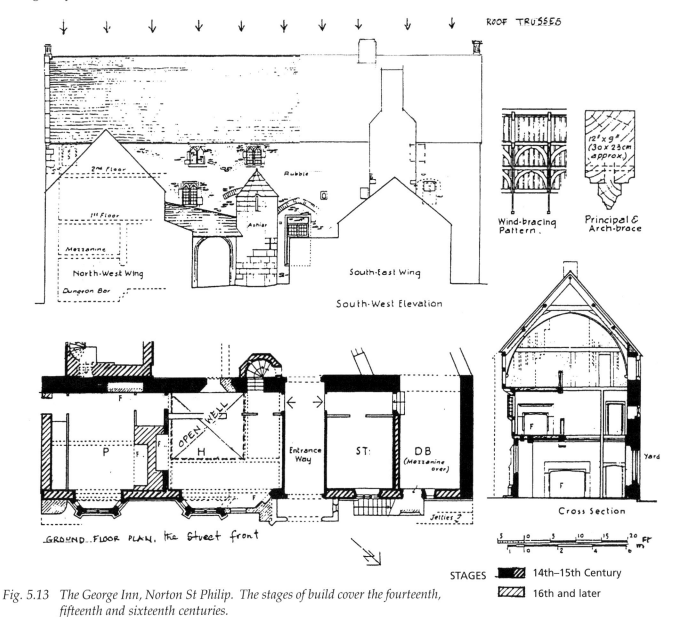

Fig. 5.13 The George Inn, Norton St Philip. The stages of build cover the fourteenth, fifteenth and sixteenth centuries.

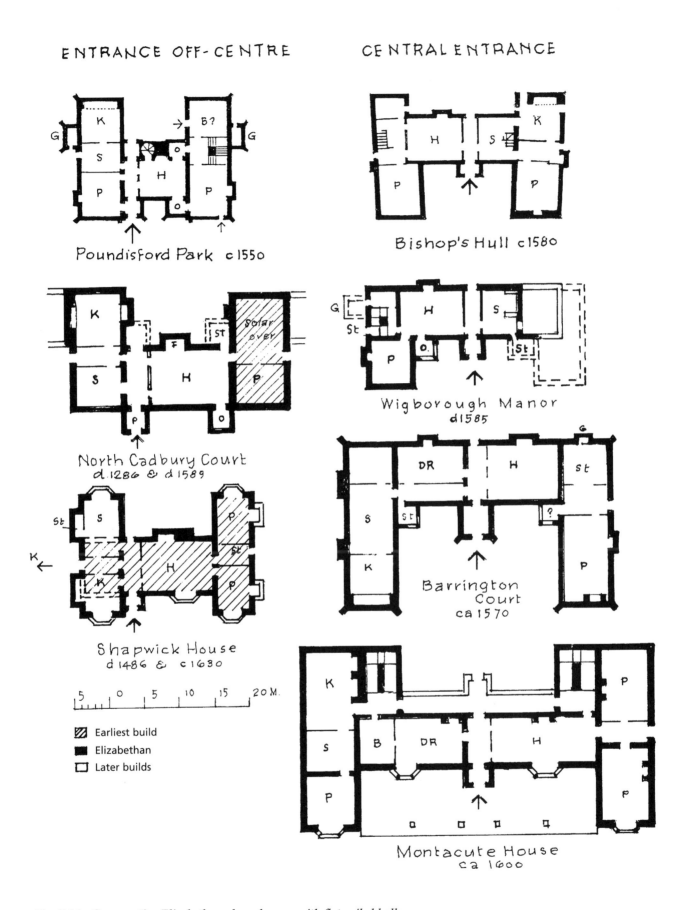

ENTRANCE OFF-CENTRE   CENTRAL ENTRANCE

Poundisford Park c1550

Bishop's Hull c1580

North Cadbury Court
d.1286 & d1589

Wigborough Manor
d1585

Shapwick House
d1486 & c1630

5 0 5 10 15 20 M.

▨ Earliest build
■ Elizabethan
☐ Later builds

Barrington
Court
ca1570

Montacute House
ca 1600

Fig. 5.14 *Comparative Elizabethan plans, houses with flat-ceiled halls.*

Manor Farmhouse, Meare, d.1325 (roof replaced).

Lodge Farmhouse, Durston.

Court House, Long Sutton, d.1328. (J. MᴄCᴀɴɴ)

The George Inn, Norton St Philip (timber façade and roof added d.1431).

Plate 9   Three fourteenth-century houses, with generous porches and large roofs.

Clockwise, starting above:
Brympton d'Evercy, c.1540: Tudor-Gothic.
Bishop's Hull, Taunton, 1589: Elizabethan.
Nettlecombe Court, c.1589: Elizabethan.
North Cadbury Court, hall range d.1586.

(J. McCann)

Plate 10   Tudor and Elizabethan buildings – magnificent opulence, c.1500–c.1600.

Poundisford Park, the former entrance front. (G. ROBERTS)

Poundisford Park hall – flat-ceiled with decorative plasterwork.

Clockwise, starting above:
Montacute House, the former entrance front. (G. ROBERTS)
The Long Gallery and oriel bay window.
Classical niches.

Plate 11   These two houses demonstrate the change of styles in the Elizabethan high status houses.

Hinton House, Hinton St George. The wing was added c.1630.

Right:
Brympton d'Evercy, wing added c.1670.

Below:
Halswell House, Goathurst, also a later wing, 1689.

Plate 12   Three Classical wings, added to earlier houses.

To end our sequence of fifteenth century structures we must look at a different type of building – a large late-medieval inn, **The George at Norton St Philip** (fig. 5.13, Plate 9). It was first built as an inn and as a market house for the sale of woollen and linen cloth by the Carthusian Monastery of Hinton Charterhouse in the fourteenth century.[28] Originally built all in stone on two tall floors, this huge building has various medieval features; very thick walls, small trefoil-headed windows to the upper floors and a vaulted cellar. The building was drastically altered, re-fronted and re-roofed in the fifteenth century to comply with the new fashion for showy timber-fronted town houses. The linen trade had blossomed, for this was an international market, and the inn was used to house both the visiting merchants and their wares during the twice-yearly fairs. So a third floor was inserted, with a new eight-bay roof over attic storage space. This new roof is tree-ring dated d.1431, the same year as the double-jettied decorative timber façade. The inn had a most unusual internal feature; a large open-galleried well, trimmed with deeply moulded beams and extending through two storeys, exposing the central arch-braced roof trusses to the ground-floor hall. By tree-ring dating the infilling joists, we know that the open well continued in use until d.1510. The building has many good features including a sixteenth-century wall painting, the whole building having recently been restored by English Heritage and Wadworth Brewery.[28]

Post-Medieval Houses

Houses of the sixteenth century illustrate the transition from medieval irregular forms to the developed classical symmetry of the late-seventeenth century, inspired by the Renaissance buildings of Italy, France and the Netherlands. Decoration too, both internal and external, began to display both classical and gothic features, the latter seen in the splendid Tudor façade at **Brympton d'Evercy** (Plate 10). Although sixteenth-century house plans begin to have symmetrical wings, the entrance porches and cross passages only become central towards the end of the century, and even then it may have been a matter of personal choice (fig. 5.14, plans). The halls became smaller and were no longer needed for public gatherings, although they were beginning to have flat decorative ceilings, which were a good deal higher than the other ground-floor ceilings. This incurred changes of level in the floor above or, in extreme cases, chambers directly over the hall being confined to the roof space (e.g Poundisford Park, Plate 11). Other specialised rooms could be accommodated in the wings – first floor courtrooms, for example, **Whitestaunton Manor** and in the **Court House, Chard**, where courtrooms were added during the seventeenth century. These rooms have barrel ceilings, the latter with lavish decorative plasterwork showing appropriate motifs suitable for a courtroom, such as 'Daniel in the lions' den' or 'the Judgement of Solomon'. Sixteenth-century kitchens were sited in a wing rather than detached from the house across a yard, as the stone-built chimneys of the period had reduced the risk of fire in the main house.

Poundisford Park, near Taunton[29] is an early experiment in regular planning, but with an off-centre entrance, combined with decorative features of the post-medieval period; arch-headed windows, corner buttresses and tall chimneys (Plate 11). The plan (fig. 5.14) is symmetrical with two cross-wings; here the two-storey porches are balanced with oriel bays and there are two identical garderobe turrets, one to each wing. This is also one of the earliest houses in Somerset with a square hall – tall but flat-ceiled rather than open to the roof. Halls were not generally flat-ceiled until the 1570s, when plaster-work ceilings were fast becoming popular to display the devices of the period, with thin-ribbed patterns and pendants, (fig. 4.23). Poundisford Park is a thoroughly Elizabethan house, compact and stylish with comfortable, well-lit rooms to suit the new class of owner/builders, who during the 1500s were coming to the fore. In this case the owner was William Hill, a prosperous Taunton merchant and overseas adventurer, who bought the estate in 1546. We do not know how soon after buying the estate he built the house, but certainly by 1570 he was displaying in the hall ceiling the initials of his second wife, Lucy Ryves, whom he married that year.

One other well-known house, **Barrington Court**[15] includes opulent early-sixteenth century features. In particular, this includes the huge windows and twisted chimneys and tall finials topping the many gables, combined here with even more rigidly symmetrical planning, with a centrally placed entrance, set between projecting wings (figs 5.14, 5.15). The house was previously thought to have been built at the beginning of the century but is now considered to be the work of a London merchant in c1570. Even this date is early in relation to other houses with central entrance porches such as Montacute, built c.1600. At nearby Wigborough Manor, South Petherton, d.1585 (fig. 5.14), a house which has lost its service wing, there is a large flat-ceiled hall. Other contemporary houses with large flat-ceiled halls still retain their off-centre entrances, such as the hall range at North Cadbury Court, tree-ring dated d.1589 (fig. 5.14, Plate 10) and at **Nettlecombe Court**, c.1599 (Plate 10). However, these three houses have much earlier documented dates or else surviving work from earlier builds, and their rather untypically large halls could well have been built on earlier foundations. **Bishop's Hull Manor**, near Taunton,[30] c.1589, has a central entrance porch with a nearly symmetrical plan (fig. 5.14, Plate 10), where the flat-ceiled hall has been balanced by the service rooms each side of a four-storey central porch. The house had an embryonic 'Long Gallery' in its attic storey – the next essential Elizabethan feature.

Both **Shapwick House** and **North Cadbury Court** in their Elizabethan rebuilding, have had long galleries imposed below their formerly open roofs. At Shapwick (fig. 5.10), the arch-braced trusses of the first-floor hall have been badly mutilated to form the gallery space, lit by two large mullioned and transomed windows in the end gables. In addition, one large bay window (now gone) was inserted into the medieval hall range (see Collinson's print c.1790, fig. 5.10). At North Cadbury Court[31] the hall range was entirely rebuilt with three storeys (fig. 5.14, Plate 10). The long-gallery roof trusses following the profile of the thirteenth-century roof of the solar wing, had to be altered drastically to allow the insertion of the end-gable window to light the new gallery. However, it was at **Montacute House**,[32] built c.1600, that the magnificent gallery was planned from the start. For Montacute is the ultimate achievement in Elizabethan manor houses, with an entirely symmetrical H-plan (fig. 5.14, Plate 11) and a central entrance; the large flat-ceiled hall to the east, balanced by attenuated service rooms to the west (a dining-room soon replacing the buttery and pantry). The balanced long wings provided two well-lit parlours and on the north side, two turret staircases, instead of oriel bays, provided improved vertical circulation. The only thing missing from this excellent plan was horizontal circulation, other than through one room to the next, on the ground and first floors. This problem was overcome very cleverly in c.1780 when a corridor and porch was built out along the west front, the structure coming from another house, Clifton Maybank. That house was originally built in the early-sixteenth century in a very elegant manner, which contrasts strangely with the more austere seventeenth-century style of Montacute.

William Arnold, a master mason from Somerset, is thought to be the designer of Montacute House[15] where he achieved a Renaissance style using enormous windows with square-headed lights, pedimented bay windows, Dutch gables and rounded oriel bays surmounted by strapwork scrolls, at each end of the immense Long Gallery. These features were derived from Flanders rather than Italy or France (Plate 11). William Arnold designed several well-known Elizabethan manor houses, and locally his influence can be seen in some arcaded porches and shell-headed niches, the latter found at the **Manor House, Charlton Horethorne**. At Montacute the niches are grouped in pairs – for conversations perhaps (Plate 11). Arnold died in nearby Charlton Musgrove in 1637.

The Classical Period

In the early-seventeenth century a purer form of Italianate classicism was emerging, following the inspiration of Inigo Jones working in the 1620s at Greenwich and Whitehall. Some of the more wealthy house owners were adding a range of state apartments to their houses in the form of large classical wings. In South Somerset, two neighbouring families, the Pouletts of **Hinton House, Hinton St George**[15] and the Sydenhams of **Brympton d'Evercy**[15] had built large mansions of the Tudor period. They added two-storey classical wings, both designed in the 1650s in the style of Inigo Jones' 'Banqueting Hall' in Whitehall, which they resembled. These buildings (Plate 12), built by Royalist families, may have been built in memory of King Charles I.[15] In the case of Hinton House, the wing could even be 'The Banqueting House', a lavish addition made in c.1650 using Hamstone and local bricks.[33] This wing is referred to as 'the State Apartments' and included a chapel by the end of the century. These spectacular additions included tall transomed cross-windows under pediments. At Hinton House (c.1630) the pediments are triangular and the parapet above has pierced gothic quartrefoils. The basically similar wing at Brympton d'Evercy, thought to have been completed some 40 years later (the Civil War having intervened), displays none of the transitional features of Hinton. The parapet is conventionally balustraded, there are no moulded string courses and the rather more generously proportioned windows have alternate triangular and segmental pediments, a richer and more assured classical design (Plate 12). A third example at **Ashton Court, Long Ashton** (c.1635) is a three-storey wing, more austere in character but still with a similar arrangement of windows. All three houses were linked by family connections.

By the end of the seventeenth century, extensions to earlier houses reached the height of classical elegance as seen at **Halswell House, Goathurst**, dated 1689 (Plate 12). This tall three-storey block, added as an entrance wing to an earlier house, has all the sophistication of the best work of the period and includes some exquisite decorative plasterwork (fig. 4.26).

This digression into classical houses is no more than a reminder that by the end of the seventeenth century the more familiar vernacular features of the smaller houses (like four-centred arches, mullioned windows, etc.). These were no longer acceptable at the higher social levels, and by the mid-eighteenth century were wholly superseded by the universally accepted simplified classicism of the Georgian good taste, shown here in the contrasting styles of **Barrington Court** (gothic) and **Tintinhull House**, (classical) both handsome houses in South Somerset (fig. 5.15).

Notes
1 Little, B., 'Saltford Manor, Somerset,' *Country Life*, 24 July 1958.
2 Williams, E.H.D. and Gilson, R.G., *Base Crucks in Somerset I*, SANHS Proc. 121, 1977.
3 Williams, E.H.D., and Gilson, R.G., *Base Crucks in Somerset II*, SANHS Proc. 123, 1979.
4 Williams, E.H.D. and Gilson, R.G., *Base Crucks in Somerset III*, SANHS Proc. 125, 1981.
5 Penoyre, J. and J., SVBRG, *Higher Broughton Farmhouse, Stoke St Mary*, VA 28, p.113, 1997.
6 McDermott, M., *Garnival's Week Farmhouse, Milverton*, VA 28, p.99, 1997.
7 Morland, S., *Glaston Twelve Hides*, SANHS Proc. 128, 1984. Also personal correspondence.
8 Penoyre, J. and J., SVBRG survey SRO 1988, 1999. VA 28, 1997.
9 Williams, E.H.D., survey, *Priest's House, Muchelney*, SRO, 1979.

10 Wood, Margaret, *The English Medieval House*, 1965.

11 SVBRG survey *Rectory Farmhouse, Stanton Drew*, SRO, 1989.

12 Williams, E.H.D. and Gilson, R.G., survey, *The Chantry, Ilminster*, SRO, 1987, and Wood, M.[10]

13 Pantin, W.A., 'Chantry Priest's Houses and Medieval Lodgings,' *Medieval Archeology III*, 1959.

14 Barley, M., *Houses in History*, Faber, 1986.

15 Dunning, R., *Some Somerset Country Houses*, Wimborne, 1991.

16 Hasler, J. and Luker, B., *Court Farm, Wookey*, SANHS Proc. 137, 1993.

17 The National Trust, *The Treasurer's House, Martock*, NT leaflet, 1998, and SVBRG survey, SRO, 1986.

18 SVBRG survey of Manor Farmhouse, Meare, SRO, 2001.

19 Nesbitt, A., 'Manor House, Meare,' *Archeological Journal* vol 10, no 38, 1853. Also Parker, J.H., *Domestic Architecture in the Middle Ages*, vol. II, 1853.

20 SVBRG, *The Vernacular Buildings of Shapwick*, 1996.

21 Costen, M., *A Survey of the Manor of Shapwick 1327*, Shapwick Project Report 2, 1989. Also Costen, M., *Abbot Bere's Terrier 1515*, Shapwick Project Report 3, 1990.

22 Gerrard, C., *Excavations at Shapwick House Hotel, 1994*, Shapwick Project Report 7, 1997.

23 We are indebted to Bob Machin for this interpretation.

24 Gilson, R.G., *Three Somerset Manor Houses*, SANHS Proc. 129, 1985.

25 Williams, E.H.D. and Gilson, R.G., survey, *Birdcombe Court, Wraxall*, SRO, 1980, 1986.

26 SVBRG and Gilson, R.G., survey *Whitestaunton Manor*, SRO 1996.

27 Williams, E.H.D. and Gilson, R.G., survey, *Gothelney Manor, Charlynch*, SRO, 1984.

28 Williams, E.H.D., Hale, B., Penoyre, J. and J., 'The George Inn, Norton St Philip,' *Archeological Journal* vol. 144, 1987. Also Rodwell, K., Mann, Fergus, handbook, published by Wadworth Brewery, Devizes, 1999. Dendrochronology in 1998–99 by Dan Miles of the Oxford Dendrochronology Laboratory.

29 Penoyre, J. and J., SVBRG survey, *Poundisford Park, Pitminster*, SRO, 1988.

30 Williams, E.H.D. and Gilson, R.G., survey, *Bishop's Hull Manor, Taunton*, SRO, 1986.

31 SVBRG survey, *North Cadbury Court*, SRO 1997. Also note [15], Dunning, R.

32 National Trust handbook, *Montacute House, Montacute*, 1988.

33 Penoyre, J. and J., SVBRG survey *Hinton House, Hinton St George*, SRO, 1989.

33 Dunning, R., *Some Somerset Houses*, Wimborne. p.73, 1991.

Fig. 5.15 Contrasting façades; Tudor Gothic and classical styles.

Below left: *Barrington Court, c.1570.*
Below right: *Tintinhull House. It has a c.1700 façade.*

SIX

Town Houses

THE TOWNS

In this chapter, although we are primarily concerned with the planning and structure of individual town houses, we are also interested to show the original street patterns where they are known to have been planned or where the original layout can be deduced from what remains. On the whole the larger medieval town layouts take the familiar form of a dominant High Street with deep, but narrow burgage plots running to a back lane. Where several roads converge on a town the High Street will usually broaden out into a market-place (e.g. Bruton, Glastonbury and Wells).

Of the many early towns in the county two have Roman foundations (Bath and Ilchester) and 11 others were listed in the Domesday Survey of 1086.[1] Smaller medieval towns whose origins date from the thirteenth and fourteenth centuries have surviving planned layouts and some of their houses are illustrated here. There are many examples of fifteenth-century houses with two-room frontages, sometimes later divided into two separate houses when the town became less prosperous, an example being Nos 26 and 28 St Thomas Street, Wells (fig. 6.13, Plate 15), which was originally one house.

Two small towns in South Somerset, Somerton and Montacute, have medieval origins but they vary in appearance chiefly because of their local building stones. Somerton was a royal Saxon town for a short time in the eighth and ninth centuries but it did not regain its importance until it became a borough in the thirteenth century when the new main street was made to bypass the old centre. The street now runs south of the church through a large market-place and turns north in a broad main street to rejoin its former course.[1] This layout is seen today, with strikingly handsome houses in Blue Lias stone with Hamstone dressings although these are mostly sixteenth century and later rebuilds. There is at least one house in West Street which has a timber jettied front, while others of similar early date may have been refaced.

Montacute is a much smaller town (figs 6.12, Plate 13), now a village, with two periods of planned development. In the twelfth century a small town called Bishopston was established there below the castle motte, then in the thirteenth century, the Cluniac Priory laid out a new borough with a prominent market-place. The houses lining the market square today were built at various dates in yellow stone from the adjoining Ham Hill, a complete contrast in appearance to the Blue Lias stones of Somerton, although the towns lie only 7 miles apart.

Another small late-medieval town, Mells, this time in the north-east of the county (fig. 6.12), was owned by Glastonbury Abbey, and in the fifteenth century Abbot Selwood, a keen builder, laid out a new street plan in the form of a cross, but only New Street, leading to the church, was actually built.

Bruton is perhaps the best example of a planned monastic small town, founded by the Augustinian Priory in the twelfth century on the north side of the River Brue.[1] An earlier Saxon town is thought to have been sited south of the river where the church and the priory were built. The present town's trade and prosperity was mostly based on the woollen cloth industry in the fifteenth and sixteenth centuries, no doubt encouraged by the Priory. It has the familiar layout of a High Street which broadens out into a triangular market-place at the east end, subsequently built over (fig. 6.1). Two back lanes are connected to the main street, on one side by steep 'bartons', footpaths leading down to the river and mills. Our surveys of six houses dated by dendrochronology show that they were all built around 1450, a surprisingly consistent date obtained from jettied timber fronts and roofs (figs 6.8, 6.9, 6.10).

Fig. 6.1   Bruton town plan.

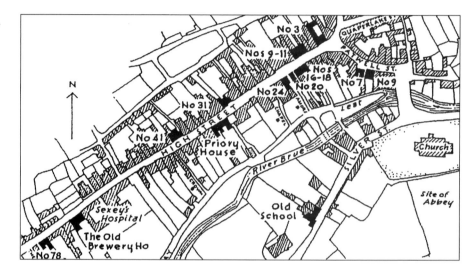

The Houses

Looking at the houses within these towns, their individual plan-forms were restricted by the limitations of the size and shapes of the original plots. They are consistently related in plan to their rural counterparts, using the one, two or even three-room frontage plans. Similarly planned town houses can be seen in adjoining South-West counties, particularly in Devon.

The number of surveyed town houses in our county is small compared to the many rural examples surveyed. Our own group's research was mostly in Bruton and Wells and to these we have added some previously published examples made in the 1960s and '70s. W. Pantin[2] is well known for his studies of town-house plans generally throughout the whole country and R. Taylor recorded many houses in Taunton.[3] The remarkable surveys of R. Gilson and the late E.H.D. Williams of some fourteenth-century structures in Taunton and Wells[4] provide a splendid basis for our later dendrochronology work.[5] Another interesting study was made for the Royal Commissioners for Historical Monuments (RCHM) by Roger Leech and local researchers on the houses of the Trinity area of Frome, which was largely built for cloth-trade workers in the late-seventeenth and early-eighteenth centuries.[6]

Taunton and Wells are both towns large enough and early enough to have had the restriction of expensive rents and narrow frontages. This restriction resulted in the adoption of the single front room plan, with a side passage leading to the rooms behind, all roofed at right angles to the street with a prominent timber-framed front gable. Such houses are of two or three storeys. The plan is type 1 in our text and was described as the 'right-angled plan' by both Pantin and Taylor (fig. 6.4). In the smaller towns with houses of the fifteenth century onwards, and where commercial pressures were less acute, the two-room frontage house with a central passage was more convenient for the use of the smaller shop-keeper or town official. Any additions could be in the form of a wing or wings behind – described as type 2 here, or the 'parallel type' in the earlier publications (fig. 6.4). Taylor himself describes type 1 as the earlier plan found in the larger towns of western Somerset and Devon, where the dividing walls were of stone and the front and back walls were more usually built of timber framing, jettied in the front. He also states that the more easterly towns like Crewkerne, Chard and Sherborne (Dorset) are less urban in character, adopting type 2 with their two front rooms and roofs parallel with the street. We have found this to be the case in surveyed houses in Bruton, Wincanton, Mells and Norton St Philip and the type is also seen in Wells, in some side streets away from the more intensely developed centre. Only the Trinity area of Frome provides a variety of plan types within one street. Here the two-room houses were favoured for the weavers, with their large looms occupying the ground-floor service rooms (fig. 6.14).

We now look at the individual houses, mostly of the fourteenth and fifteenth centuries, plan type 1. **Vicars' Close, Wells** (fig. 6.2, 6.3), is a well-known mid-fourteenth century scheme planned by Wells Cathedral to house 42 'Vicars' Choral' in small individual units within two parallel terraces. It is probably one of the earliest and most elegant groups of priests' dwellings in England, built to a high standard of design. The Bishop of Bath and Wells, Ralph of Shrewsbury, began to build the houses in 1346 and finished them after the Black Death, c.1363.

No. 20 Vicars' Close[7] has been examined in detail and the first-floor joists were tree-ring dated to d.1349. The vicars lodged in their houses, eating their meals in a separate communal first-floor hall, and it is possible that they had a servant or relative living in the house. The entrance opened directly into the ground-floor hall, heated by a small lateral fireplace; adjoining the entrance was a post-and-panel screen defining a small service area (with a small front window). In the hall were two trefoil-arched mullioned and transomed windows, an ogee-arched laver-niche and two doorways which led to a turret stair and the back yard, formerly with a garderobe below the stairs. Upstairs, a large heated chamber was open to a decorative roof. By looking at several houses in the Close it was possible to recognise original features which have been lost in some of the other houses, such as the squinted doorway through the thick back wall to the yard, which was often blocked in later alterations. No. 20 had its mullioned windows replaced by sashes, but No. 22 still has its stone arched windows (fig. 6.2, 6.3).

In the next century, Bishop Beckington unified the terraces, originally built piecemeal over a period of time. He (or his executors) built a continuous sloping roof running down the Close, with arch-braced and windbraced trusses, tree-ring dated d.1466 in No. 20, (the form of the earlier fourteenth-century roof is not known). At the same time he extended the lateral chimneys with tall decorative octagonal stacks. Altogether Vicars' Close is an exceptional build and forms an important part of the whole cathedral complex.

Next we look at town houses, which were often built by the Church for leasing to commercial or domestic tenants. These houses of the fourteenth and fifteenth centuries are variations of plan type 1, with single front rooms facing the High Streets in Wells and Taunton where they occur on narrow fronted plots, their roofs end onto the street. These houses display magnificent and inventive roofs over their internal open halls. Later in the fifteenth century, the upper chambers became the most important rooms, also built open to the decorative roofs.

A small house in the High Street, the **King's Head Inn, Wells,**[8] has an extremely ornate truss over the hall (fig. 6.4, 6.5), tree-ring dated d.1318. It is very similar to that in the Priory of St John, also in Wells (fig. 5.4, 5.5). The Priory is unusual for Wells with its roof parallel with the street, the medieval building probably being free-standing originally. The King's Head Inn is

Above: *High Street, Rode, a town involved with the woollen cloth industry.*

Above: *No. 22 Vicars' Close, Wells, once two terraces, built near the cathedral, 1349.*

Fig. 6.2 *Street scenes from North Somerset.*

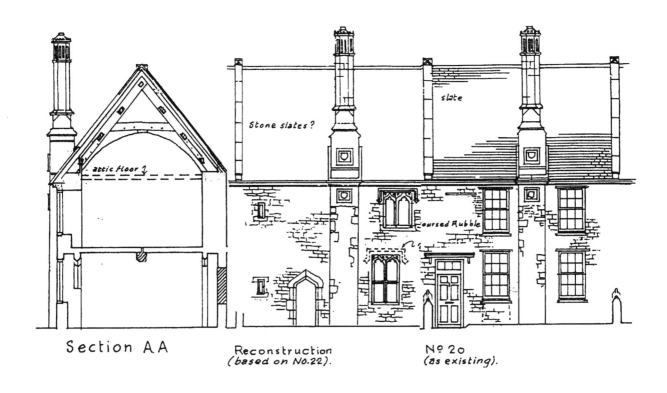

Section AA

Reconstruction
(based on No.22).

No 20
(as existing).

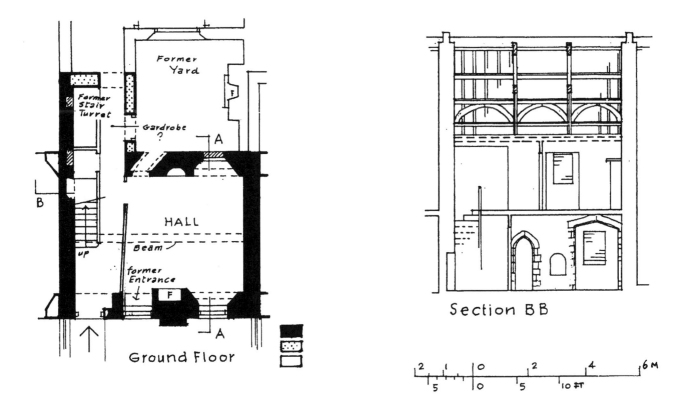

Ground Floor

Section BB

No 20, VICARS' CLOSE, WELLS

Fig. 6.3   Ecclesiastical houses of the fourteenth and fifteenth centuries.

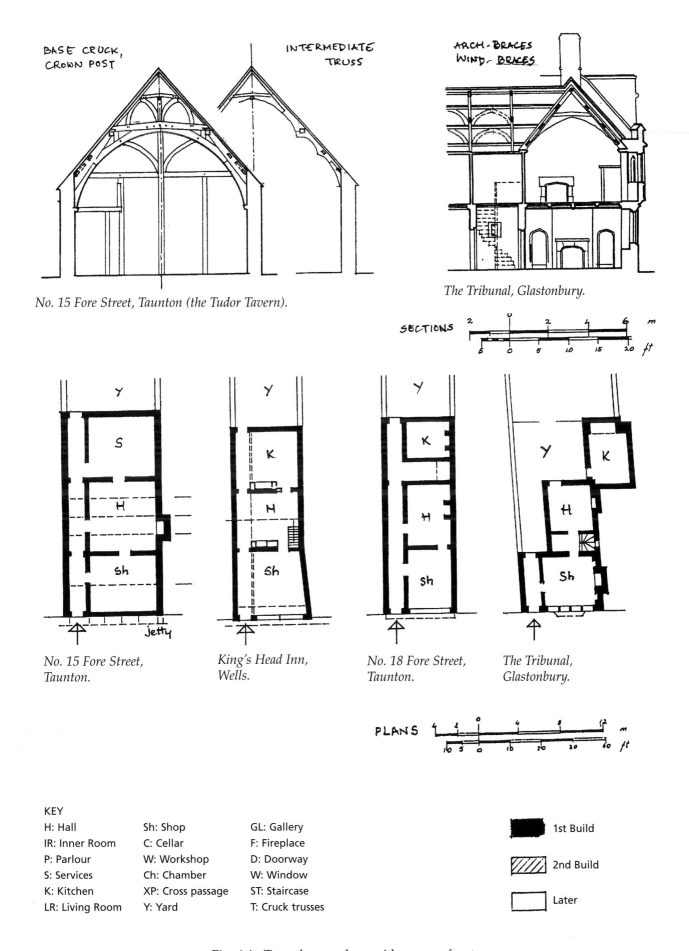

BASE CRUCK, CROWN POST

INTERMEDIATE TRUSS

ARCH-BRACES WIND-BRACES

No. 15 Fore Street, Taunton (the Tudor Tavern).

The Tribunal, Glastonbury.

SECTIONS

No. 15 Fore Street, Taunton.

King's Head Inn, Wells.

No. 18 Fore Street, Taunton.

The Tribunal, Glastonbury.

PLANS

KEY

H: Hall

IR: Inner Room

P: Parlour

S: Services

K: Kitchen

LR: Living Room

Sh: Shop

C: Cellar

W: Workshop

Ch: Chamber

XP: Cross passage

Y: Yard

GL: Gallery

F: Fireplace

D: Doorway

W: Window

ST: Staircase

T: Cruck trusses

1st Build

2nd Build

Later

Fig. 6.4   Town house plans with narrow frontages.

sited on the main street so is a type 1 plan; at the front is a single room, perhaps a shop, and behind it is a central open hall and a back service room (later a kitchen), all connected by a lateral passage within the house. A gallery in the hall over the passage is also a feature and there was an open hearth originally in the hall.

The smoke-blackened roof truss has a moulded cinquefoil arch-brace, with a trefoil arched upper cruck, flanked by three tiers of windbraces, also cusped (fig. 6.5). The hall end trusses are missing, replaced by stone cross walls when fireplaces were added in the seventeenth and eighteenth centuries. The three-storey front section of the house was partly rebuilt in the seventeenth century with an axial partition supporting a pair of gables facing the street (now under one roof). On the ground floor the medieval ceiling joists in the front room show mortices for a former timber-framed jettied front wall (now replaced by a modest nineteenth-century brick façade). However, the main glory of the house is the hall roof, still visible from the bar of the inn. (The hall roof has recently been tree-ring dated at d.1313.)

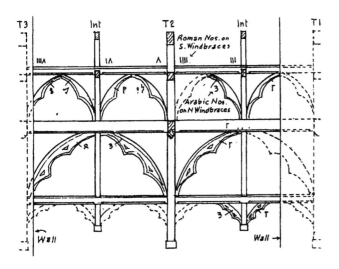

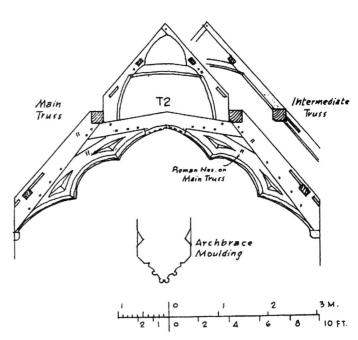

Fig. 6.5   The King's Head Inn, Wells, the hall roof.

Fig. 6.6 The open hall in the Tudor Tavern, Taunton.

No. 15 Fore Street, Taunton,[4] formerly the Tudor Tavern, is a larger version of the same type 1 plan (figs 6.4, 6.6). It is an early-fourteenth century house of secular ownership occupying an important central position in the town, its elaborate gable and jettied timber-framed façade facing down the main street, the frontage having been extended forward in 1578. The plan is the same as that of the King's Head Inn, but the span of the spectacular hall roof (d.1323–4) is larger at 8.5m (28ft) compared to the 6.0m (20ft) at Wells. Here there are three base-cruck trusses with crown posts on top (an unusual form for Somerset), the central truss an open arch-braced cruck flanked by delicate cusped intermediates. The end walls of the hall also have base crucks forming decorative closed partitions (fig. 6.6). This is a truly magnificent survival of an imaginative fourteenth-century design, until recently on view from the public bar of the inn.

A later version of a type 1 plan at **No. 18 Fore Street, Taunton**[3] was built in the late-fifteenth century and has no open hall. The plan (fig. 6.4) differs from the previous examples in having a small yard between the ground-floor hall and the back room (later a parlour). The yard was perhaps introduced for better lighting, as it was always a problem to light the central hall when there was no adjoining open space or light well. A first-floor gallery in the yard connects the two-storey back block with the hall chamber, which was open to a cruck roof in the fifteenth century. In the 1600s the hall chamber was ceiled with an ornate plaster ceiling. This late-medieval plan is found in some Devon town houses, in Totnes and Dartmouth, and is usually planned with a detached kitchen in the yard.[9]

One other well-known house, **The Tribunal, Glastonbury**[10] (fig. 6.4), is a much rebuilt fifteenth-century house, with a type 1 plan, but differs from the last in that the roof of the front rooms is parallel with the street (usually a feature of type 2 plans). The arrangement of the rooms is also different, the main ground-floor room and chamber above being at the front rather than in the centre of the house. This may be because the fifteenth-century owner, a rich merchant, converted an earlier house to his own commercial use, the front shop becoming more like a parlour, with two chambers above open to the roof. The middle block consists of rooms for family use, a hall and chamber above, also with an arch-braced roof. In this house the side passage is partly external, and a mullioned window to the parlour, facing the open part of the passage, has a hood moulding terminating in carved portrait heads, perhaps depicting the owners (fig. 6.7).

At the back there is a detached kitchen with a large gable fireplace. But it is the street elevation which causes the most speculation, as it appears to be a conglomeration of stone features put together and ill suited to a street frontage. It is possible that these fine features are all post-medieval additions reused from the Abbot's Lodgings when the latter was demolished in the eighteenth century (see Stukeley's *Prospect of Glastonbury*, 1712, showing many long mullioned windows and bays in the lodgings[10]).

Fig. 6.7 Fifteenth-century carvings, at The Tribunal, Glastonbury.

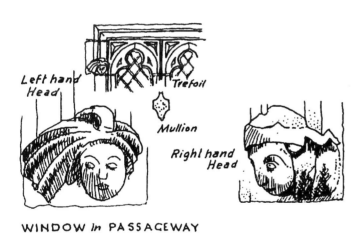

The next two groups of houses in the **High Streets of Bruton** and **Rode** are of the fifteenth century and were probably built for commercial use (fig. 6.8). The two groups are rather similar in plan, that comprising Nos 23–25 High Street, Rode, being the more traditional, possibly having open halls (they compare well with the terrace in Spon Street, Coventry)[11]. The Rode terrace is now three houses, but we suggest it was first built as a row of four or five units, with part of the ground floor open to the roof. The extensive windbraced roof running along the length of the terrace has tie-and-collar trusses, smoke-blackened and tree-ring dated d.1428/9, the same date as the dividing first-floor beam. There were large tall windows overlooking the small back yards at regular intervals (see blocked opening in unit B, fig. 6.8). This, combined with the position of the cross partitions gives four units in the present terrace. It is suggested that each unit consists of a narrow open hall, from front to back, next to a first-floor chamber over an entrance passage alongside the hall, the dwelling units being 5.5m x 4.5m wide (17ft x 15ft). The depth of the chamber is not established, but a loft floor only extends to

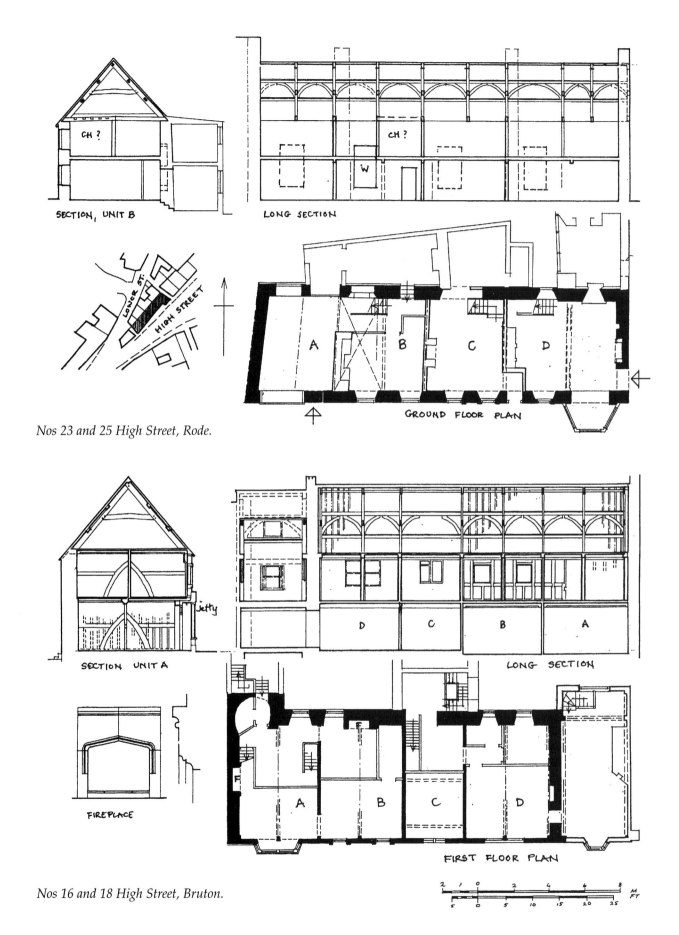

SECTION, UNIT B

LONG SECTION

CH ?

CH ?

W

GROUND FLOOR PLAN

Nos 23 and 25 High Street, Rode.

SECTION UNIT A

Jetty

LONG SECTION

FIREPLACE

FIRST FLOOR PLAN

Nos 16 and 18 High Street, Bruton.

Fig. 6.8   High Street terraces of the fifteenth century.

half the depth of the house. The plan arrangement is similar to Spon Street, Coventry, but without a jettied front. It differs from the well-known row in Tewkesbury where the hall is at the back, with a front chamber over a shop. Rode is in the north-east of Somerset, right on the Wiltshire border and the area was renowned for the production of high-quality woollen cloth in the late-Middle Ages, the parish having four fulling mills and associated dye works. It is therefore quite possible that the Rode terrace was built as artisan workshops-cum-dwellings, the unit at the east end being slightly larger, perhaps for an overseer (fig. 6.8).

The Rode terrace can be compared to **Nos 16 and 18 High Street**, Bruton (fig. 6.8).[12] The Bruton group, built only 24 years later is now divided into two houses, but could have been built as three or four units in the late-medieval period. Tree-ring dated to d.1453, each two-storey house consisted of two bays. The houses had their main rooms heated by stone fireplaces at first-floor level, indicating that this was the main domestic level with a shop below (some with cellars) and an attic floor above. The terrace had a timber-jettied front with stone walls at the gable ends and back (for stability on the slope behind the houses). This construction is seen at other jettied houses in the town.

Priory House, High Street, Bruton[12] (fig. 6.9, Plate 15), on the south side of the High Street is a house of much higher status with a three-room frontage and two street entrances, the extensive cellars entered from the street and from the sloping ground behind. The structure is virtually the same as Nos 16 and 18 High Street, but the façade is highly decorative with three carved stone corbels, one to each gable wall and one in the centre, the two separate jettied fronts between suggesting two original houses (fig. 6.9). (These corbelled stone walls can still be seen in some towns, indicating the presence of earlier jettied fronts, such as the County Stores, Taunton). The Priory House corbels are carved with medieval animals and the coats of arms of Bruton Priory's founders (Mohuns) and Prior Henton's rebus (a hen sitting on a tun or barrel). His father is thought to have been a clothier or mercer in the town and he may have built the house. The central hall had a lateral fireplace and no stone central cross wall and could have been used earlier as a courtroom or municipal hall but there is no documentary record of either use. Only a nineteenth-century painting by William Wheatley, titled 'The remains of the Old Town Hall and Market House,' and its likely building date of mid-fifteenth century might suggest it could have been a predecessor to the Market Hall opposite, built in 1684.[13] Quite another sort of painting in the form of an overmantel panel (like a Dutch scene complete with Glastonbury Tor in the background) is part of the panelled parlour which replaced the service room in the eighteenth century (fig. 4.21).

Throughout the late-medieval period Bruton was in the hands of the Augustinian Priory, becoming an Abbey in 1511. The Priory planned the medieval town (fig. 6.1) on the north side of the River Brue where the land rises steeply, the houses on the south side of the High Street having sloping yards or 'bartons' behind. The type 2 plan with a two-room frontage suited the small shopkeepers, who had a shop, a kitchen and a central passage-way leading to the yards, which gave access to large cellars, presumably for commercial use. In our surveys of Bruton we found eight out of the twelve houses surveyed had type 2 plans, all with similar structures and all of the mid-fifteenth century. It is therefore possible that the Priory was then developing the town, as it was known for its association with the booming cloth trade of the region.

No. 3 High Street, Bruton (fig. 6.10), another fifteenth-century house, now a shop with a handsome Georgian front, is a good example of the type 2 plan, in this case with a contemporary kitchen in a rear wing incorporating a smoke-bay at the gable end. In the sixteenth century the house was extended across the back to form a three-sided courtyard with a later version of a jettied timber building and an arched stone doorway. This led to yet another yard which again was extended with a fine eighteenth-century 'gothick' style coach-house next to the back lane. The house almost certainly made commercial use of its large plot.

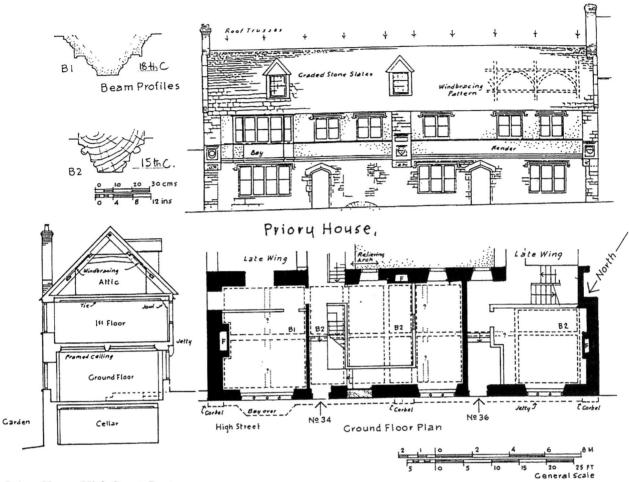

Priory House, High Street, Bruton.

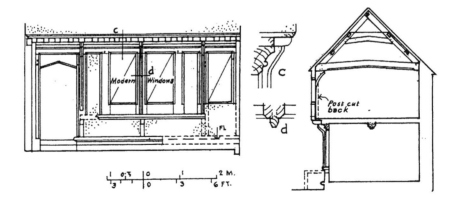

No. 24 High Street, Bruton, a shop front to Amor's Barton.

Fig. 6.9 Bruton houses, with stone back and end walls and jettied timber fronts.

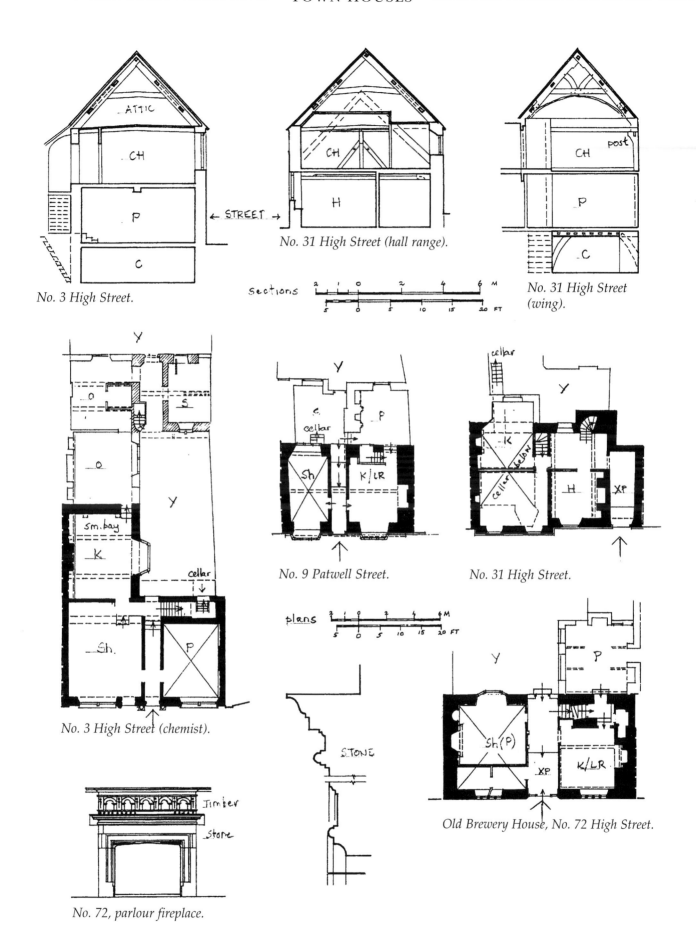

No. 31 High Street (hall range).

No. 3 High Street.

No. 31 High Street (wing).

No. 3 High Street (chemist).

No. 9 Patwell Street.

No. 31 High Street.

No. 72, parlour fireplace.

Old Brewery House, No. 72 High Street.

Fig. 6.10   Bruton houses, the smaller two-room plans.

A smaller version of the type 2 plan is found in **No. 9 Patwell Street, Bruton** (fig. 6.10) where the house would have faced the market-place before it was built over, hence its decorative jettied front. A mid-fifteenth century build is suggested by its similar roof design to those of the tree-ring dated houses. The two-room plan has a small shop with cellar underneath, and a central passage-way next to the family kitchen/living-room (a parlour wing was added in the eighteenth century). The plot runs down to a mill leat taken off the River Brue.

Among the many buildings of the fifteenth century in Bruton, a small jettied timber-fronted shop faces Amor's Barton, as part of **No. 24 High Street** (the front part of the house was rebuilt in the nineteenth century). The shop front and jettied chamber over were tree-ring dated to d.1430, the shop having a typical medieval frame and the remains of a display counter for goods outside the windows (fig. 6.9).

A later version of the two-room plan is the **Old Brewery House, Bruton** (fig. 6.10), which was built with some style probably by Hugh Sexey in 1629 when he built the adjoining almshouses, Sexey's Hospital. The house has a wide central entrance passage lined with post-and-panel screens each side. The parlour may have been used as a business room for a merchant clothier. The room has excellent seventeenth-century detailing and is panelled throughout (fig. 4.15). There were many outbuildings at the back adjoining the river and the house is known later to have been a maltster's house and then a silk factory in the eighteenth century.

One other building should be looked at here, **No. 31 High Street, Bruton** (fig. 6.10). This was probably originally a three-room house parallel with the street, but now has only a two-room frontage, with a wide cross passageway, the low end later blocked by the adjoining house. The central hall has a similar roof to the other houses (tree-ring dated d.1453/4) with the same tie-and-collar truss construction and a timber cross partition between the hall and parlour wing, the latter having a jettied gable onto the street. The wing has a more delicate arch-braced roof of about 1400, but the real pointer to the age of the building is in the cellar under the wing, where a heavy square-sectioned beam with supporting curved braces has been tree-ring dated d.1294–98 (fig. 6.10). This early date is substantiated by a scarf joint of an early type used in the beam.[14] So this interesting town house indicates the presence of a late-thirteenth century building in Bruton High Street.

In other parts of the county only the occasional timber-framed town house can be seen, such as the well-known house, the so-called **'King John's Hunting Lodge' Axbridge** (figs 6.11, Plate 15). This is really a handsome fifteenth-century merchant's house sited at the corner of the market-place and the High Street, so two façades are timber-framed and jettied (with three gables onto the High Street) and with stone walls between the adjoining sites. The medieval building included three lock-up shops with separate doors to the street, the merchant's house being behind and above it.[15]

Next we look at two planned layouts in small Somerset towns, both built by monastic owners in the fourteenth and fifteenth centuries, the groups intended to be part of larger developments. The houses are built in limestone rubble, with freestone dressings and stone-tiled roofs.

Nos 4, 8 and 9 New Street in Mells[16] (fig. 6.12), a Glastonbury Abbey owned village, are in the only street built by Abbot Selwood, c.1460. The pleasing group included two earlier houses and the Talbot Inn, leaving room for six new houses. Only three remain today, the others having been replaced in the nineteenth century. The fifteenth-century houses of some quality were perhaps built for clothiers and merchants, having wide-fronted three-room plans (type 3) and half-octagonal turret stairs at the back. The surviving houses have changed very little although some of the arched doorways and trefoil-headed windows have been replaced. However, the roughly coursed stonework and stone-tiled roofs help to unify the terraces. Even without the original complete group this remains a very attractive street and a good example of fifteenth-century planning.

The Market Square, Somerton.

Middle Street, Montacute.   *(J. McCann)*

Plate 13   Small medieval planned towns.

Tudor Tavern, Taunton, d.1323, with later frontage.
(G. Roberts)

The Church House, Chew Magna, c.1500.

Cheap Street, Frome.

Plate 14 Medieval town houses, gable end to the street.

Nos 26 and 28 St Thomas Street, Wells.

'King John's Hunting Lodge' Axbridge.

Priory House, Bruton with a timber jettied front. (J. McCANN)

Plate 15   Town houses of the mid-fifteenth century.

Above, left and right: *The Trinity area of Frome, developed for cloth-trade workers.*

Right: *Castle Street, Bridgwater.*

Plate 16   Early-eighteenth-century terraces.

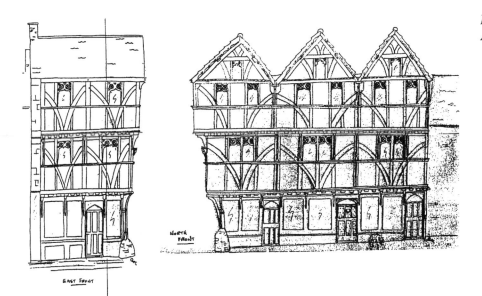

Fig. 6.11. 'King John's Hunting Lodge', Axbridge.

(CHRISTINE GILSON)

No. 1, The Borough, Montacute (fig. 6.12) is one of the earliest houses in the town square, which was part of the planned borough made by Montacute Priory in the early-twelfth century. Of this only the large market square and South Street remain, North Street having been swept away by Sir Edward Phelips when he built Montacute House in about 1600. Most of the present houses in The Borough have two or three-room frontages, the houses built at different dates but all with Hamstone walls and stone-tiled roofs (the latter now reduced to a few courses at the eaves). No. 1 is a little earlier than the Mells houses, with a stone arched doorway and two-light ogee-arched windows of c.1400. (fig. 6.12). The eaves have been raised but irregular masonry on the façade indicates a former lower eaves line with a stone gable over the hall chamber window, not a common feature so far south in Somerset.

Returning to the cathedral town of Wells, we look at Bishop Beckington's 'New Works' built c.1450 (fig. 6.13). This is a planned L-shaped group of houses comprising the north side of Market Street and part of Sadler Street, both backing onto the Cathedral Green.[17] **No. 18 Sadler Street** (fig. 6.13) has been surveyed and similar arch-braced roofs can be seen in Market Street, both terraces having their large roofs running parallel with the street. These roofs and their two prominent lateral stacks at the back, can be best seen in a modern aerial view[18] showing six large roofs in Market Street and two roofs in Sadler Street (Nos 18 and 20) next to Brown's Gateway leading to the Green. The plots taper and get very narrow in Sadler street and are described in a Grant of 1451 giving dimensions, the more regular plots being in Market Street. The two-storey houses were built to a high standard with wide frontages (12m or 40ft) using type 2 plans, with a central passage between hall and service room. The most important room in these houses is on the first floor, the main chamber, open to the decorative roof. This room is unusually placed centrally, rather than the more common arrangement with the chamber directly over the hall below (see long section). The large room had a turret stair access and a lateral fireplace and stack on the back wall. Most of the other rooms have framed ceilings. Later extensions on the back yard included a kitchen and date from between the seventeenth and nineteenth centuries.

The street façade in Sadler Street is plain, the walls rendered and windows replaced. A small bay window at first-floor level is the same as the repetitive bays in Market Street, the sash windows replacing earlier mullioned casements. This exceptional group of houses has almost lost its identity due to later subdivisions, particularly in Market Street.

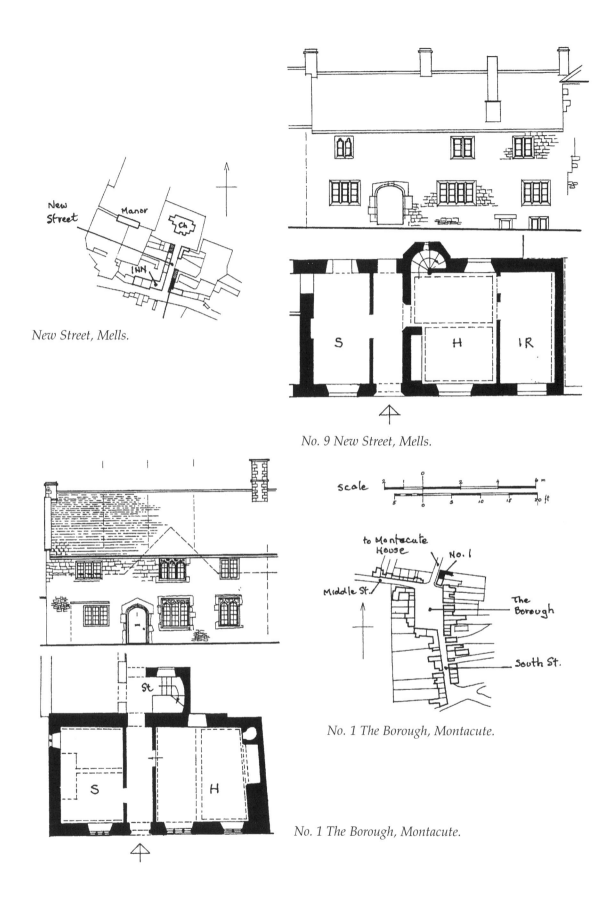

New Street, Mells.

No. 9 New Street, Mells.

scale

No. 1 The Borough, Montacute.

No. 1 The Borough, Montacute.

Fig. 6.12 Planned town groups, fifteenth century.

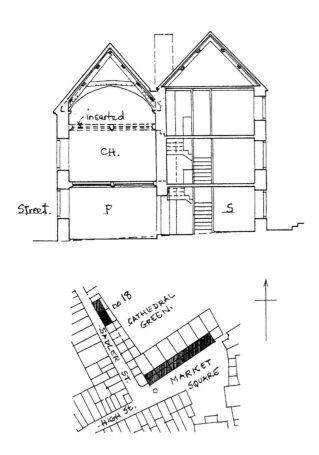

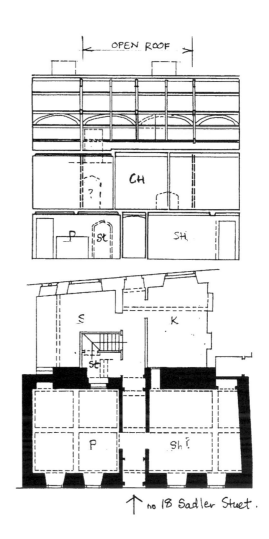

Location map and No. 18 Sadler Street, Wells.

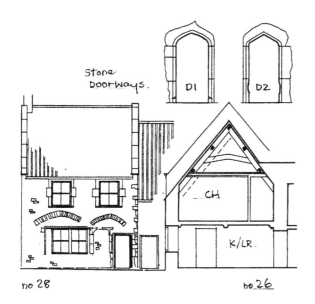

Nos 26 and 28 St Thomas Street, Wells.

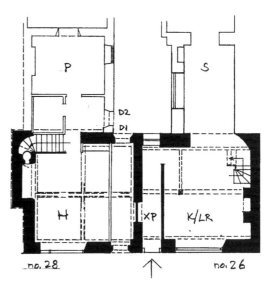

Fig. 6.13   Houses of the fifteenth century in Wells.

Starting at the same time as Bishop Beckington's experiments in the centre of the city, a mixed group of medieval houses were being built on the eastern outskirts. **Nos 26 and 28 St Thomas Street**, Wells (fig. 6.13, Plate 15), is a late-fifteenth century two-roomed house, but is now subdivided into separate ownerships with very different outside appearances. After surveying the houses, however, it became clear that they had been divided sometime in the sixteenth or seventeenth centuries, when No. 28 was raised to two and a half storeys and a back wing was added to the front hall. The service room and passage remained in No. 26, so a new passage for No. 28 was carved out of the medieval hall, still with its large fireplace and newel staircase, its four-panelled framed ceiling being interrupted by the partition to the new passage. There are signs of blocked mullioned medieval windows in the front and there are two fine stone arched doors at the back of No. 28, the passage doorway having a full four-centred arch with wide plain chamfers and a diagonal stop, all of the fifteenth century. The other door to the new wing has a similar doorway with a more depressed arch of the late-sixteenth or seventeenth century. No. 26 has a lower roof, a replaced door and windows and a rendered front wall (fig. 6.13). There are many houses of different dates in St Thomas Street, representing piece-meal development of plots in post-medieval Wells.

To conclude, we turn to a planned suburb, built between c.1660 and 1750, on the outskirts of **Frome**, with varied sized houses, all grouped together as terraces in the tightly packed streets of the **Trinity area**.[6] Local clothier families such as the Yerburys, Barnards and Whitcombes planned this part of the town for their workers, their factories being built on the edge of the town. The grid pattern of roads was built on former open fields, expanding street by street for nearly a century, its builders choosing the local vernacular style of the late-seventeenth century. The terraces (fig. 6.14, Plate 16) varied both in width of plots and number of storeys, with one or two-room frontages, many with an added wing at the back. The houses are two or two and a half storeys high, the earlier ones with attic windows in stone gables, often removed when a third storey was added. The two-room plans compare with contemporary village houses, with two rooms in front and the entrance passage next to the family living-room (with a large fireplace and newel stair beside it – a very traditional arrangement). The smaller unheated room is thought to have been a workshop for cottage industry. The attics are described in an inventory of 1724, as 'garrotts and wool lofts'.[6] The rubble stone walls, pantile roofs and sash windows, with occasional ovolo moulded windows in the earlier houses, all contributed to a 'natural development' look that the builders wanted rather than that of the new regular Georgian town streets which were starting to be fashionable in the larger towns at the time (Plate 16).

We have now reached the end of our prescribed study period, c.1700, but it would be a great pity to ignore any reference to the Georgian and Victorian town houses in the county, particularly the brick terraces in towns such as Taunton and Bridgwater, where the use of new local brickwork was fully exploited. A good early example is to be seen in **Castle Street, Bridgwater** (Plate 16), one of several streets built by the Duke of Chandos in 1730 on the site of the former castle. Each terrace comprises double fronted three-storey brick houses built for well-to-do townsfolk, the houses having heavy segmentally arched sash windows and elaborate classical entrance doorways, each house to a different design.

Like any county town in the south of England **Taunton** has its quota of Georgian terraces, one of the best being, **The Crescent**, facing west opposite the County Council Offices. Brick built, simple, elegant and sophisticated this long terrace with restrained arched doorways and recessed sash windows can be seen in towns throughout the country, built at the beginning of the nineteenth century. We cannot however, claim its urban elegance as peculiar to Somerset.

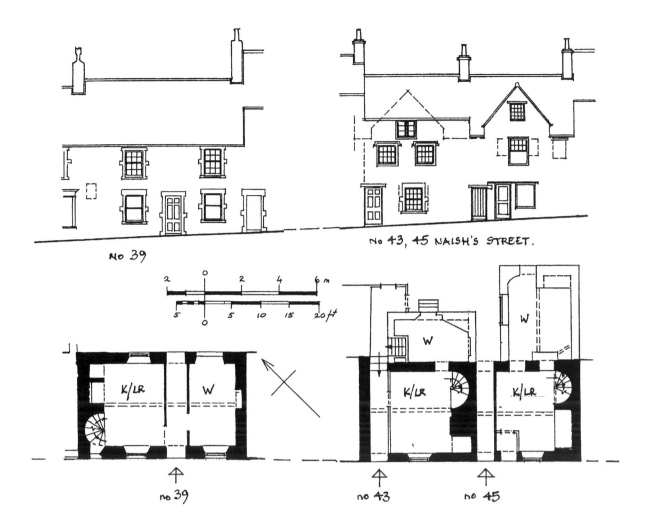

*Fig. 6.14   Houses in Naish's Street, the Trinity Area of Frome, a comprehensive
build, c.1700. (RCHM SURVEY, R. LEECH, 1981)*

Notes
 1 Aston, M.A. and Leech, R. Historic Towns in Somerset – Archeology and
Planning, Bristol, 1977.
 2 Pantin, W.A., 'Medieval English Town-House Plans,' *Medieval Archeology*,
vol. 16–17, 1962.
 3 Taylor, R. *Town Houses in Taunton, 1500–1700*, Somerset Local Studies
Library, Taunton.
 4 Williams, E.H.D. and Gilson, R.G., *Base Crucks in Somerset, III*, SANHS
Proc. 125, 1981.
 5 SVBRG's *Somerset Dendrochronology Project 1997–99*. Dendrochronology
by Dan Miles and Michael Worthington of the Oxford Dendrochronology
Laboratory, SANHS Proc. 141, 142, 1998, 1999.   Also in *Vernacular
Archeology Journal*, vols 28, 30. 1997, 1999.
 6 Leech, R., *The Trinity Area of Frome*, HMSO, 1981.
 7 SVBRG survey, *No. 20 Vicars' Close, Wells*, SANHS Proc. 142, 1999.
 8 Williams, E.H.D. and Gilson, R.G., *Base Crucks in Somerset I*, SANHS Proc.
121, 1977.
 9 Laithwaite, M., 'Town Houses up to 1600', in *Devon Buildings*, ed.
Beacham, P., Devon, 1990.
10 Dunning, R.W. and Penoyre, J. and J., *Glastonbury Tribunal* handbook,
Tourist Information Office and Museum, Glastonbury, 1997.

11 Dallimore, J., Nos 23–25 High Street, Rode, *Vernacular Architecture* vol. 30, 1999. Also Jones, S.R. and Smith, J.T., *Spon St, Coventry, the Wealdon Houses of Warwick*. Birmingham Archeology Society, 1960.

12 Penoyre, J. and J., *Some Bruton Houses*, surveyed by SVBRG, SANHS Proc. 140, l997. Our work in Bruton was greatly helped by John Bishton, whose knowledge of the houses and history of the town was invaluable.

13 Dunning, R.W., ed. *Victoria History of Somerset*, vol. vii, p.34.

14 Hewett, C.A., *English Historic Carpentry*, 1980. No. 31 High Street, Bruton, timber structure identified by John McCann.

15 Survey of 'King John's Hunting Lodge' Axbridge, by Gilson, R. and drawing by Gilson, C.

16 Williams, E.H.D. and Penoyre, J. and J., *New Street, Mells*, SANHS Proc. 130, 1985/6.

17 Scrace, A.T., *Wells, a Study of Town Origins*, Town and Country Planning Working Papers, Bristol, 1982.

18 Croft, R. and Aston, M.A. *Somerset from the Air*, p.84, SCC, 1993.

SEVEN

Farm Buildings and Farmsteads

by John Dallimore

With thanks to Isabel Richardson, who kindly supplied information on Cloutsham Farm, Luccombe and photographs for figs 7.1, 7.10, 7.19, 7.20 and 7.22.

Fig. 7.1   A pastoral farm group in West Somerset. East Lynch Farm. Selworthy.

The soil, topography and climate – with some modification due to aspect – are the prime elements, which have been the key to Somerset farming over the centuries. These factors, together with the availability of building materials have determined the type of farm buildings that developed. With these considerations in mind, Somerset can loosely be divided into six areas (fig. 7.2), each of which, over the centuries, has developed differing agrarian activities and characteristics.

Fig. 7.2 Areas of study.

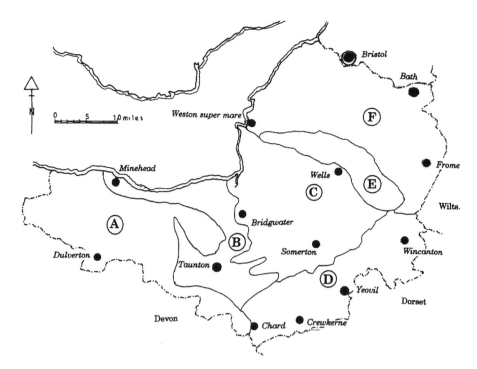

(A) West Somerset, comprising a part of Exmoor, the Brendon, Quantock, and Blackdown Hills, is a predominantly pastoral area much of which had been the subject of enclosure in the late-Saxon and medieval period resulting in scattered farmsteads. Cattle and sheep were reared and a small quantity of cereals grown for domestic needs.

(B) The vale country of Taunton Deane and the Coastal Plain (between Bridgwater and Porlock) historically included some outstanding fertile arable and stock-rearing areas.

(C) The Levels, with extensive commons subject to regular flooding, provided rich summer grazing for cattle – a situation which did not change until the extensive drainage schemes in the nineteenth century. Dairying and horse-breeding were also important; sheep and cereals less so.

(D) The Southern Arc, extending from Chard and Crewkerne through Yeovil and beyond towards Frome was, until the modern period, an area of open fields and nucleated villages with the farmsteads located within the villages. The region was well suited to dairying, arable crops and sheep rearing; cheese, pigs and wool were significant by-products. Apple orchards are still planted.

(E) The Mendip Hills, until the late-eighteenth century enclosures, was mostly an area where sheep production predominated, although the fertile land on the southern slopes became suited to market-gardening and dairying.

(F) The Northern Arc of undulating land stretching from Weston-super-Mare to Frome was suited to dairying and the growing of cereals and was favoured, being close to the cities of Bristol and Bath.

Cider orchards, for which Somerset became noted, were much in evidence over most of the county.

The differing natural characteristics of these regions created substantial variations in the quality of the land and hence the amount of investment potential, so ultimately reflecting the financial return derived by the landowner and/or occupier over the centuries. The result, in the context of farm buildings and farmsteads, is that the better quality and more durable buildings are generally found in the regions with the more favoured physiography, particularly in South Somerset and the vale country of Taunton Deane.

Researches by the Somerset Vernacular Building Research Group and others have shown that, in the main, there were few farm buildings of any substance before the middle of the eighteenth century. The exceptions, of course, are the Tithe Barns which were built by the Monastic estates, some of which date from the thirteenth and fourteenth centuries.

A number of factors gave rise to an increase in the number of farm buildings which occurred in the period from the mid-eighteenth century through until the last quarter of the nineteenth. Firstly, the change from the life-hold leasing to the rack-rent system enabled the landlord to exercise control and encouraged him to invest and to improve the land and the building of the farmsteads. At the same time open fields were being enclosed and as a result some new farmsteads were created (again by the landlords) outside the perimeter of the nucleated settlements. It was also the period of the Agricultural Revolution when new and progressive ideas in husbandry, stock rearing and farming practices were being promulgated. A significant development was the establishment of the Bath & West of England Society in 1777 which had a great impact throughout the region; it organised shows, meetings, lectures, practical demonstrations and publications. The period of 'High Farming' followed, which resulted in further advances in farming practices reflected in the improved quality and design of farm buildings – outstanding examples being the creation of a number of planned farmsteads such as Manor Farm, Chiselborough and Manor Farm, Stratton-on-the-Fosse (fig. 7.37).

Vale Farm.

BUILDING MATERIALS AND TECHNIQUES

The ready availability of stone throughout the county, although of variable quality, made it the most common building material for farm buildings. It was superseded to some extent in the mid-nineteenth century by brick which was mostly produced in the Bridgwater and Wellington areas. Some cob and/or timber was used where stone was not readily available, although sometimes in combination with stone. Inscribed datestones are rarely found, the few examples are associated with farmsteads built by gentry landowners.

Thatch was the most common roofing material but stone tiles appear in the northern and eastern sectors of the county, a prime example being the Abbey Barn at Doulting (tree-ring dated d.1288–90). Clay tiles produced in the Bridgwater area became widely used from the mid-nineteenth century particularly in central Somerset.

Slate had been used to a limited extent up until the early-nineteenth century in the west of the county but Welsh slate subsequently became available and was used particularly on the higher-status farm buildings – probably brought in via the Bristol Channel ports and the growing canal or rail system.

Roof construction (fig. 7.3) tends to mirror that of farmhouses, although relatively archaic styles tended to continue in farm buildings long after their use in houses had been discontinued. Crucks, jointed crucks and sling-braces lend themselves to use in buildings where unobstructed headroom was a requirement. In the late-eighteenth and nineteenth-century period bolted queen-post and scissor-braced trusses were used in the larger buildings and king-post trusses became common, particularly in cowsheds and cartsheds. Fig. 7.3 shows typical roof structures and Higher Hill Farm at Butleigh c.1700, is a good example of different roof types in one farmstead.

To avoid racking (lengthwise movement) of the roof structure windbraces were used. Straight windbraces continued in use much later in the larger barns than in houses. In the relatively rare timber-framed buildings the structure is of the jointed-cruck and/or tie-beam truss construction – the walls being clad with weatherboarding.

Bundle-thatch – where brushwood is piled on top of flat joists and then thatched – may have been more common but only one example of this simple roof structure is known to survive in the county.

Examples of barn roofs: a former barn in West Chinnock (post-medieval) and scissor braces at nineteenth-century Yeabridge Farm, South Petherton.

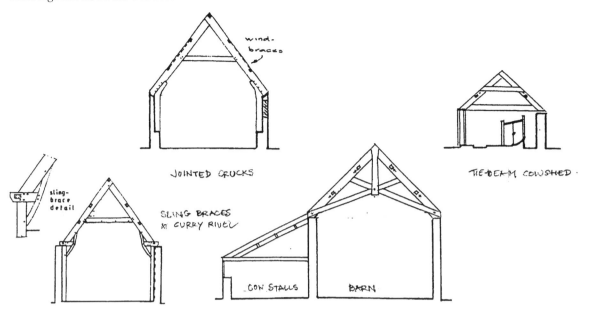

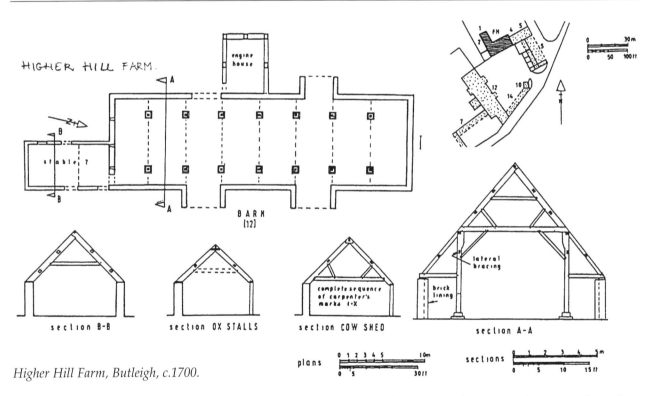

Higher Hill Farm, Butleigh, c.1700.

The farmhouse formerly overlooked the main ox yard; the cow yard – perhaps a secondary enterprise – was relegated to the western side of the barn. The farmhouse dates from c.1700 with the wing, which included a dairy, cider house and a below-ground cellar being added c.1780. It is probable that the farmstead was built at this time. The farm then amounted to 636 acres at an annual rental of £350. Although the acreage remained unchanged in 1819 the rent had increased to £850 – this may relate to the fact that the ox stalls and bull's house had been built c.1848. By 1884 the holding (then within a ring fence) had been reduced to 350 acres of which 282 acres were arable, 77 pasture, 20 wood and 4 orchard. The buildings are of excellent quality, the principal building, the barn, is of aisled construction – one of the few of this type in Somerset. The seven aisled trussees have carpenter's marks in sequence. Also noteworthy is the fact that the Lias stone walls are lined internally with brick as an original feature.

Fig. 7.3 Somerset barns.

TYPICAL FARM BUILDINGS

The period 1750–1880 saw a gradual proliferation of farm buildings, many of a relatively specialised nature, typically, corn barns, engine houses, field barns, mixing house barns, cattle and cowsheds, shippons, linhays, stables (for both hack and cart-horses), pigsties, granaries, corn-drying kilns and maltings, hay barns, dairies and cheese rooms, brewhouses, cider houses, implement and cart houses, and wagon houses.

Corn Barns   (figs 7.4–7.9)

A number of such buildings which had been used for the storage and processing of grain crops or legumes survive, although many have been converted to non-agricultural usage and have lost their intrinsic character. The larger examples are sometimes erroneously called Tithe Barns, often without supporting documentary evidence. Such buildings were, in fact, exclusively for the storage of the tenth part of the annual produce of land or labour levied in a parish to support its priest, to maintain the fabric of the church and to provide relief of the poor of that parish.

Generally barns are the dominant structure of the farmstead, usually being the equivalent of two storeys in height. They vary in size according to the needs of the particular holding. Since the barn was used for threshing as well as storage of the crop there were usually two large opposing doorways, to give through-draught for winnowing and to give access to the threshing floor which was often formed with planks 5cm (2ins) or 7.5cm (3ins) thick. The large entrance doorways were often protected by porches or canopies, sometimes large enough to accommodate a loaded wagon. Very large barns may have more than one threshing floor as well as a number of pitching doors usually in the gable ends. Ventilation slits are provided at intervals along the length of the building and owl holes often feature in the gable ends. Both features may be cut from a solid piece of stone.

Internally, part of the barn may be fitted with an upper floor, probably at one end; the lower-floor area in such instances was probably used to house stock during the winter. There may also be a small corn-hole – a timber-framed structure for the storage of threshed corn. Near the doorways there may also be recesses where lamps can be placed in safety.

In South Somerset some barns have a wagon shelter as a continuation of the main range with a pitching door in the gable end of the barn. This allowed a loaded wagon to be put under cover and the contents pitched directly into the barn.

Stock Yard Barns   (fig. 7.8)

These two-storey buildings are a combination of byre, threshing-barn and granary and have been found in the cattle-rearing areas of the vale country of Taunton Deane and further west. The ground-floor byre is open-fronted with direct access to a stock yard and shelter shed. The upper floor is supported on posts or solid arcaded structures; the front of this upper floor is sometimes timber-framed with weatherboarding or brick infill.

Less sophisticated two-tiered versions with similarities to the bank-barns found elsewhere in hilly areas have also been identified in the area around Taunton.

Sources of Motive Power   (figs 7.10–7.11)

With the advent of the mechanical threshing machine c.1786 a power source became a necessity. If a reliable water-supply was available a water-wheel could be utilised but the most common power source was the ubiquitous horse. This involved the provision of a horse engine (or gin) which was

Fig. 7.4 *Abbey Barn, Glastonbury, d.1334–44.*

Fig. 7.5 *Seventeenth-century Spargrove Manor Farm, Batcombe, incorporating a stable and shelter shed.*

Fig. 7.6 *Eighteenth-century Newton Farm, Newton St Loe.*

Fig. 7.7 *Eighteenth-century Estate Farm, Pitney, incorporating a wagon shed.*

Fig. 7.8 *Amberd House Barn, Pitminster, a first-floor threshing barn and granary.*

Fig. 7.9 *Flax barn, Hayes End Farm, South Petherton, since converted to domestic use.*

commonly contained in a purpose-made building added to a barn. Such buildings were open sided and varied in shape, some being round, others polygonal, apsidal or square. If, for any reason, such a building was not feasible, by the middle of the nineteenth century an outdoor portable sweep type horse-gin became available.

Later, drive-shafts, etc., were introduced which enabled the horse-engine to power other equipment such as root and chaff cutters or cider-apple mills.

Portable steam engines became available by the mid-nineteenth century and together with traction engines they provided the power for threshing and, on the largest farms, fixed steam engines were installed. These mechanical aids were not as readily available on the small hill farm, due to the difficulties of terrain and access, so that the horse-engine continued in use until the small petrol-driven tractor and the electric motor became available.

Mixing House Barns   (figs 7.12–7.14)

These buildings developed in the mid-nineteenth century mostly in the planned farmsteads. By then it was possible to discontinue using the large barn for threshing purposes. They were two storey with a granary and straw store on the upper floor; the engine, winnowing, chopping, chaff cutting and milling machinery was kept below, located immediately adjoining cattle stalls so that the food could be fed directly to the stock.

Shelter sheds   (figs 7.15–7.16)

The provision of housing for cattle until the nineteenth century was sparse. During the winter months shelter was simple and in the summer cows were often milked in the field, particularly if the grazing was some distance from the farmstead, a practice which continued in some areas until the mid-twentieth century.

In the nineteenth century beef cattle were kept loose in open or only partially covered yards. Such shelter sheds were single storey and open-fronted but had a solid back and end walls, the open front facing away from the prevailing wind.

Cow Sheds and Shippons   (figs 7.17–7.18)

By the nineteenth century dairy cows were being provided with single storey sheds with numerous doors or openings along the frontage, the cows standing side-by-side in double bays facing away from the doors – perhaps with a feeding passage at the head. The layout varied according to the number of animals, the topography of the site, the space available and the particular method of feeding and mucking-out favoured by the farmer.

Shippons occur in the west of the county and vary from the conventional cowshed since they have a hayloft on an upper floor with three or four doors along the frontage. The cows were often tethered in two rows across the building with a manure passage between, accessed from the central doorway. Feeding was by way of the other doors. This type of building passed out of favour as the excessive heat generated by the animals could give rise to respiratory problems.

Housing for oxen is documented in the sixteenth century and again in the nineteenth century but no details survive.

Linhay   (figs 7.19–7.21)

This is a combination of an open-fronted shelter shed beneath an open-fronted hayloft which mostly occur in the area to the west of Taunton. The building usually has three walls with the open-front being supported by piers.

Fig. 7.10 West Lynch Farm, Bossington. A round house engine house.

Fig. 7.11 Horse engine and steam engine houses.

Above: Fig. 7.13 A sack hoist, Yeabridge Farm, South Petherton.

Above left: Fig. 7.12 Yeabridge Farm, South Petherton. A mixing house barn.

Left: Fig. 7.14 A two-storey mixing house and stock yard, Pennsylvania Farm, Newton St Loe.

Fig. 7.15 Shelter sheds, New Farm, Shapwick.

Fig. 7.16 Shelter shed, Moortown Farm, Fivehead.

Fig. 7.17   Cow sheds, Spargrove Manor Farm, Batcombe.

Fig. 7.18   A shippon with a loft above in West Somerset.

Fig. 7.19   A hay loft in linhay, Bossington Farm, Bossington.

Fig. 7.20   A linhay with stock yard, Bossington Farm, Bossington.

Fig. 7.21   Longforth Farm, Wellington, linhay with byre.

Fig. 7.22 Hay stable, West Luccombe Farm, West Luccombe.

Fig. 7.23 Cart-horse stable, Manor Farm, Sparkford.

Fig. 7.24 Seventeenth-century riding horse stables, The Manor (School), Shapwick.

Fig. 7.25 Hack stables, Spargrove Manor House, Batcombe.

Fig. 7.26 Pigsties, Milton Farm, Ash.

Stables   (figs 7.22–7.25)

Being highly valued and relatively expensive to maintain, horses have always been well treated and well housed. Stables usually occupy a prominent situation in the farmstead often close to the farmhouse. The building was normally two storeys high with well-proportioned windows and external steps or a ladder rising to the hayloft above. Working farm horses and hackney horses had separate stables; the latter often combined with a trap house and perhaps a harness room. The size of the stalls was commensurate with the particular type of horses being accommodated, stalls being divided by substantial partitions. The partitions in stables belonging to the gentry were often formed with elaborate ironwork. Each stall had its manger and hayrack (served by a hay-drop from the loft) and close by were wall brackets to hold the harnesses. On higher status holdings there may be a harness room – perhaps with a fire for the comfort of the groom. In contrast to cowsheds, stables were well supplied with windows for light and ventilation. There were keep-holes in the stable walls to allow the safe storage of grooming tools and lamps or candles.

Floors were covered with stone-sets or purpose made durable bricks, all cut or moulded to give a non-slip surface laid with falls to a drainage channel.

Calf Houses

These were small buildings on dairy farms sited near to the farmhouse and dairy. In some instances (e.g. Batcombe) they were used to house calves which were to be raised for 'white' veal. One of the requirements was that the animals should be kept in the dark, the housing therefore only had narrow arrow-slits for ventilation and there were no window openings.

Pigsties   (fig. 7.26)

From the eighteenth century, as a result of the restrictions arising from the enclosure of common land, pigs no longer had free range. This led to pigsties becoming a feature of the farmstead. The standard pigsty was a low lean-to building, large enough to accommodate one or two pigs and having a small yard with a trough and feeding chute. The walls were often built with orthostatic slabs of stone which would have been resistant to the gnawing habit of pigs. The floor was laid with stone flags for ease of cleaning.

Unfortunately, as such structures were of minor significance, few pigsties have survived.

Cart Sheds, Implement and Wagon Houses   (fig. 7.27)

These buildings were usually simple structures, although sometimes part of a more substantial granary building. Generally the cart shed was completely open on one side and in order to avoid the timber of the carts or implements being warped by the sun and any metal parts rusting due to rain it was preferable to orientate the building with the open side facing north.

Often integrated with a barn, wagon houses are, of necessity, substantial structures of sufficient height to accommodate a loaded wagon.

Manure Midden   (fig. 7.28)

The need to improve productivity and hence the fertility of the soil led to the need to prevent loss of nutrients due to dilution by rain. To this end, in the mid-nineteenth century, covered manure middens were built. The example illustrated had a curved segmental-shaped roof of corrugated iron supported on iron trusses and purpose-made cast-iron stanchions bolted to a low stone wall.

Dovecotes   (fig. 7.29)

These were being built from medieval times until the eighteenth century. A comprehensive review is included in *The Dovecotes of Historical Somerset* by John and Pamela McCann (2003).

Granaries   (figs 7.30–7.32)

Until the seventeenth century most grain – especially seed for use the following season – was stored in the lofts of farmhouses. Later, when granaries were built they may have been free-standing or alternatively forming the upper floor of a cart shed or stable. Within the building the floor was divided by low timber partitions between which the grain could be stored loose or kept in sacks. The boarded floor was tongued-and-grooved to avoid loss – sometimes a metal strip was inserted in the grooves between the boards. The walls were also lined with close-fitting boarding.

Externally, a gap was left at the doorway which was spanned by a 'draw-bridge' to prevent access by vermin. For the same reason the building was usually raised above the ground on staddle-stones. Nineteenth-century examples combine granaries with mixing houses and cow sheds.

Corn-Drying Kilns and Maltings

In the hilly and wetter western half of the county corn drying kilns have been recorded. Where only small amounts needed to be dried they are sometimes built alongside the hearth in the farmhouse. Such kilns might equally have been designed to allow the roasting of barley to make malt. Free-standing kilns have rarely been found.

Hay Barns

These are usually free-standing structures comprising a roof with trusses supported on piers of brick or stone – later examples having columns of timber or iron. They began to be built at the turn of the nineteenth century.

Flax Barns   (figs 7.9, 7.33)

More frequently seen in South Somerset, these buildings were used for the storage and drying of flax. They are similar in proportions to hay barns but have a number of distinctive features – in particular there are usually two floors, the lower floor is of stout timber and raised about 60cm above ground level. The roof is supported at intervals on substantial stone or brick piers – the intervening spaces being infilled with weatherboarding with gaps between the boards to allow ventilation.

Dairies, Cheese Rooms and Cheese Lofts   (figs 7.34–7.35)

These are usually within or adjacent to the farmhouse. Cheese lofts were provided with hoists and racks for the storage and the ripening of cheeses.

Cider Houses and Cellars

Most farms had their own orchards and made cider, this beverage being part of a labourer's wages. A typical cider house is a two-storey building – the apple-loft occupying the upper floor with a shute to the milling machine. The ground floor is divided into two parts, one section housing the apple mill and crusher – which may be powered by hand or horse engine. After crushing, the apple pieces were collected and transferred to a screw press which needed adequate head room; the resultant liquid was put into barrels

Fig. 7.27   Cart shed and wagon house, Yeabridge Farm, South Petherton.

Fig. 7.28   Manure midden, Higher Rocke's Farm, Butleigh.

Fig. 7.29   Dovecote, Rectory Farm, Stanton Drew.

Fig. 7.30   A granary, Yeabridge Farm, South Petherton.

Fig. 7.31   A granary over a cart shed, Bossington Farm, Bossington.

Right: Fig. 7.32   Corn bins, Eastwood Manor Farm, East Harptree.

Fig. 7.33   Flax barn, Milton Farm, Ash.

Fig. 7.34   Cheese house, Pennsylvania Farm, Newton St Loe.

Fig. 7.35   Cheese loft with hoist and cheese racks, Brue Farmhouse, Lovington.

Fig. 7.36   Bee boles, Charity Farm, Lovington.

in an adjoining cool cellar to ferment and be stored. The cellar needed to be large enough to accommodate a year's supply.

Farmyard Features

Modernisation for one reason or another has caused the loss of many features which would have been commonplace until the middle of the twentieth century.

For example a wagon-wash was used for expanding the wooden wheels and to wash the horses at the end of the day. The wash may also have been adapted as a sheep-dip at certain times of the year.

Drinking troughs were formed from solid pieces of Ham or Doulting stone or made from Lias slabs held with iron links. They could not be adapted to take a piped water-supply so are now sought-after ornamental garden features. Circular apple-crushing troughs are similarly utilised.

Cob boundary walls are occasionally seen – they may be capped with thatch or tiles.

Gate-posts of monolithic slabs of Ham stone, Blue Lias and Draycott conglomerate sometimes survive although many have given way to steel posts where it was necessary to widen gateways to allow the passage of modern farm equipment.

Staddle-stones – usually in two pieces each cut from the solid. They formerly supported the platform on which a corn stack, hay rick or granary was built.

Mounting blocks built of local stone were located alongside the hack stable.

Bee boles – the niches for the straw skips which preceded the modern beehives – are still to be found occasionally, usually in a south-facing wall close to the farmhouse (7.36).

Kent Farm.

FARMSTEAD LAYOUT

Where open fields and common grazing lands had existed the farmsteads would have been congregated in the nucleated villages, each having a toft which was entered from the village 'street'. As the frontage of the toft was often of limited width it is commonly seen that the farmhouse abuts the village street with the access to the farmstead running immediately alongside it. In the late-eighteenth and early-nineteenth century, when the open fields had been enclosed and the rack-rent regime had become prevalent, additional and improved buildings were provided by the landlord. This development often resulted in a random layout. However, the revisions which resulted from the enclosures enabled new 'ring-fence' holdings to be established and in such instances it was possible to create a farmstead, often outside the village and more conveniently located relative to the new holding. Many of these new farmsteads had the advantage of being planned and built for efficient and economic operations.

Key to layout of buildings diagrams

☐ Farmhouses

▨ Barns

▨ Other Buildings

a   corn barn (cross-hatched)
b   barn – hay (cross hatched)
c   calf house
d   cart shed
e   cattle shed or bullock house
f   cowshed
g   dairy/cheese room
h   granary
he horse engine
j   implement shed
k   linhay
l   midden (covered building)
m   pigsties
n   shelter shed
o   shippon
p   stable
q   food store/processing
r   trap house
s   wagon shed
t   water mill
u   yard
v   cider house
w   well

In the hill areas the landscape is mostly of a moorland character and hamlets and isolated farms predominate with the density of settlement being low. The quality of the farm buildings was likely to have been poor until the late-eighteenth to early-nineteenth century period when parts of the moorland were enclosed and subsequently new farmsteads were created which contained the basic accommodation for pastoral farming. One of the outstanding examples of this development was the building, between 1844 and 1852 by John Knight and his son Frederick of 11 farms (totalling 20,000 acres) with farmsteads, in the parish of Exmoor, within newly enclosed fields.

The diverse nature of farmsteads in the widely differing parts of the county makes it impossible, within the context of this volume, to cover all the different types which exist. Accordingly a selection has been made which is, as far as possible, representative of the agrarian influences in the six areas referred to earlier and shown in fig. 7.37.

The plans are based mostly on first edition Ordnance Survey maps and are drawn to a uniform scale. Note that many of the buildings shown no longer survive, have been much altered or converted to domestic use.

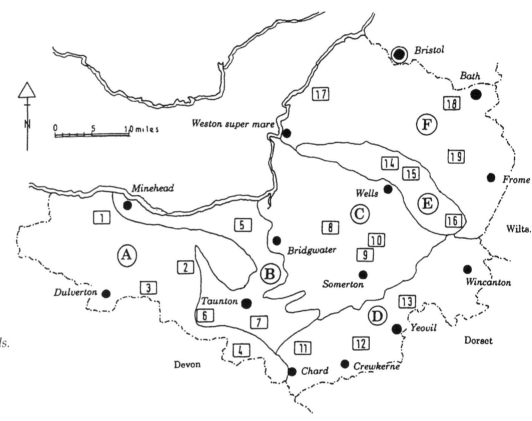

Fig. 7.37   Location of farmsteads.

Area A
1.   Cloutsham Farm, Luccombe
2.   Lower Wedcombe Farm, Brompton Ralph
3.   Little Wilsecombe Farm, Raddington
4.   Major's Farm, Churchinford

Area B
5.   Roobies Farm, Fiddington
6.   South Gundenham Farm, Langford Budville
7.   Amberd House Barn, Pitminster

Area C
8.   Beerway Farm, Shapwick
9.   Willey's Farm, Compton Dundon
10. Higher Rocke's Farm, Butleigh

Area D
11. Dunpole Farm, Sea, Ilminster
12. Manor Farm, Chiselborough
13. Parsonage Farm, West Camel

Area E
14. Chancellors Farm, West Harptree
15. Whitnell Farm, Emborough
16. Lower Farm, Batcombe

Area F
17. Bullock Farm, Kingston Seymour
18. Newton Farm, Newton St Loe
19. Manor Farm, Stratton-on-the-Fosse

FARMSTEADS – AREA A

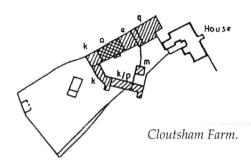

Cloutsham Farm.

1   CLOUTSHAM FARM, Luccombe

The farmstead is at an elevation of 850ft (226m) and overlooks the East Water valley immediately to the north of Dunkery Hill on Exmoor. The farmhouse has seventeenth-century origins; the barn range is eighteenth century and the other buildings are of nineteenth-century build. All are constructed of local red sandstone rubble with clay-tile roofs, probably thatched until the twentieth century. In the mid-nineteenth century it was a sheep- and cattle-grazing holding totalling 320 acres and part of Sir Thomas Acland's extensive Holnicote estate.

2   LOWER WEDCOMBE FARM, Brompton Ralph

The holding is in a well watered deep valley on the eastern edge of the Brendon Hills at an elevation of 525ft (160m). The farmhouse dates from c.1400 and incorporates a dairy and corn-drying kiln. In the nineteenth century it was a mixed farm of 114 acres. The farm buildings probably date from the early nineteenth century and are built of local rubble stone and formerly would have been thatched. The barn is two storey, the lower part housed stock and the upper floor was used for the storage and threshing of corn.

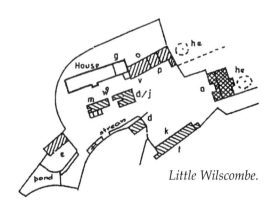

Lower Wedcombe Farm.

3   LITTLE WILSCOMBE, Raddington

In the nineteenth century this was a mixed arable and grazing farm totalling 141 acres. The farmhouse probably dates from the sixteenth century and most of the buildings from the eighteenth century. Although isolated, the site of the farmstead had probably been determined by the availability of the spring water-supply and the lie of the land in a hollow with a southerly aspect in the lee of Heydon Hill. It is at an elevation of 260m (850ft). Advantage was taken of the topographical features when the house and buildings were arranged: the house is elevated giving an overview of the farmstead, the buildings for housing cattle and horses mostly face south, the pigsties (now gone) were close to the dairy, the threshing floor of the barn is aligned to the prevailing wind and the cart-sheds and linhay have openings on the side away from the prevailing wind and sheltered from the sun. The 1889 edition OS map shows that there was a horse-gin associated with the shippon and another adjoining the barn. The buildings are all built of local rubble stone.

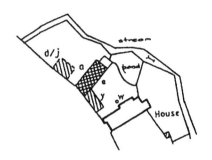

Little Wilscombe.

4   MAJOR'S FARM, Churchinford

The farmstead is close to the centre of the village in the undulating land-scape of the Blackdown Hills at an elevation of 284m (800ft). In 1802 it totalled 25 acres and this remained unchanged until c.1920. The modest farmhouse probably dates from the sixteenth century. The bank-barn may date from the late seventeenth century, the linhay with its sling-braced roof being added late in the seventeenth century. The cowshed was built c.1900. The buildings have walls of local chert and cob and would be once been thatched.

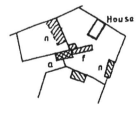

Above and left: *Major's Farm.*

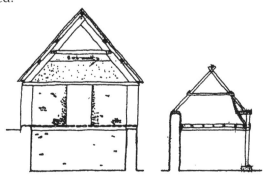

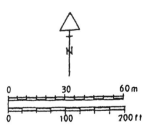

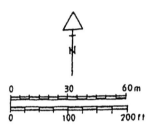

Above and right: *Roobies Farm.*

FARMSTEADS – AREA B

5   ROOBIES FARM, Fiddington

A mixed ring-fenced farm of 190 acres, in an isolated location on the gently undulating fertile lowland of the coastal strip north of the Quantock Hills. The farmhouse and the buildings of the farmstead probably date from the early-seventeenth century with additions in the early-eighteenth. They are mostly of rubble stone and tile although the threshing barn is timber-framed and of jointed-cruck construction with ship-lap board cladding. In the early-nineteenth century it belonged to the extensive Acland-Hood estate.

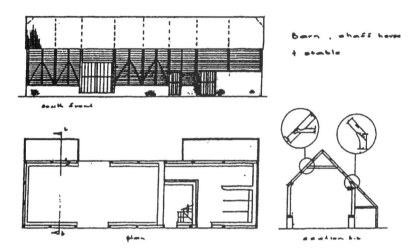

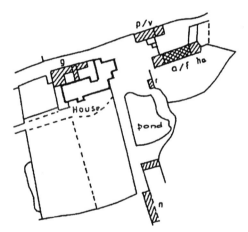

South Gundenham Farm.

6   SOUTH GUNDENHAM FARM, Langford Budville

Located in the vale country of Taunton Deane, in the nineteenth century this was a mixed farm which averaged c.100 acres. Emphasis was placed on milk and cheese production later in the nineteenth century. The farmhouse dates from the late seventeenth century and the buildings of the farmstead date from the eighteenth and nineteenth centuries – all are built of rubble stone with some brick voussoirs and tile roofs. The dominant building is a two-storey barn which has two threshing floors at first-floor level and accommodation for cattle below. A horse-engine house was added in the nineteenth century. It was owned by the Haviland family from the mid-seventeenth century until it was sold to E.A. Sanford in the mid-nineteenth century.

7   AMBERD HOUSE BARN, Pitminster

This building is contemporary with Amberd House built by Col J.M. Vibart c.1801 as part of his 53 acre estate – the majority pasture and meadow. The building is on two floors, the ground floor is open on the S-front and gives access to a walled stock yard; a rick yard adjoins. The upper floor was a threshing barn and granary, the threshing floor supported by heavy beams. The barn is built of a mix of local sandstone and has rubble with brick voussoirs; the upper part of the front is timber-framed with brick infill, probably previously clad with timber boarding. The roof is tiled. The E-gable contains 24 nesting holes.

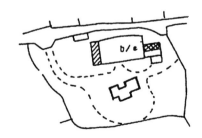

Amberd House Barn.

FARMSTEADS – AREA C

8   BEERWAY FARM, Shapwick

This farm was built c.1861 in an isolated position on well-drained pasture/arable land outside the village. The uniformity of the layout and design of the buildings show that the farmhouse and farmstead were a comprehensive planned development (probably by Mr George Warry) with emphasis on milk and cheese production. The farm totalled 220 acres in 1871.

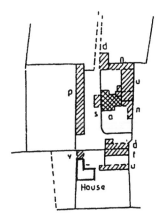

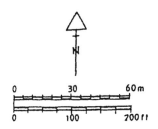

Above and left: *Beerway Farm.*

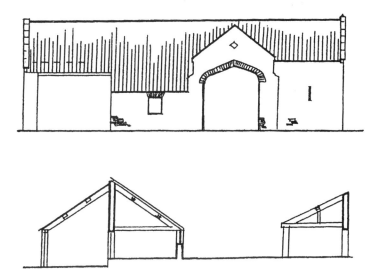

9   WILLEY'S FARM, Compton Dundon

Situated in the centre of the village all the farmstead buildings are built of local Lias stone with thatched or tiled roofs. The land is gently undulating and in 1841 comprised 17 plots dispersed in a number of parts of the parish and totalled 89 acres. The farmhouse dates from the late sixteenth century; the threshing barn has remnants of jointed-cruck trusses and probably dates from the seventeenth century. The remainder of the buildings are of nineteenth-century date.

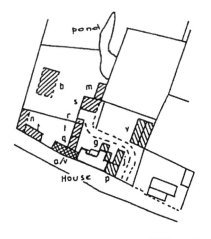

Willey's Farm.

10   HIGHER ROCKE'S FARM, Butleigh

The farmstead was arranged in two yards, that immediately south of the farmhouse (which dates from the sixteenth century) being the earlier of the two. The second yard was probably built all of a piece in the mid-nineteenth century as a dairy unit with accommodation for 42 cows. Centrally positioned was a covered manure midden with a corrugated-iron roof supported on cast-iron stanchion posts. The buildings all have walls of local Lias stone with tiled roofs. In c.1874 it comprised 214 acres which included 81 acres meadow and pasture, 109 acres arable and 22 acres of orchard.

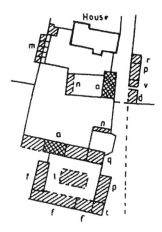

Higher Rocke's Farm.

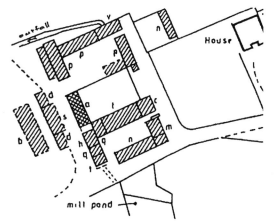

Dunpole Farm.

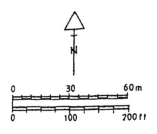

Above: *Manor Farm.*
Right: *Manor Farm, c.1861.*

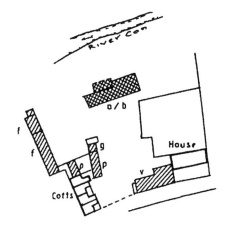

Parsonage Farm.

FARMSTEADS – AREA D

11   DUNPOLE FARM, Sea, Ilminster

The name appears as 'Dunepole' in a charter of King Ine, AD725. The mixed farm and farmstead is remotely located on the gentle slopes of Herne Hill; the ring-fenced land is well drained with direct access to the River Isle. It totalled 155 acres in 1869. The comprehensive set of buildings are of local rubble limestone with tiled roofs. Until demolished c.1983 the cider house was thatched. There had been an associated horse-gin which was still in use in 1945. The house and buildings probably all date from the eighteenth century.

12   MANOR FARM, Chiselborough

This is a planned farmstead complete with an elegant farmhouse built in 1861 at the edge of the village astride a small spring-fed stream which was impounded to provide power for a feed mill – the outfall being utilised as a water-borne effluent disposal system. In 1871 it was a mixed farm totalling 411 acres employing 24 men and three boys. At the end of the nineteenth century, emphasis changed from mixed and arable to dairying – the dairy being in a nearby house. The buildings were of local Ham Hill stone and roofed with Welsh slate. The development was commissioned by the landowner, the Earl of Ilchester, to the design of Robert H. Shout.

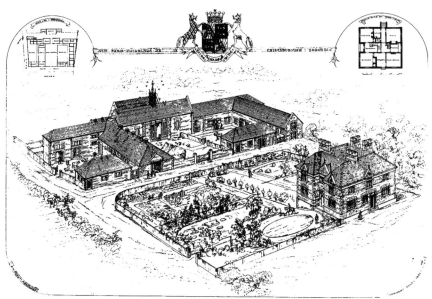

13   PARSONAGE FARM, West Camel

Located in the middle of the village close to the River Cam, the farmhouse dates from the seventeenth century and the major farm buildings, in particular the large cider house and the threshing barn/granary from the eighteenth century or earlier. There are four farm cottages. In 1881 it was a mixed farm totalling 240 acres, the land being remote from the farmstead. In the late-nineteenth and twentieth centuries concentration was on dairying and cider production. The buildings are of local Lias stone with clay tiled roofs (formerly thatched). The ground floor of the two storey threshing barn/granary has stone walls but the upper floor is clad with ship-lap boarding on a framework of jowl-posts which support the tie-beam and collar trusses.

FARMSTEADS – AREA E

14 CHANCELLORS FARM, West Harptree

This farm is located on an exposed site high on the Mendip Hills with only a shelter-belt of trees for protection. There may have been a holding on the site since at least medieval times as a map c.1570 shows the then 'Chanceller's (sic) House' in pictorial form. The present farmhouse probably dates from the seventeenth century but remnants of an earlier medieval house are thought to have been incorporated into an eighteenth-century dairy extension. The buildings have rubble stone walls and tile roofs, formerly thatched, and/or slated. The stables and the threshing barn date from the mid-seventeenth century. It was a substantial holding in the eighteenth century, then owned by the MP for Wells. By 1829, probably as the result of enclosure, it comprised 272 acres, predominantly pasture and all ring-fenced. It totalled 463 acres in 1851, 640 acres in 1861 and 362 acres in 1871.

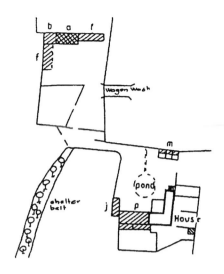

Above and left: *Chancellors Farm.*
Drawing left by Marion Hall.

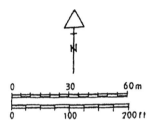

15 WHITNELL FARM, Emborough

The farm is at an altitude of 225m (738ft) on the Mendip Hills. The farmhouse has medieval origins and was upgraded in the sixteenth century. The planned farmstead probably dates from the early-eighteenth century. It was then part of the estate of the Hippisley family who had owned it since at least the seventeenth century. The land which had previously been six small estate farms was enclosed and totalled 124 acres in 1764. It totalled 233 acres in 1840. The buildings are of rubble limestone with some brick dressings and with tiled roofs.

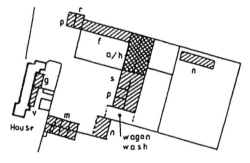

Whitnell Farm.

16 LOWER FARM, Batcombe

Located at the foot of a well-watered steep valley; the enclosed land in 1841 totalled 143 acres of mixed arable and pasture. The buildings which probably date from the eighteenth century are of rubble limestone with some Doulting stone dressings and tiled or slate roofs. A horse-gin is shown c.1885. Dairying predominated in the nineteenth century; in 1851, four labourers and a dairymaid were employed.

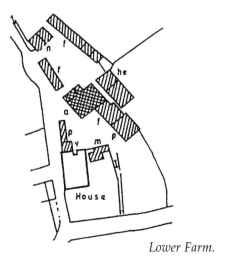

Lower Farm.

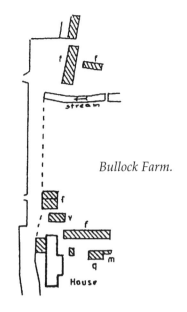

Bullock Farm.

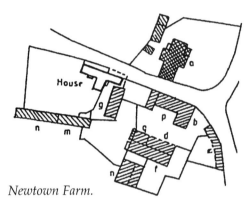

Newtown Farm.

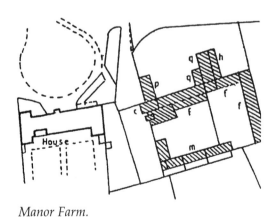

Manor Farm.

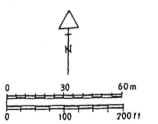

FARMSTEADS – AREA F

17   BULLOCK FARM, Kingston Seymour

A purely pastoral and dairy farm of about 140 acres this farm is located away from the village and close to the Bristol Channel, the land being at sea level. High tides are kept out by a sea wall. The River Kenn forms the northern boundary and was the main water-supply for stock. The farmhouse has seventeenth-century origins; the buildings near the house are of a late-eighteenth century date, while others are from the nineteenth and early-twentieth centuries. The house and buildings are of rubble stone with tiled roofs. The house contained a dairy with cheese store above and cider cellar. The stable building has 11 dove holes in the gable-end.

18   NEWTON FARM, Newton St Loe

Located in the centre of the village and according to the suggested date for the farmhouse the holding was possibly well established by the late-seventeenth century. By 1840 the holding comprised 231 acres with about 30 per cent being arable. The buildings are of local waste Lias stone with some Bath stone embellishment. The threshing barn has a datestone inscribed 'WL 1796' – William Gore-Langton owned the manorial estate at that time. Late in the nineteenth the granary-cum-shelter-shed-cum-roothouse had been built and is distinguished by having a series of round-sectioned cast-iron pillars to support the upper floor.

19   MANOR FARM, Stratton-on-the-Fosse

The farmstead is outside the village but close to the Fosse Way. The manor has been owned by the Duchy of Cornwall since the fourteenth century and the land was leased to gentry families over the centuries. The farmhouse, then separate from the farm, was classified as a mansion when built (or rebuilt) c.1700 and was then known as Stratton House. The farm was recorded in 1736 as comprising 27 acres, in 1841 as 157 acres, increasing to 250 acres by 1861 when seven men and three boys were employed. Soon afterwards the Duchy took the property in hand and c.1882 a new comprehensive farmstead, Dairy House and two labourers cottages were built all to the design of Samuel Hooper of Hatherleigh, Devon.

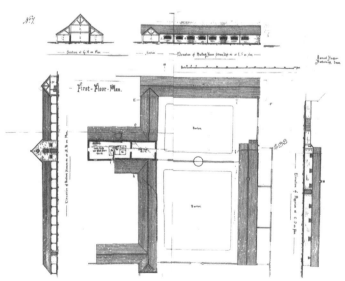

Manor Farm, c.1882.

EIGHT

Conservation

by Russell Lillford

The distinctive and unique character of Somerset is largely derived from its countryside, landmark churches and traditional buildings, especially the houses which collectively shape and define the appearance of towns and villages. Their importance is increasingly recognised but at the same time there is growing awareness that their architectural and historic integrity is being surreptitiously eroded.

Earlier chapters investigated the ways and means, the how and when historic houses were built, altered and extended. This invaluable understanding of the past can be viewed merely in an academic context or for more practical and conservation purposes. Indeed, the need for better informed conservation and planning decisions has led to a marked increase in the extent of building recording undertaken by English Heritage, and that commissioned by others from professional consultants. Local study groups, such as the Somerset Vernacular Buildings Research Group and individual building owners have also added to a growing level of appreciation and understanding that can only be beneficial in the future for the care and maintenance of our traditional buildings.

Most, if not all, the buildings in this publication have been formally recognised for their special architectural or historic interest and, as such, are included on the Statutory Lists issued by the Secretary of State on the advice of English Heritage. The main purpose of these Lists is to ensure that historic buildings of all types and designs are not demolished or irreparably altered before such proposals have been carefully examined and their full impact understood.

The first survey in Somerset to identify buildings suitable for listing was completed in 1962. Since that time the criteria for selection has changed to reflect, for example, the importance of nineteenth- and twentieth-century architecture and a greater awareness and understanding of local traditional buildings. To this end in the 1980s most of the county was resurveyed and new lists issued. In turn, these lists are added to and amended from time to time, often as a result of new information from research and recording.

For administrative convenience, the Statutory Lists are compiled on a Civil Parish basis and the individual entries are classified into one of three grades as an indication of their relative importance. By 2004 there were 11,580 listed buildings in Somerset with 308 in Grade I, 789 in Grade II* and 10,483 in Grade II. Whilst these numbers would, on the face of it, appear to be significantly large it should be remembered that in fact they represent less than 1 per cent of the total building stock of the county. Details of listed buildings can be viewed at the offices of the local authorities or online at www.somerset.gov.uk/heritage.

The great majority of traditional houses, whether listed or not, are still capable of beneficial use and, with skill and understanding, they can be successfully adapted to meet the needs of modern living. The onus of keeping all buildings in a reasonable state of repair rests, in the first instance, with the owner. With a listed building, however, the local authority can ultimately prevent its destruction from neglect, decay or redundancy by serving a Repairs Notice.

Today, with the market value of most historic houses at such a high level they are understandably well looked after and cared for by their owners. But at any given time a small percentage are found to be at risk. In order to draw wider attention to their plight details are regularly published and updated by English Heritage and some local authorities.

In Somerset, an independent charity, the Somerset Building Preservation Trust was established in 1988 to help save threatened buildings. The Trust publishes a county-wide Buildings at Risk register and has successfully rescued historic buildings that had no other realistic chance of survival. The repair and conversion schemes undertaken by the Trust are carried out in an exemplary manner and are designed to set standards for other building owners to follow. To reinforce this practice the Trust, together with the local authorities, organise public training days and conservation craft fairs to encourage the more general use of local materials and traditional building techniques.

Grant-aid for the repair of historic houses can be made in exceptional circumstances to individual private owners. English Heritage can help with funding for works to the most important buildings, listed Grade I or II*. Owners of Grade II buildings should enquire of their local authority to see if financial assistance is available. Also, in some situations, Value Added Tax (VAT) can be reclaimed for listed houses (of all grades) when consent has been granted for certain specified works. Details can be obtained from Customs and Excise.

Even if funding is not forthcoming to help with the repair and maintenance of the property, local conservation officers (at either the County or District Council) will be able to offer a wide range of help and advice. Often the most crucial decision that an owner has to make will be the selection of accredited professional advisors and suitable contractors. From their collective experience over the years conservation officers can offer much-needed guidance drawing upon informal registers that they have compiled of local specialists in all aspects of building conservation work. In addition, *The Building Conservation Directory*, published annually by Cathedral Communications, lists specialists from farther afield, but also gives details of trade organisations that can put owners in touch with skilled local craftsmen.

In 1877, William Morris spoke of the need to 'stave off decay by daily care, to prop a perilous wall or mend a leaky roof.' Maintenance is important to traditional houses of all ages and types and is as vital today as it was in Morris' time.

In recent years, many books and leaflets have been published on the subject of building repair, maintenance and conservation. A particularly helpful resource is the English Heritage publication *The Repair of Historic Buildings: Advice on Principles and Methods*, which is both succinct and informative and especially valuable for listed houses. The Society for the Protection of Ancient Buildings (founded by William Morris) produces the most authoritative and useful range of inexpensive pamphlets covering such issues as the use of lime, repairing historic joinery and dealing with damp. In 2002 the Society, in association with the Institute of Historic Building Conservation, published a comprehensive booklet, *A Stitch in Time: Maintaining Your Property Makes Good Sense and Saves Money*. Available from the Society or local authorities, this indispensable publication provides a detailed checklist of all the do's and dont's when repairing and maintaining traditional buildings.

Other more specialist and technical books are available through the County Library Service; libraries should be able to obtain them via inter-library loans.

In summary, whichever course of advice and expertise that is followed certain cardinal conservation rules are common to all situations:

- In the first instance get to know the property, study its history and record how it has changed over time.
- Move slowly, respecting the building's character, appearance and age-old patina.
- Avoid guesswork, conjectural restoration and unnecessary work – concentrate on essential repairs based on a thorough understanding of the causes of defects.
- Use only tried and tested materials, traditional techniques and finishes.
- Always reuse sound materials salvaged from the building.
- Repairs should usually be low-key, reinstating or strengthening the structure only where appropriate.
- New work should be fitted to the old to ensure the survival of as much historic fabric as is practical.
- Extensions should not dominate the existing house in either scale, detailing, materials or situation.
- Planning controls apply to all work to a listed house, both external and internal, that would affect its special interest, but consent is not normally required for repairs unless such works involve alterations which would affect the character of the building.
- Finally, carry out regular inspections and maintenance observing the old adage of doing little and often.

Four House Surveys

This appendix includes four representative examples of surveys of houses by the Somerset Vernacular Building Research Group over the past 25 years.

House surveys are undertaken with full consent and co-operation of the owners. Dependant upon the size and complexity of a house a survey is undertaken by a team of between two and ten members and usually takes one day to complete. During the survey internal and external features are recorded and a sketch plan of the ground floor made, together with details of construction, etc. A composite report is subsequently prepared which contains scale drawings, a description and an interpretation of the house's development. Whenever possible the report is supported by documentary evidence researched at the County Record Office and elsewhere. A copy of each report is supplied to the owner or occupier and, with his or her permission, is deposited at the Somerset Record Office and the National Monuments Record in Swindon.

The examples chosen are from different areas of the county, two of them with cruck roofs and two with later more sophisticated features:

Flaxpool Cottage, Crowcombe is in Taunton Vale and is a small farmhouse of the 1500s;

Lower Grant's Farmhouse, Ford, Wiveliscombe Without CP is a medieval house in the western hills;

Old Bell Farmhouse, Woollard, Publow, is a late-medieval house in the north of the county;

Manor Farmhouse, Middle Chinnock, is a house of the sixteenth/ seventeenth century in the farming country of the south-east of Somerset.

SURVEY 1: FLAXPOOL COTTAGE, CROWCOMBE

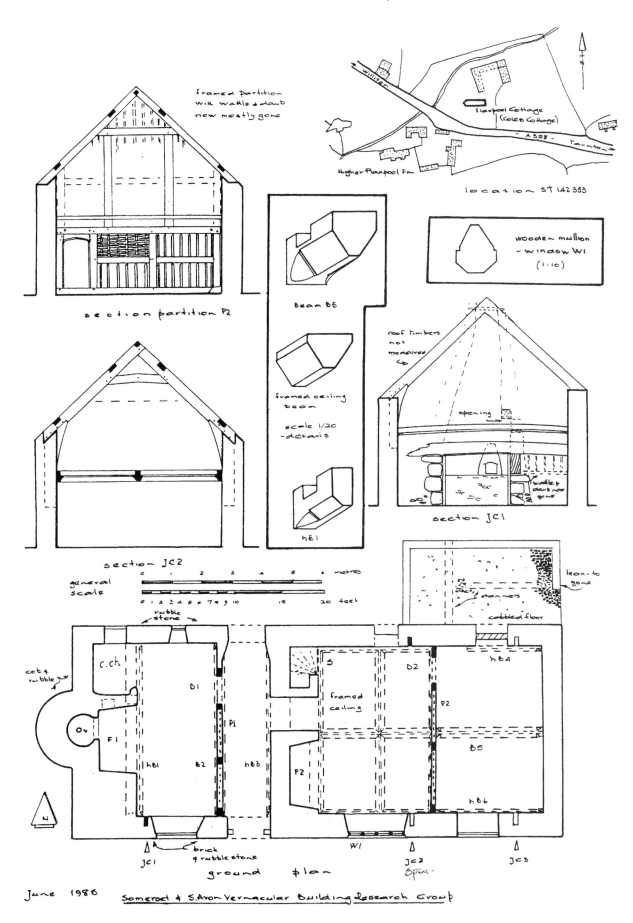

FLAXPOOL COTTAGE

(earlier, Coles Cottage)

CROWCOMBE

---

1. Grid ref. ST142 353. Crowcombe parish. Williton & Freemanors Hundred. West Somerset District Council area; previously Williton R.D.C.

2. Listed by the Dept.of Environment as of Architectural or Historic interest, Grade II, ref.10/64 and described: " Late 16 - earlyC17. Roughcast, probably over cob, thatched roof, half hipped right, brick stack left gable end and to right of entrance. 3 cell and cross passage plan. 1½ storeys, two 3-light dormer casements, ground floor 3-lt. casements in outer bays and 4-light C17 octagonal mullioned window to right of entrance, plank door. Tiled bread oven projecting on left return; brick outshot at rear. Interior: not viewed..."

3. Exterior:
During recent renovation work the walls were shown to be substantially of cob with some brick and stone. The lean-to on the NE corner (now gone) had brick walls and a cobbled floor.

4. Interior:
Beams: (a) hB1,B2 and hB3 have flat chamfers (7cm deep) with step and run-out stops;
     (b) the framed ceiling beams have deep flat chamfers (16cm);
     (c) HB4,B5 and hB6 also have deep flat chamfers (16cm) with step and run-out stops.

Partitions:
P1 (until recently) was of timber frame construction with wattle and daub infill It contains doorway D1 which has peaked head. P2 is similarly framed but in this case it extends up to the roof - although not integral with it. Doorway D2 also has a peaked head and is chamfered on the hall side.

Fireplaces:
F1 is an open-hearth fireplace with an oven built into and projecting from the W.gable. To the right of the fireplace is an area which was probably previously used as a curing chamber - there is a blocked opening in the jamb - 60 x 50cm at floor level and a return flue set at 240cm above floor level, the walls show some smoke-blackening but there is no characteristic shelf - as seen elsewhere. The wall between the chamber and the room was earlier formed with wattle and daub - presumably with a door?
A bressummer extends the whole width of the room and a slight arch at the S.end suggests that there may have been an earlier oven in the corner.
F2 is an open-hearth fireplace with a very worn freestone surround, flat chamfer and cambered wooden bressummer.

Stairs Until recently a newel stair existed at position S in the hall.

Trusses:
Three trusses, each of jointed-cruck construction: JC1 has a joint on the S. principal only and this extended down into the wall - the N. principal is a later replacement - probably when the N.wall was raised. JC2 and JC3 are both side-pegged jointed crucks, vertical legs extend well down into the walls. Pair of trenched purlins each side, notch for square ridge purlin, cambered collar tenoned into principal rafter - all wood pegged.

Windows:
W1 is a 4-light window with wooden mullions and surrounds, all flat chamfered.

5. Interpretation:
The framed ceiling beams in the hall, the beams in the inner room, partition P2 and the jointed crucks JC2 & 3 suggest a late C16th date for the E. 'half' of this 1½ storey house. It is probable that this was the extent of the original dwelling - particularly as the wall which forms the E. side of the cross-passage continues for its full width up to roof level so forming the gable-end. This hypothesis is particularly viable as the beams in the cross-passage and the kitchen indicate a C17 date and are identical to one another

July 1985

Somerset and South Avon Vernacular Building Research Group

SURVEY 2: LOWER GRANT'S FARMHOUSE, NEAR FORD, WIVELISCOMBE WITHOUT CP

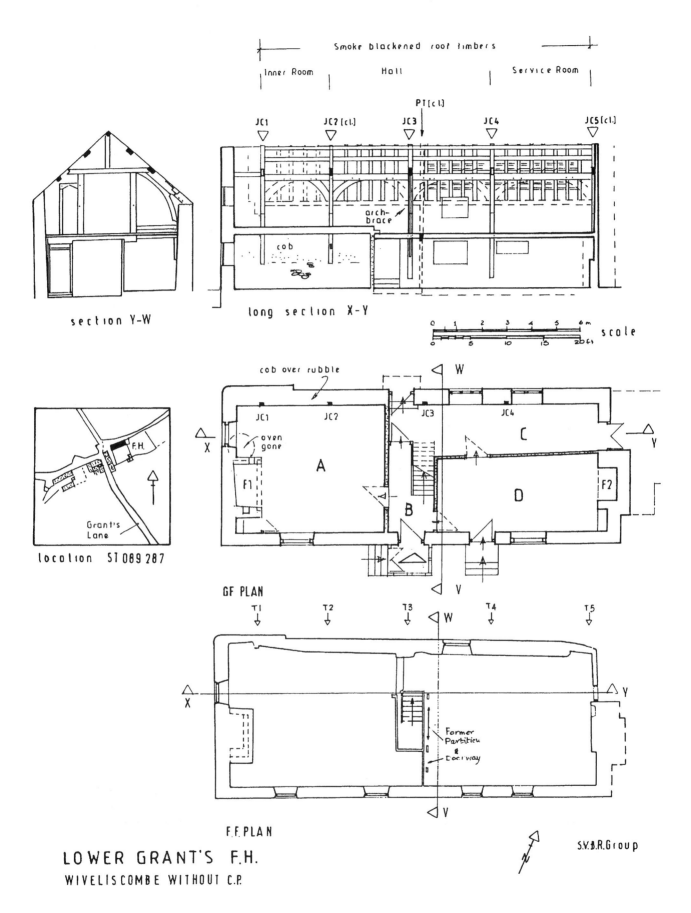

Smoke blackened roof timbers

Inner Room   Hall   Service Room

PT [cl.]

JC1   JC2 [cl.]   JC3   JC4   JC5 [cl.]

arch-brace

cob

section Y-W

long section X-Y

scale

cob over rubble

F.H.

Grant's Lane

location ST 089 287

oven gone

JC1   JC2   JC3   JC4

A

F1

C

B

D

F2

GF PLAN

T1   T2   T3   W   T4   T5

X   Y

T1

Former Partition & Doorway

V

F.F.PLAN

LOWER GRANT'S F.H.
WIVELISCOMBE WITHOUT C.P.

S.V.B.R.Group

Somerset Vernacular Building Research Group

Affiliated to the Somerset Archaeological and Natural History Society
and to The Vernacular Architecture Group

S V B R G

SURVEY

Lower Grant's Farmhouse,
Grant's Lane, near Ford,
Wiveliscombe Without Parish
JD, TM, MMcD, JR

LOCATION
NGR ST 089287. Wiveliscombe Without CP. Taunton Deane BC area. Located on the S side of Grant's Lane in an area of dispersed settlement approx. 1 mile to the NE of Wiveliscombe.

Recorded during renovation when much of the roof and part of the internal face of the N wall were exposed. The listed-building description seems to have been based on external observation only.

LISTING
Listed grade II, ref. 8/126. 'Farmhouse. C18. Cob and rendered rubble, gabled thatched roof, external rendered stepped stack right, brick stack left. 2 storeys, 1:1:2 bays; sashes with glazing bars ground floor, 2-light casement windows with weatherboarded gables breaking through eaves, C20 glazed brick porch with corrugated iron roof and C20 door centre, next bay left gabled wooden porch with corrugated iron roof and plank door.'

PLAN
A rectangular building, aligned approximately E-W, with a ground plan of two main rooms (A & D) on either side of a cross-passage (B), but D has been reduced in size by the creation of a narrow axial passage (C). Each of the main rooms has an axial fireplace at the end wall. At the E end of the house is a low extension. The wide cross-passage includes a straight flight of stairs, and below the landing there is an internal doorway across the passage. To the N of this doorway the E partition of the cross-passage has been removed, so that the N end of the cross-passage now forms part of axial passage C. In addition to the two 'opposing' external doorways, there is an external doorway on the S side of room D and another at the E end of C.

EXTERIOR
The N wall (c.66 cm thick) and both gable-end walls are rendered; where visible internally, the building-material is cob on a rubble plinth, but there is some patching in rubble, and there is brickwork on the W side of the post of JC1. The S wall (c.50 cm thick) has been rebuilt in exposed red sandstone rubble. Changes of alignment and wall-thickness at the W end of the N wall and at the NE corner of the house have resulted from alterations or repairs. The roof is thatched. The doorways and windows have no early features. In the S wall there are sash windows on the ground floor, and tall casements (now altered) on the first floor rising through the eaves to dormers. The N elevation includes a solitary first-floor window beneath the eaves. The gable-end stacks (the E stack projects externally) have late brick chimneys. There is a modern porch at the S entrance to B.

INTERIOR
Beams
The only visible beam is a medium-chamfered half-beam (HB), underbuilt by a brick partition wall, at the W end of room D. No stop is identifiable at the S end. There are redundant joints in the soffit (exposed above a later doorway at the S end) for a panelled partition. (Half-beams are normally positioned *against* a wall or partition.) The N end of the beam has been cut away: the beam now projects a short distance into the axial passage, the butt-end supporting a partition-stud above, whilst in the soffit there is a redundant joint for a stud or door-post below. Tall, narrow joists visible above A, C & D are late features, but the E side of the half-beam has 11 cm wide slots for earlier joists.

Partitions
The inserted partition wall forming the S side of C is built of brick, as is the partition (replacing earlier panelling) beneath the half-beam. Where visible, the structure of the partition on the W side of B is also of brick.

On the first floor, truss JC2 has redundant joints underneath the collar for two studs and wattle-and-daub infill, and there is a redundant joint for a beam or rail at the top of the N jointed-cruck post. Wattle-and-daub infill remaining above the collar is clean on the W side but smoke-blackened on the E, whereas the truss is blackened on both sides: the partition was therefore inserted into JC2. On the ground floor, another mortice in the face of the N post must either have been associated with the lower part of this partition or with an earlier 'low partition' (see Phase 1 below).

The remains of another inserted partition survive on the first floor above the half-beam (see drawing of cross-section). The framing includes two studs (with redundant mortices for former rails at mid-height) rising to a collar which supports a king-post and has a bird-mouth joint at each end for attachment to the roof-purlins. The lower ends of the studs are joined to the half-beam below by slip-tenons. There are redundant stake-holes beneath the collar, and a groove in the top of the half-beam, for wattle-and-daub infill. Some surviving wattle-and-daub above the collar is clean on both sides.

Doorways
On the first floor a doorway with a cranked head has been inserted near the S end of the second partition, but is now blocked. No other doorways have early features.

Fireplaces
F1 occupies a substantial stack which projects into the building and is stepped on the upper floor. The S jamb is built of sandstone rubble, but a 7cm plain chamfer on the wooden lintel overlaps the N jamb, which includes brickwork and rubble and replaces an earlier jamb, thus reducing the width of F1. The entrance to a brick-lined bread-oven survives in the N jamb, but the body of the oven has been removed.
F2 has rubble-built jambs and a slightly-chamfered wooden lintel: it is probably later in date than F1. On the floor above is a small cast-iron fireplace.

Stairs
The present stairway is a late feature. There is no clear evidence for an earlier stairway in the house, but there may have been a winding stair to the N of F1 before the bread-oven was built.

Roof
This is of four bays and includes remains of five jointed-cruck trusses (JC1-JC5), although the S posts are entirely missing. All that survives of JC5 in its original form is the N principal (the NE corner of the house, where the N post would have been, has been rebuilt) and the collar.
The cruck joints are of the side-pegged long-tenon type: the surviving collars are tenoned and cranked; and the ridge-piece is set diagonally in a V-notch (but supported by an inserted king-post in JC5 and by another king-post in the inserted partition above the half-beam). Each bay has at least one surviving windbrace, but the windbracing was always confined to the lowest tier of the roof. The purlins (three tiers on each side, now incomplete) are trenched, and the surviving common rafters are broad and flat. A number of original laths (also broad and flat) survive, as does some original wheat under-thatch, with thatching ties made from thin plant stems. All the original roof-timbers and under-thatch are smoke-blackened.

Central truss JC3 has a chamfered archbrace and clearly occupied the centre of a medieval open hall. The N post can be seen to descend almost to ground-level; and the archbrace descends far down the post, although mutilated on the first floor. The N post of JC4 also descends to a low level, and those of JC1 and JC2 descend to what appears to be a rubble plinth (exposed during renovation work) at c.1m above the floor-level of room A.

The curved tops of the posts of JC2 and JC4 protrude rather than merge smoothly into the undersides of the principals. The same 'step' also occurs in JC3, but not in the integral archbrace.

Much of the S side of the original roof has been destroyed, but at one point the top of the S wall obscures a surviving part of it: this indicates that the wall is a replacement, built immediately inside the line of the original S wall (which was presumably built of cob like the N wall). This rebuilding of the S wall would have been associated with the disappearance of the S cruck-posts.

JC5 has remains of wattle-and-daub infill inside the E gable, suggesting that the house may formerly have had a timber-framed gable or wall at this end. Within the roof-void the W side of JC1 can be seen to be clean, indicating that the truss was built against an earlier W gable wall which was demolished when the present stack and gable-end wall were built. The house has thus been slightly lengthened at the W end and possibly the E end also, but it has been made narrower by the rebuilding of the S wall.

INTERPRETATION

Phase I: medieval

The building was originally a single-storeyed medieval farmhouse (15C?), in which the accommodation was very possibly divided by low partitions into three rooms, including a central hall with an open hearth. It is unlikely that the original entrances were in the same position as the opposing doorways of the present cross-passage, which is positioned centrally within the former medieval hall rather than at one side as in a screens passage. The roof, which is windbraced in all bays, gives no indication of which was the 'upper' or 'lower' end of the medieval house. The insertion of a first-floor chamber or solar into the W end of the house in Phase II (see below) suggests that this was regarded as the upper end. On the other hand the bread-oven in F1 indicates that this was the service end at a much later date (the oven itself is probably 19C), perhaps resulting from a reversal of the upper-lower orientation of the house at some stage during its history.

Phase II

The fact that the wattle-and-daub infill inserted into JC2 is clean on the W side but blackened on the E indicates that a first-floor chamber was created between JC1 and JC2, but that the hall remained open to the roof. This alteration probably occurred towards the end of the medieval period (perhaps late-15C or early-16C).

Phase III

The chamfered half-beam at the W end of room D is associated with the ceiling-over of the hall and the E end of the house, probably in the 16C. The remains of the wattle-and-daub partition above the half-beam are clean on both sides, indicating that by this stage one, and possibly both, of the present gable-end stacks had been built, superseding the open hearth of the former hall. The deeper chamfer on the lintel of the W fireplace suggests that this fireplace was built first.

The fact that the half-beam only has joist-sockets on the E side suggests that cross-passage B (which was presumably created in this phase) was unceiled: conceivably this part of the house remained as a vestigial open hall, but, if so, it was unheated. More probably, the presumed three-room plan of the medieval house had now been transformed into a two-room ground-floor plan with a central cross-passage, forming the basis of the present plan.

Baghay Farmhouse near Milverton also has a two-room plan of early date, but one of the rooms has a fireplace backing onto the cross-passage in contrast to the end-stacks at Lower Grant's Farmhouse.

Phase IV

Later in the 16C or in the 17C a doorway with a cranked head was inserted into the S end of the partition above the half-beam, indicating that the S end of the cross-passage had been ceiled over or that a stairway had been inserted here.

Later Phase or Phases

In the 18C or 19C the S wall was rebuilt, with sash windows and prominent dormers (the latter now refenestrated): there are no signs of earlier blocked windows in this wall. At about the same time axial passage C, with a gable-end doorway, was created by the insertion of a brick partition wall, and similar walls replaced earlier partitions on either side of cross-passage B. Other changes included the insertion of a cast-iron fireplace on the first floor, the laying of patterned tiles in B and the construction of the present stairway: these probably occurred in the 19C. It is possible that most or even all of the above features were part of a wholesale updating of the house in one operation during the 19C.

November 2001

SURVEY 3: THE OLD BELL FARMHOUSE, WOOLLARD, PUBLOW

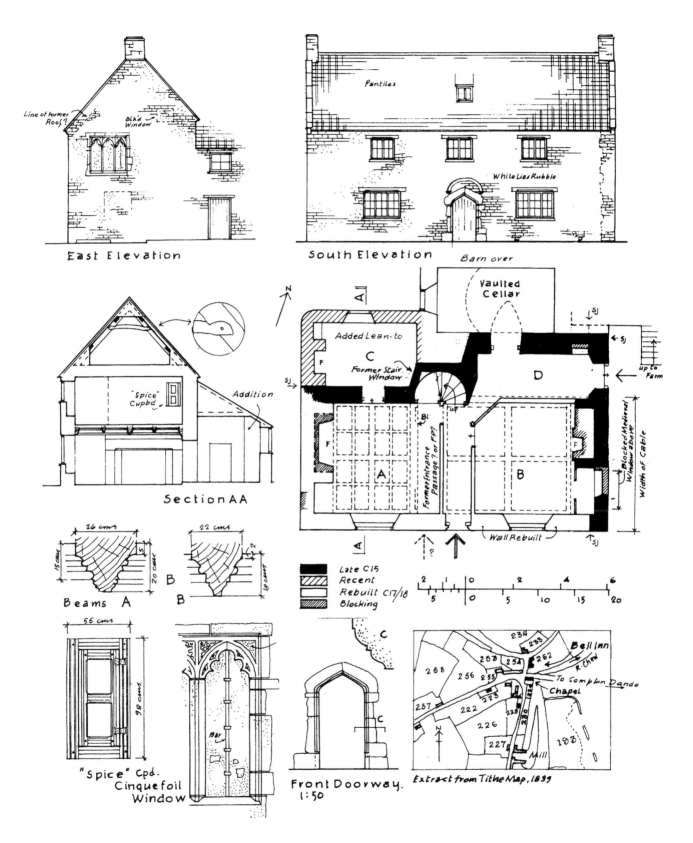

East Elevation

South Elevation

Section AA

Beams A

B   B

"Spice" Cpd.
Cinquefoil
Window

Front Doorway.
1:50

Extract from Tithe Map, 1839

Somerset Vernacular Building Research Group

SOMERSET VERNACULAR BUILDING RESEARCH GROUP

**The Old Bell Farmhouse
Woollard, Publow**

Parish   Publow
Local Authority N.E Somerset
Grid reference ST 632645
Listed Building Grade 2

Surveyed by members of
SVBRG (B & JB,J & JP,JD,
SH,DS,SS)

August 1997

GENERAL. The Old Bell Farmhouse stands next to the bridge over the River Chew where five roads meet on the parish boundary. Formerly the house was the Bell Inn (1839 Tithe Map) and in a 1776 Popham Estate survey it was called "the Tanyard House, stable and tanning office"; the tannery itself lay some 300m away to the south. There is a painting in the Bristol University Library, dated also 1864, in which it is called "Priest's House, Woollard" and the caption also refers to a Chapel opposite (now a dwelling).

PLAN.
    A 2½ storey two-room central entry house facing south, small hall or parlour (A) to the left, larger service and kitchen (B) to the right. A stair turret at the back of the passage and back premises are built into rising ground comprising a rear entrance (D), a vaulted cellar and an added lean-to (C). The farmyard and buildings lie behind the house at a higher level (ca.1.5m) with the main barn roof extending over the staircase to give access to the attics.

EXTERIOR.
    Walls. White lias rubble stone, coursed and squared. A conspicuous joint at the SE corner indicates that the front wall has been rebuilt. Masonry on the East gable is rough and shows that the roof has been raised.
    Doorway. Entrance door has a high 4-centred arch in stone, arch and jambs with narrow shallow mouldings, ogee step ovolo; a late segmental timber hood above.
    Windows. Timber casements under ovolo moulded timber lintels. At 1st floor level, East elevation, a 3-light blocked stone-mullioned window with arched heads and cinquefoil cusping, but no dripstone; one central iron bar survives. Spandrels intricately carved (late C15 early C16?). A small late dormer lights the attic.
    Roof. double roll pantiles, coped gables. Stone chimneys.

INTERIOR.
    Beams. Room A, a fine 16-panel framed ceiling, C15 mouldings. Room B, a 4-panelled framed ceiling, more simply moulded (see drawing no 1). A late beam B1 probably inserted when a wall or partition was removed.
    Roof. Tie and collar trusses, cambered collars lap-dovetailed to principals; apexes concealed; 2 butt purlins in line each side.
    Stairs. timber newel stairs to 1st floor; winding stairs to attics.
    Fireplaces. Gable fireplaces. Room A with a flat timber bressumer, plain chamfered; room B blocked with a modern fireplace.
    Fittings. A panelled wall cupboard in West chamber has C17 moulded panels and butterfly hinges (see drawing).

INTERPRETATION

There are two recognisable C15 features in the house:
a) the opulent framed ceiling in room A (and possibly the plainer one in room B as well).
b) the 3-light cinquefoil window. The unusual carved spandrels, each one a different floral pattern, have the appearance of later rather than earlier C15 work. The window is set in the East gable wall which is of rougher masonry than the rest of the house and is original; although the window lacks a hood mould it is probably in its original position.

In addition, it is probable that the newel stair is sited in the remains of a C15 turret, now partly lost in the later rear premises.

The stone entrance doorway is less certainly of the C15 as the mouldings include an ovolo and may be a C16 substitute.

It seems that the C15 **plan** was much as it is to-day, two rooms with a central entry. It is difficult to establish the use of the two rooms. <u>Either</u> the space between the two framed ceilings was formerly an entrance passage and room A was a Parlour with a gable fireplace, <u>or</u> the space was filled with a fireplace backing onto the present entrance passage, in which case room A would be a small Hall, the gable fireplace being substituted when the walls were rebuilt.

On balance we believe the former to be more likely, with room A the Parlour and room B the Hall where the cooking was done. In either case, straight joints in the masonry indicate that room D was in the original build; it would have been a service area. Room C is a late addition and the vaulted cellar, having no dateable features, could be original or introduced later to support the floor of the farmyard barn at the higher level. At this stage, with the entrance between the two framed ceilings, the stair would have wound in the reverse direction.

The principal chamber was evidently over the Hall, B, lit by the 3-light window and probably heated by a gable fireplace in the hall stack, now blocked.

There is no evidence for a third room other than the small service room D. Surviving examples of C15 two-room plans are a rarity but they do more often occur in ecclesiastical dwellings (ref. M.Wood in 'the English Medieval House'), which might reinforce the idea of this being a priest's house.

2 **Late C17 or early C18;** a major conversion. The front and west walls were rebuilt with new windows, the entrance was moved and an new entrance passage was created to make a larger Parlour A and a smaller Hall B, which then became a Kitchen. The direction of the stair was reversed and perhaps the cellar was introduced. The parlour fireplace was rebuilt with the west wall, the roof was raised to improve the bedroom accommodation and the medieval east window was blocked in favour of the new front windows.

SURVEY 4: MANOR FARMHOUSE, MIDDLE CHINNOCK

SOMERSET VERNACULAR BUILDING RESEARCH GROUP

Manor Farm   November 1983, survey by
Middle Chinnock   J & J Penoyre

Parish   West Chinnock, County of Somerset
Grid reference   ST 472 133
Local Authority   Yeovil District Council
Listed Building   Grade II ref 14/15 West Chinnock, Yeovil RDC

PLAN   A three storey house with a two storey wing, a cross
                passage, stair turret at the back and a single storey range
                of outbuildings and lean-to at the rear. The house stands
                well back from the road and faces North West. It is the most
                imposing of the older houses in the village.

EXTERIOR
Walls   Hamstone ashlar for the whole of the 3-storey part of the
                house and the front of the 2-storey wing; elsewhere coursed
                and squared rubble; a large buttress (four weathered offsets)
                in the centre of the front of the 2-storey wing. The wall to
                the left of the entrance at ground floor level is about 80cm
                thick. The front of the 3-storey wing has plinths, string and
                cornice mouldings (early classical) with a fluted frieze.
                The gable coping corbels are extended as an eaves moulding in
                the gables as well as the main roof. A short section of similar
                eaves moulding occurs above the buttress.

Windows   Hamstone mullioned windows of ovolo and hollow chamfer
                section, marked on the drawings 'O' and 'H' respectively. A
                very small pierced stone round headed window occurs in the
                N facing spandrel of the W gable above the slates of the
                main roof. Other windows are late timber casements.

Front doorway   Wide (134cm) depressed "four-centred" arched lintel
                with incised spandrels, ogee and ovolo mouldings and flask
                stops. The two internal stone doorways to the stair turret,
                at ground and first floors are similar. The boarded ground
                floor doors are heavily studded and have fine iron furniture.

Roof   Welsh slates, presumably replacing stone slates on the 3-storey
                wing.
Chimneys   A group of 3 tall diagonally set ashlar stone chimneys
                with base and single cap mouldings dominates the house.
                Other chimneys, brick above roof.

INTERIOR
Roof trusses   3-storey wing; three tie-beam trusses with vertical
                struts and heavy purlins. Roof space inaccessible.

Fireplaces   All modern except for a small hamstone fireplace (depressed
                four centred arched lintel, plain chamfers) on the third floor.

Staircase   Solid timber spiral stair in rectangular turret, with
                round (14cm diam.) continuous timber newel with ball finial
                at top; no handrails.

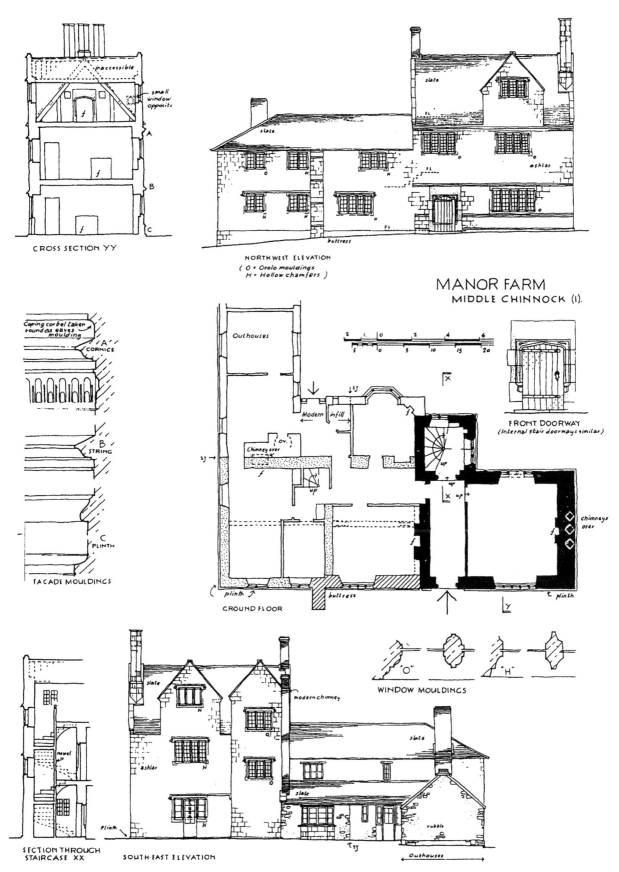

CROSS SECTION YY

NORTHWEST ELEVATION
(O = Ovolo mouldings
H = Hollow chamfers)

MANOR FARM
MIDDLE CHINNOCK (1).

Coping corbel taken
round as eaves
moulding

A
CORNICE

B
STRING

C
PLINTH

FACADE MOULDINGS

Outhouses

Modern infill

Chimney over

up

up

up

FRONT DOORWAY
(Internal stair doorways similar)

chimneys
over

plinth

buttress

plinth

GROUND FLOOR

"O"   H

WINDOW MOULDINGS

newel

slate

modern chimney

slate

ashlar

slate

rubble

plinth

Outhouses

SECTION THROUGH
STAIRCASE XX

SOUTH-EAST ELEVATION

Survey by EVBRG, 1983

Beams   One exposed beam only, ground floor 2-storey wing, narrow
         chamfer and plain stops, probably late 18C.

INTERPRETATION

Three builds:

First a three-room house extending at least as far as the
buttress with a large chimney backing onto the cross passage, probably
16C. The thick wall on the left of the entrance and the wide space
between the fireplace wall and the window where the former fireplace
would have been, make this a strong probability.

Second, the principal build, probably early 17C, comprising
the whole of the 3-storey wing.

The third build comprised the 2-storey part of the house, the
remaining first build wall to the left of the entrance being refaced in
ashlar. The beam section, the rationality of the structure and the wide
span indictate a (late?) 18C date. This part of the house may have
been re-roofed in the early to mid-19C and it is probable that the
outhouse range was added at that time. The lean-to at the rear is
itself in 2 builds and is of 19 and 20C date.

A more precise estimate of the date of the second build is made
very difficult by the absence of any decorative plasterwork or exposed
beams and the inaccessibility of the upper roof space.

There is no visible evidence to suggest that the three-storey wing
ever extended to the left of the entrance.

In an estate survey of 1651 there is a reference to a farm called
"Stafford East Court" occupied by Giles Hodges. There is no proof that
this is Manor Farm although the Lord of the Manor in 15C was Sir Humphrey
Stafford.   A survey of the Ilchester Estate in 1730 refers to the
occupier as Samuel Hallett. In 1813, it is Robert Harding and in 1824
it is George Bishop. The tithe apportionment of 1839, calls the
house 'Lower Farm' and gives the owner as Martha Templeman and occupier
as herself.

Glossary

Arch:	Shape of arch often used as a dating indicator, fig. 4.2.
Archbrace:	Curved braces to collar truss, forming an arch shape.
Architrave:	Moulded frame round doors and windows.
Ashlar:	Masonry of finely cut rectangular stones and fine joints.
Bay:	The space between roof trusses, as in a 'two-bay hall'.
Bressumer:	Large timber beam spanning a fireplace opening.
Camber:	The slight arching (or cranking) of a horizontal member, e.g. collar.
Cellar:	A store room for beer, cider, etc., not necessarily below ground.
Chamfer:	A 45 degree splay across the edge of a beam, mullion, etc.
Cob:	Walling of compacted earth, gravel, straw, etc.
Collar:	Horizontal member of an A-shaped truss.
Coping:	Capping of a wall, especially a gable.
Cross Passage:	A transverse entrance passage with external doors at either end.
Cruck:	A pair of curved or elbowed principal rafters extending from near the ground to the apex of roof. A 'jointed cruck' is made in two pieces (fig. 3.15).
Curing Chamber:	A smoking chamber for curing bacon, etc., adjoining a kitchen fireplace.
Dendrochronology:	A scientific method of dating timbers.
Double pile:	A type of house plan with two parallel ranges (fig. 3.2).
Dripstone:	Or hoodmould; a projecting stone moulding above an opening to shed the rain.
Finial:	A decorative feature on top of a gable.
Framed ceiling:	Panels formed of cross beams and edge beams.
Garderobe:	An internal privy, sometimes in a garderobe turret.
Hall:	The principal room of a medieval or post-medieval house. An open hall is the room open to the roof timbers.
Half-hip:	As a hipped gable, but starting half way up the roof.
Inner room:	A private room beyond the hall, remote from the cross passage.
Jamb:	The side of the opening.
Joist:	Small beams supporting the floor boards.
Lap-dovetail:	A halved and shaped joint between collar and principal rafter (fig. 3.15).
Lintel:	The head beam of an opening.
Mortice:	A rectangular recess to receive the tenon of a timber joint.
Moulding:	Linear carved decoration of various sections (fig. 4.2).
Mullion:	A stone or timber post dividing a window of two or more lights.
Pediment:	A low-pitched triangular feature above classical openings, etc.
Purlin:	Longitudinal roof timbers spanning between trusses supporting rafters.
Quoins:	Large, usually rectangular corner stones.
Rafters:	Small sloping timbers supporting the roof finish.
Rubble:	Rough masonry ('coursed' or if irregular 'random') with wide joints.
Stop:	The termination of a chamfer or moulding, often decorative (fig. 4.19).
Saddle:	Small horizontal timber joining two principal rafters at the apex.
Service room:	A buttery, pantry, storeroom or kitchen.
Straight joint:	A vertical joint in a wall denoting stages of build or blocked opening.
Tie-beam:	A horizontal transverse timber joining the feet of a roof truss.
Transome:	A stone or timber member dividing a mullioned window horizontally.
Truss:	An assembly of timbers forming the structural divisions of a roof (fig. 3.15).
Verge:	The sloping edge of a gable where there is no coping.
Wall plate:	Lengthwise timber along wall top to receive roof loads.
Wattle and daub:	Mud and plaster on timber woven backing between vertical studs (fig. 3.16).
Windbrace:	Longitudinal bracing between roof purlins and principals, usually curved.
Yoke:	Short triangular timber joining two principals at the apex.

Further Reading

GENERAL

Ayres, J., *The Home in Britain*, Faber & Faber, 1981.
Barley, M., *Houses and History*, Faber & Faber, 1986.
Clifton Taylor, A., *A Pattern of English Building*, Faber & Faber, 1987.
Cook, O., *The English Country House*, Thames & Hudson, 1974.
Girouard, M., *Life in the English Country House*, Penguin, 1978.
Quiney, A., *Traditional Buildings of England*, Thames & Hudson, 1990.
Quiney, A., *Medieval Town Houses*, Yale University Press, 2003.

SOMERSET

Aston, M.A. and Burrow, I.C., eds, *The Archeology of Somerset*, SCC, 1982.
Aston, M.A., ed. *Aspects of the Medieval Landscape of Somerset*, SCC, 1988.
Bettey, J.H., *Wessex from AD1000*, Dovecote Press, 1994.
Bush, R., *Somerset, the Complete Guide*, Dovecote Press, 1994.
Costen, M., *The Origins of Somerset*, Manchester University Press, 1992.
Dunning, R.D., *The History of Somerset* (third edition), Somerset Books, 2003.
Dunning, R.D., *Some Somerset Country Houses*, Dovecote Press, 1991.
Hardy, P., *Geology of Somerset*, Ex Libris Press, 1999.
Leach, P., *Roman Somerset*, Dovecote Press, 2001.
Penoyre, J. and J., *Decorative Plasterwork in the Houses of Somerset*, SCC, 1994.
Pevsner, N., *The Buildings of England*, 2 vols North Somerset, 1958 & South Somerset, 1979.
Prudden, H., *Geology of the Landscape of Taunton Dean*, TDBC, 2001.

HOUSES AND FARM BUILDINGS

Alcock, N.W., *Cruck Construction*, CBA Research Report 42, 1981.
Beacham, P., ed., *Devon Buildings*, DCC, Devon Books, 1990.
Brunskill, R.W., *Illustrated Handbook of Vernacular Architecture*, Faber & Faber, 1971.
Hall, L.J., *The Rural Houses of North Avon and South Gloucestershire 1400–1720*, City of Bristol Museum and Art Gallery, 1983.
Slocombe, P., *Medieval Houses of Wiltshire*, Wiltshire Buildings Record No. 1, Alan Sutton, 1992.
Slocombe, P., *Wiltshire Farmhouses and Cottages 1500–1850*, Wiltshire Buildings Records No. 2, 1988.
Slocombe, P., *Wiltshire Farm Buildings 1500–1900*, Wiltshire Buildings Records Nos 3, 1989.
Slocombe, P., *Wiltshire Town Houses, 1500–1900*, Wiltshire Buildings Record No. 4, 2001.
SVBRG, *The Vernacular Buildings of Somerset Villages: Alford and Lovington* (1986), *Batcombe* (1988), *Butleigh* (2001), *Chiselborough* (1993), *Compton Dundon* (2004), *Haselbury Plucknett* (1994), *Long Load & Knole* (1982), *Shapwick* (1996) and *West Chinnock* (1980).
Dallimore, J. and Newton St Loe Vernacular Building Research Group, *Newton St Loe, NE Somerset*, Bath and North East Somerset Council, 2001.

Index of Named Houses

Listed under parishes with page numbers, figure numbers and colour plates